Appraising & Developing
MANAGERIAL PERFORMANCE

T. V. Rao
Chairman
T V Rao Learning Systems Pvt. Ltd.
&
Academic Council, Academy of HRD

T V Rao Learning Systems Pvt. Ltd.

EXCEL BOOKS

T V Rao Learning Systems Pvt, Ltd.
12, Cosmoville, Satyagraha Marg
Post. Thaltej Road, Ahmedabad 380 054

The earlier edition of this book was published as "Performance Appraisal: Theory and Practice" under AIMA-VIKAS Management Series in 1984, and by the Academy of HRD in 1992 (reprint of second edition)

ISBN: 81-7446-169-8

First Edition: 1984
Reprint of Second Edition: 1992
Excel Books Reprint: New Delhi, 1999

Published by
EXCEL BOOKS
A-45 Naraina, Phase I
New Delhi - 110 028

Printed at
Excel Printers
C-206 Naraina, Phase I
New Delhi - 110 028

To

Ravi J. Matthai
In rememberance of the
learning spaces
he created for several people

PREFACE TO THE FIRST EDITION

The basis of appraisal system described here was evolved jointly by Professor Udai Pareek, Larsen & Toubro Professor of Organisational Behaviour at the Indian Institute of Management, and the author during 1974-75 when they were working with Larsen & Tourbo Limited. During their discussions with a large number of executives of this company, the managers themselves wanted such a development-oriented system. The objectives and components suggested by a number of them were put together and the objectives, framework and components for a developmental performance appraisal system were evolved. Subsequent discussion and interviews with supervisors, officers, and managers at various levels from various organisations (private sectors, medium-sized and large industries, public sector industries, banks, government departments in health, education and such other sectors, corporations) with whom we worked reinforced, modified and developed the system into the form described in this book. During our discussions for evolving such a system we were looking for evolving different systems for different organisations as organisations differ in their culture. But we were surprised at the consistency with which various groups of people from varying backgrounds suggested very similar things. We were also surprised at the similarity of the doubts raised by a section of managers from every organisation at the time of implementing such a system - a system that they wanted! These are largely dealt with in chapter 15.

In early stages we were reluctant to propose a system applicable to all organisations. But with the consistency with which we heard managers say similar things about the existing appraisal formats and about what they want, we were convinced about the universal need for such a system. Professor Iswar Dayal argued elsewhere that appraisals should be designed to suit the culture. We have taken a different point of view. We feel that appraisals can be used as instruments of change towards a desired culture rather than waiting for culture to change and changing appraisals to suit such change.

Changing organisational culture through appraisal systems alone may be too high an objective to achieve. We do not think that it is impossible. First of all we must be clear about the culture we want to develop. Today we feel that starting with our educational institutions, in every organisation, work place and the society itself, there is need for a definite and positive culture to be developed. A culture that values human beings and their capabilities that enable them to be proactive and develop and apply their capabilities; a culture that encourages collaboration and team work; a culture that encourages openness that trust and makes the place of work a happy place; and most importantly a culture that promotes work ethic through all these. We believe that the appraisal system presented in this book could be an instrument to move in that direction.

A few details of this system were brought out by us in the form of performance appraisal manuals in 1978. The appraisal system presented here evolved first as a subsystem of an integrated Human Resources Development System (HRDS). Experiences of organisations attempting to introduce HRDS indicated that introducing HRDS is a long-drawn process and in the process Performance Appraisal stands out distinctly as an important part. Hence we decided to make available some in-depth details of this system to the world of practising managers as well as fellow professionals and students. The details of the place of Performance Appraisal in HRDS are presented elsewhere.

I am happy to bring out this book at this point of time. My own experience of working with a few organisations in Malaysia, and discussions with several executives, administrators and educationists from several Asian countries in my visits to a few of these countries and my participation in UNESCO (Bangkok) organised workshops and seminars indicate that they are also looking for such a system. In one of the chapters in this book I have described briefly the appraisal mechanisms existing in some of these countries.

At the end of the book there are 51 references given. Of these only 9 are Indian. Why this adoration of Western researches? Is there no Indian work on this topic or am I promoting American Systems in India? Answers to these questions are important to be given here because we have seen practising managers who did not have a say in evolving the system described there, those who are ignorant of Western systems, those who see good things in this system which are also present in Western systems and those who are not yet emotionally prepared to accept this system, sometimes, tend to call it an "American System" to suit their purposes. I have compared and distinguished elsewhere the HRDS in India and the USA. I have also argued elsewhere how managers who reject such systems because they think that these are American systems borrowed by Indian Business Schools (as though only American Professors have the copyright to do useful things for their country) tend to sabotage unknowingly their own development opportunities.

There are 42 foreign references in this book because after I started writing this book, I became curious to know what is happening in the Western front on this topic. In fact, the first understanding I gained about HRD in the Western front prompted me to write the first article "HRDS: the new approach" (originally titled as "HRDS : an old wine in a new bottle?" in 1981. At the time I referred mainly to the Training and Development Journal. Prompted by the suggestions given my colleague Prof. Ramadhar Singh at IIMA, I read a few other journals and particularly the recent issues of the Journal of Applied Psychology. I read to the point that I got convinced that any additional investment in reading is not going to give me a proportional increment in my understanding about what is happening in the USA. After having come to that point I have decided to communicate the understanding I have gained to the readers of this book. To me it is valuable because this reading has given me a few new insights and at the same time it has reinforced some of the stereotypes I have about Behavioural Science Research in the West (e.g., that most of them are not generalisable beyond the laboratory settings in which they were conducted). The insights I gained relate to the 'performance appraisal ratings' and most of the research studies I read dealt with this issue. I have chosen a few studies that struck me and summarised them in Chapter 6 on performance appraisal ratings. The reader may notice that most of these appeared in the last 5 years. Indian researches are rather few and quite a few of these are not published as they are conducted for internal consumption by companies. I am aware of a few other contributions to this area, but I may not have used them as my intention is not to present an exhaustive review of published literature in our country on each and every aspect of appraisals. Where I am aware of some in-company researches, an attempt has been made to use them in Chapter 13 to give an over view of the Indian scene. In one or two cases I have not given any indication of the source in order to maintain the confidentiality the companies desired. Of course, in a way it is also true that there is very little available in India on performance appraisal and hence this book.

T.V. RAO.

PREFACE TO THE SECOND EDITION

More experiences have become available in the last seven to eight years since the time I first wrote this book. Many organisations have started changing their executive appraisals to make them more open and more development-oriented. However, the difficulties and the dynamics involved in initiating and managing this change seems to be the same whether it is in 1970s or now. Executives want open and development-oriented appraisal systems until they come. When they come they seem to see the unexpected additional time investments required for development and get scared or neglect it.

Development needs investment of time, effort and emotions. If learning culture or HRD culture already existing in the company, such investments may become less.

A few more organisations have shown the courage to change. Some of these with whom the author has familiarity includes Larsen & Toubro Ltd., L&T (ECC) Construction Group, Voltas, State Bank of India, Sundram Fasteners, National Dairy Development Board, Life Insurance Corporation, Crompton Greaves Ltd., etc. These have been included in this book.

A chapter indicating the movement from Performance Appraisal to Performance Planning, Analysis and Development has also been included. Some possible movement towards ratingless appraisals and subordinate appraisals have also been discussed in a separate chapter. The detailed case on Performance Counselling has been dropped and only a part of it has been included for illustration.

January 27, 1992 T.V. Rao

ACKNOWLEDGEMENTS TO THE FIRST EDITION

Many people have contributed directly and indirectly to what is in this book. The first among them is my colleague, Professor Udai Pareek who is now in Indonesia as a consultant to the Ministry of Health. It was through a number of years of close association and working together with Udai on designing and implementing new appraisal systems, that I learnt a lot of what is reflected in this book. Such a learning was also made possible by organisations like Larsen & Toubro Ltd., Bharat Earth Movers Ltd., State Bank of India, Petrofils Cooperative Ltd. and lately Crompton Greaves Ltd. who invited us to look at their appraisal systems and had the courage and commitment to experiment with something new for Human Resources Development. Professors Ravi Matthai, Samuel Paul and V.S. Vyas of IIMA provided the right climate and encouragement at IIMA which enabled me to experiment with new appraisal systems. I particularly thank Prof. S Paul who was directing IIMA during my initial years there for all the encouragement he gave.

I also thank Mr. S.R. Subramanyam, Vice-President, Personnel & OD of Larsen & Toubro Ltd., Mr. K.N. Randeria, Vice-President, Personnel, of Voltas Ltd., and Mr. T.P. Raman, Chief Officer (HRD) of State Bank of India for their kind permission to describe and reproduce their performance appraisal systems in this book. By giving permission Mr. Subramanyam, Mr. Randeria and Mr. Raman have not only showed their own and their organisations' commitment to professional management but have demonstrated their faith in HRD philosophy.

Several people have contributed to the generation of experiences reported in this book through their commitment to experimentation and other HRD values. Notable among these, with whom I had innumerable interactions and have learnt a lot, are : Dr. D.F. Pereira, Dy. General Manager, HRD of L & T: Mr. T. Shanmugam, Managing Director, State Bank of Patiala; Mr. C.R. Vijayaraghavan, Chief General Manager, SBI; Gen. O.M. Mani (ex-Chairman and Managing Director of BEML); Mr. L.C. Joshi (ex-Director Finance, BEML), Late Brig. G.K. Gokhale (Chairman and Managing Director, BEML), Mr. C.N.S. Rao (AGM, HRD of BEML); Brig. M.Y. Mudabidri (G.M. BEML); Mr. J. Swaminathan (Executive Director, Rail Coach Division of BEML); Mr. K. Shankara Narayanan (SBI); Mr. P.M. Pattabhi Raman (SBI), and many other managers of L & T, BEML, SBI and Petrofils and more recently a few managers from Crompton Greaves. My understanding of the Appraisal Systems in other countries was made possible through the opportunities provided and materials supplied by my friends like Md. Iqbal Kuppa (Director of IBBM, Malaysia); Dr. Tun Lwin (UNESCO, Bangkok); Dr. M.M.A. Bukhari (Allama Iqbal Open University, Pakistan); Dr. Subhash C. Mehta (National University of Singapore); Dr. J.E. Jayaruriya (Sri Lanka); and Dr. Peter Sheppard (SIDO, Malaysia).

I must make a special mention of the indirect contribution made by Jaya, Raju and Nandini who showed a high tolerance for my repeated and prolonged absences from home in my pursuits to complete this work.

I would also like to thank V.S. Ravi Kumar for typing most parts of this manuscript.

Professor S.K. Bhattacharya, Chief Executive of Management Structure and systems probably does not know that he has a share in this work. It was at his suggestion that Mr. Narendra Kumar of Vikas contacted me and persisted that I should complete this work faster. My thanks to both of them. Of course, Professor Bhattacharya had contributed in other ways by constantly communicating his high expectations from me.

When a management professor works with an organisation, or suggests a new scheme, one of the questions often asked is: "Do you follow in your own institute what you are teaching us"? In some areas the question may not be fully relevant as an educational institution may not be comparable completely to an industrial enterprise. In those areas where comparisons do make sense, the management professional has more confidence and credibility if he knows and sees that what he preaches is also being practised in his own institution in spirit or format or both. The develoment-oriented performance appraisal described and outlined in this book has been evolved through a process of participation of executives. But much before this, a development-oriented appraisal system was evolved and established by the great institution-builder Professor Ravi Matthai at the IIMA. Experiencing this system as a faculty member at IIMA has added greatly to my understanding and conviction. Ravi was the architect of a similar system at IIMA and has been the propagator of HRD philosophy in everything he did. He invested himself for creating learning spaces for developing several people including villagers of Jawaja, students and faculty of IIMA, and others institutions, heads of government departments and chief executives of companies. He has been the greatest source of inspiration for me during the last ten years of my work at IIMA. I have learnt a lot from him. I used to have several discussions with him about my work on performance appraisal and counselling. The setting used to be mostly the rural Jawaja between 1975 and 1978. As this book was in press, I got the shocking news of his death in London on February 13, 1984. In remembrance of the innumerable learning spaces he created, I dedicate this book to Ravi.

T.V. RAO.

ACKNOWLEDGEMENTS TO THE SECOND EDITION

The entire manuscript of this book was word processed by my Secretary at IIMA, Mr. P.G. Muraleedharan. It is his hard work that enables me to bring the second edition out in a record time. I thank Murali for all his effort and hard work.

I would particularly like to acknowledge the support given by the following individuals and organisations for including their experiences with appraisals:

1. Mr. C.R. Ramakrishnan, Joint Managing Director and Mr. S. Chandrasekar, Deputy General Manager (HRD) of Larsen & Toubro Limited (ECC Construction Group), Madras;

2. Dr. Amrita Patel, Managing Director and Shri Shailendra Kumar, Manager (HRD) of National Diary Development Board, Anand;

3. Shri K.K. Nohria, President and Managing Director and Ms. Susan Varughese, Manager (HRD) of Crompton Greaves Limited, Bombay;

4. Shri S.R. Jain, Chairman; Shri Arvind Pande, Director (Personnel & Corporate Planning) of Steel Authority of India Limited, New Delhi and Shri M.R.R. Nair, Managing Director, Steel Authority of India Limited, Bokaro Steel Plant; and

5. M/s. Life Insurance Corporation of India and particularly Shri K. Kalyanaraman, Secretary (HRD Cell)

CONTENTS

Chapter 1

PERFORMANCE APPRAISAL : THE PAST AND THE FUTURE

THERE is a great degree of unhappiness all around with performance appraisals. Rarely does one come across managers who are happy with the appraisal systems in their organisations. When such a great degree of unhappiness exists about them, why should we continue to have them? But managers find it difficult to do without them because in the absence of an appraisal mechanism, howsoever weak it may be, it is difficult to get work out of people. It is a good mechanism to control people. Employees want promotions, they want salary increments, they want good work conditions, they would like to be placed in prestigious positions, and would like to be transferred to places of their choice and like jobs giving them maximum satisfaction, and so on. Therefore, if people get what they want, they should give what their bosses want. And performance appraisal is one mechanism to make sure that people at every level do things the way their bosses want them to do. Thus the bosses at every level strive for better ratings of their own performance by assessing the performance of their subordinates and thus controlling their behaviour.

What is stated in the above paragraph is precisely the problem with our performance appraisals. That is why they are under attack from every corner. The subordinates complain that their bosses try to rate their performance without really knowing what they are doing and the constraints under which they are working. They are also not satisfied since given the same performance levels, different bosses rate the performance differently. They are also not happy because their bosses rate their performance confidentially rather than communicating and trying to help them improve. The bosses are unhappy because the form-filling has become a ritual. Year after year they have to fill the same forms for employee after employee and there is no improvement in their performance. They are also not happy because they really do not know what happens to those forms after they rate and send them to the personnel departments and dont even come to know what happens to the various recommendations they make for their subordinates' training, promotions, increments, transfers, etc. The personnel departments are unhappy because most of the forms are never received on time. The personnel departments are also not happy because managers keep on making liberal recommendations and placing demands on the personnel departments without looking into the organisational constraints. The top managements are unhappy because in spite of their efforts the quality of personnel seems to be declining day by day.

Objectives of Performance Appraisals - The Past

This situation exists today in most organisations because of lack of understanding of the potential uses of performance appraisal systems by everyone and improper designing of performance appraisals. The appraisal systems in most organisations are designed today to meet the following objectives:

1. To control employee behaviour by using it as an instrument for rewards, punishments and threats.
2. To make decisions regarding salary increases and promotions.
3. To place people to do the right kind of jobs.
4. To identify the training and developmental needs of the employees.

These objectives though appearing very good suffer from a major disadvantage. That is, they are all, at least give the impression of having been, framed from the "management" point of view rather than the "employee" point of view. This is because there seems to be the following assumptions made in these objectives:

1. Employee behaviour needs to be controlled and monitored by their bosses.
2. Rewards, punishments and threats are mechanisms of controlling employee behaviour.
3. Employees want mainly promtions and salary increments and therefore, by using performance appraisals as a basis for them, employees can be motivated to give their best as they need to get good appraisal ratings.
4. Their motivation levels are likely to be high when they do not know how their boss has rated them. This enhances the control value of appraisals.
5. The boss is in a good position to rate the appraisee and he does not need any inputs from the appraisee. In fact, the appraisee should not provide any inputs at the time of appraisal because most employees would like to put themselves in the best possible light and therefore may bias the ratings of their bosses.

6. The appraisers alone can generate objective data about employee for placement and promotion decisions.
7. Training needs can be decided through confidentially rated appraisals.
8. The reviewing authority (normally two levels above the appraisee) is in a good position to moderate the appraisal ratings and decisions of the appraiser by virtue of his position and authority and therefore, may be able to bring in objectivity through his review.
9. Assessment on a few standard dimensions like honesty, sincerety, drive, job-knowledge, dependability, leadership, etc., is sufficient to know about an individual.

Unfortunately most of these assumptions are not true or only partially true.

1. Who controls the behaviour of whom? This is not an easy question to answer. Certainly every manager has the responsibility to ensure that his subordinates perform the tasks they are required to perform and also exhibit the behaviours (attitudes, orientations, adherence to organisational values and norms, skills, qualities, etc.) that are considered desirable for them as well as for the organisation. How does he fulfil this responsibility? It is presumptuous if managers think that only they can control the behaviour of their subordinates. Every employee controls or modifies his own behaviour if he sees the need for it. The manager, as an appraiser, therefore, may provide standards and frames of reference, may increase awareness, may point out consequences of certain behaviours, may give feedback, may educate, and may take executive action wherever certain undesirable behaviours are being shown. Thus, more than an instrument for controlling employee behaviour, the appraisal should provide an opportunity for the manager to create conditions for employees to control their own behaviours by continuously examining its appropriateness for themselves and for the organisation.

2. Rewards and punishments can be effective if they are seen as rewards and punishments. If performance appraisal has direct links with rewards and punishments then it can have the potency to control behaviour. Rewards and punishments will have the desired effect if they are followed immediately by the desired undesired behaviour exhibited by the individual. On both these counts appraisal systems fail. Firstly, most employees fail to perceive the value of the rewards they get. Most public sector organisations do not have any visible mechanisms of

rewarding better performing employees. They are restricted from giving salary increments. Even in those organisations where rewards are available, quite often there is a gap of perceptions. For example, in one organisation the top management wanted bright and capable managers to be posted in the training department. As they considered training as a relatively light job, provided a lot of opportunity for professional growth and at the same time benefitted the organisation they thought it as a reward for high performing managers. However, when these managers got transferred to the training department most of their colleagues started sympathising with them because they were being sent to positions that had no power and authority. As a result, the high performing managers, who were posted as trainers, started feeling this as a punishment posting and got quite demoralised. When tangible rewards like salary increments and promotions come, they come so late that quite often managers fail to see them as rewards linked to their performance. They may just attribute it to their seniority.

Threats have very little value as they normally result in counterthreats and vitiate the work atmosphere.

3. Salaries and promotions are still viewed as symbols of recognition and status and therefore, are good mechanisms of motivating people to perform well. However, since there are limits to which any organisation can give these, they have motivational value only for a small section of employees. With an overstress on these forms of rewards, other satisfying factors like improvement in work conditions, welfare measures, personal touch, job-challenge, etc., as mechanisms of motivation are being neglected. If taken into consideration, providing these would require different formats of appraisal.

4. Researches in behavioural sciences suggest precisely the opposite of the assumption that "confidentiality has motivational value". Researches suggest that knowledge of the consequences of one's own activities and inputs helps in behaviour modification. If a person has to change his behaviour he must see the need for it and should be aware of the direction in which he should change. Confidentiality brings down the value of appraisals. In fact, uncertainty about the results of one's own effort causes a great degree of dissatisfaction in people. In a research study conducted by the author, school teachers were found to change their classroom behaviour dramatically when feedback was given to them after observations of their class performance on objective measures and they were helped to examine the implications of their own behaviour (Pareek and Rao, 1971).

5. It is true that the boss of every employee is normally in a good position to rate the employee. This is because he is likely to be more knowledgeable and experienced and at the same time has the opportunity to observe the performance of his subordinates continuously through various transactions. However, he has limitations imposed by his own time constraints, the number of people he has to supervise and the various responsibilities he carries with him. Hence he may not have sufficient opportunities to observe each of his subordinates thoroughly. Hence he has to rely on someone else to increase his objectivity. That someone else could be none other than the employee himself. It is true that the employees are likely to present themselves in the best possible manner. There is no harm in doing so because the bosses do get to know the weak spots of their employees easily and reminding the boss about the strong points of the appraisees probably does not do any more harm than leaving it entirely for the boss to rate on limited data of his observations.

6. Appraisers are certainly in an advantageous position to generate useful data about their subordinates for placement and promotion purposes, provided they know how to do it and they are provided with necessary instruments for this purpose. Generating data for promotion and placement purposes requires a thorough job analysis and assessment of individuals on the capabilities they have to perform different functions. Since performance on any given job may not give enough data about the potential of an employee for higher jobs or for future jobs, different systems of appraisal may be required. To the extent the performance on a given job is assessed in a detailed way with respect to different functions, the appraiser will be generating useful data for placement and promotions.

7. Certain training needs require no assessment. For example, when new functions are being added, new capabilities may need to be developed. These may not require any assessment in most cases. However, to bring about improvements in performance, training needs can be assessed better through the involvement of the employee. This is particularly because any training will be effective only when the trainee wants to get trained. Unless the employee himself feels the need for training, giving it may be a wastage. Secondly, unsatisfactory performance may not always be due to lack of capabilities that require training. In such cases the appraiser would do well by having a dialouge with the appraisee and then both of them jointly determining the training needs.

8. In some organisations the reviewing officer is also required to rate the assessee and the average of the ratings given by the boss and his

boss (reviewing officer) are taken into consideration. The purpose is to bring about objectivity. Normally, reviewing officers go by whatever ratings are given by the immediate boss. In those cases, where he does not agree, his feelings may be based on limited data as the opportunities he has to observe the subordinates' subordinates are rather limited. Even in case his observations are data based, by moderating or changing the ratings of the immediate superior in the form he is creating problems of credibility for the first rater which is not healthy for the organisation. Therefore the role of the reviewing officer should be more in terms of helping the reporting officers to do a good job of appraisal by pointing out their biases (if he notices any), by pointing out areas of improvement, by supplementing the data of the reporting officers, by observing the trends in appraisals and giving feedback to the reporting officers on their rating behaviour, by supplying information on training needs, etc. His own ratings of people two levels below would put constraints on his time as well as objectivity.

9. Unfortunately even today some organisations appraise the performance of their employees on traits. The trait-based system of appraisal has serious limitations. It neglects the review on direct job-related dimensions. Secondly, some of the traits take a long time to be developed and year after year unless something is done the employee may keep on showing the same behaviours and get similar ratings. It is possible to do a good job in some managerial roles without exhibiting all the traits on which the personality is being assessed. For example, a maintenance manager may do an excellent job of managing the maintenance function without exhibiting qualities like leadership, initiative, sociability, etc. Subjectivity is likely to be very high and "hale effect" (the tendency to rate the person high or low consistently on all the dimensions on the basis of an overall impression) operates.

Having examined the partial truth in some of the assumptions underlying traditional systems of appraisal, we are faced with the problem: "What kind of formats are therefore desirable for appraising managerial performance?" To answer this question we may start with a restatement of the need for performance appraisals, identify all possible objectives the appraisals can serve and then derive components of appraisal system that help in achieving these objectives.

Organisation's Philosophy on Human Resources

The nature of the performance appraisal and its effectiveness depend a great deal on how Human Resources are viewed and treated in the organisation. If the organisation believes that people do not work unless they are closely supervised and controlled, it may tend to have a confidential report form of appraisal. If the organisation believes that every individual has potential and strengths and that human capabilities can be sharpened, developed and utilised better by providing a healthy climate, then the organisation would have an appraisal system that attempts to identify, sharpen, develop and utilise the potential and capabilities of its employees.

Every employee spends a major part of his working life for the organisation. In some organisations managers spend as much as about 80 per cent of their working life for the organisation (inclusive of the time they spend at home thinking about, planning, discussing, etc., of things related to their work). An average manager of an average organisation is bound to spend at least 60 per cent of his time for his work. If the organisation and its tasks form a major part of an employee's life, shouldn't the organisation take upon itself the responsibility of making the work-life an enjoyable life? Generally, every top level manager agrees with this. However, the problem arises when it comes to the question of operationalising this. The question is: "How can you make the work-life enjoyable?" To make the work-life enjoyable, one must have some understanding of human nature. The following are some of the insights provided by behavioural science researches in the past. These should be kept in mind in designing any appraisal systems.

1. Employees would work hard when they feel that they are "wanted" in the organisation.
2. Employees would work better when they are "clear" about what they are expected to do and when they have some say periodically in modifying these expectations.
3. Employees would work better when they start "experiencing" success in the tasks they are performing.
4. Employees would work better when they feel that the organisation provides opportunities for their performance to be recognised and rewarded.
5. Employees would work better when they see that their organisation is providing them an opportunity to develop and utilising their capabilities to a large extent.
6. Employees will have a high level of commitment when they see

that their organisation is willing to inviest time and other resources for the development of its people.

7. Employees would work better when they are being trusted and treated with dignity.

Performance appraisals can serve very useful purposes if they recognise the above and take them into consideration in their purposes and processes.

New Objectives of Performance Appraisal

Performance appraisal systems can serve the following purposes, if designed properly:

1. They can help each employee to understand more and more about his role and become clear about his functions.
2. They can be instruments in helping each employee to understand his own strengths and weaknesses with respect to his role and functions in the company.
3. They can help in identifying the developmental needs of each employee with respect to his role and functions.
4. They can increase mutuality between each employee and his supervising officer so that every employee feels happy to work with his supervisor and thereby contributes his maximum to the organisation.
5. They can be mechanisms of increasing communication between the employee and his supervising officer so that each employee gets to know the expectations of his boss from him and each boss also gets to know the difficulties of his subordinates and attempts to solve them; and thus they together accomplish the tasks.
6. They can be instruments to provide an opportunity for the employee for self-reflection and individual goal-setting so that individually planned and monitored development takes place.
7. They can play a role in helping every employee internalise the culture, norms and values of the organisation so that an organisational identity and commitment is developed through out the organisation.
8. They can help in preparing employees for performing higher level jobs by continuously reinforcing the development of behaviours and qualities required for higher level positions in the organisation.
9. They can be instruments in the creation of a positive and healthy

climate in the organisation that drives people to give their best and enjoy doing so.

10. In addition they can assist in a variety of personnel decisions by generating data about each employee periodically.

A Suggested Format

In order to achieve these objectives the appraisal format should have the following components:

- Identification of key performance areas (KPAs) and target setting through periodic discussions between each employee and his boss.
- Identification of qualities required for the present and future jobs (higher level) in the company.
- Self-appraisal by the appraisee.
- Performance analysis to identify factors that have facilitated and factors that have hindered performance.
- Performance discussion and counselling to understand each other and assist each other.
- Identification of training needs.
- Action planning and goal-setting for future.
- Final assessment by the supervising officer for administrative purposes.

Each of these components is explained in some detail below.

• Identification of Key Performance Areas (KPAs)

Every job has a set of functions to be performed by its holder. In manual jobs generally these are clear and specific. As one goes up in the organisational hierarchy, for supervisory and managerial jobs, the activities and functions become complex and many keep on changing priority from time to time. For example, a marketing manager may need to focus more on market surveys during a certain period, on training his salesmen in another period and may have to spend his time mostly on promotional activities during another time. In view of these changing priorities and complexity it is necessary to identify, review, recapitulate and reflect upon the key functions periodically. Researches across the world in the past have demonstrated the existence of role-ambiguity in several jobs leading to poor performance. Hence periodic joint discussions may enable each employee to become more clear about his important functions. This helps also in subsequent appraisal of performance on these functions. In the confidential form of appraisal the employee never gets to know if he is being rated low on some functions for which he is giving less importance.

In addition to the identification of KPAs, it is useful to set targets for the period of appraisal. These targets should deal with the tasks expected to be accomplished by the appraisee under each KPA during the period that will be reviewed later. Such target setting helps the appraisee to be clear of the expectations and also provides an opportunity for his to ask for the assistance required from his boss in order to accomplish whatever was set for him. The target setting should be done through a process of mutual consultations and discussions. This itself may become an educative process in terms of understanding each other. A trusting climate should be established. It is not fair to assess the performance of any employee on tasks and targets that have not been made clear to him and that do not take into consideration his own difficulties and capabilities.

- **Managerial and Behavioural Qualities**

Another important aspect of employee performance is the extent to which each employee exhibits the qualities desired for the employees of that organisation. These qualities may be managerial qualities or behaviour constellations. These qualities are also the qualities that are increasingly required for performing functions associated with the higher level jobs in the company. Some such qualities include: creativity, initiative, contribution to team spirit, organisation ability, perseverance, etc. Every organisation should identify a list of such qualities desired to be shown by its employees and include these in the performance appraisal formats. Appraising the employees periodically on these will enable the employees to strive for these.

- **Self-Appraisal**

At the end of the year or the appraisal period the appraisal process should begin with self-appraisal by every employee. To appraise one's own self on KPAs, targets, and qualities, the appraisee would go through a process of reflection and review. Behavioural scientists have established beyond doubt that change is faster when it is self-initiated. If any employee has to improve or do better, he must first feel the need to do so. Reflection and review is a process that enables him to feel the need. Besides, when one reviews one's own performance, he also gets an opportunity to become more aware of his own strengths and weaknesses; if the review is systematic and guide. Self-appraisal sets the stage for this. For example, a salesman may say to himself that he has done well in contacting a record number of potential customers, but failed very much in selling the product. On analysis he may discover his lack of convincing skills and interpersonal communication skills. Thus self-assessment may help people to discover their developmental needs and plan for development that also helps the organisation.

- **Performance Analysis**

As a result of performance appraisal the communication between the appraisee and the appraiser should increase. The appraiser should know more and more about the circumstances under which his appraisee is working, the difficulties he is experiencing and the contribution he is making. The appraisee should also understand how he himself is responsible for some achievements or non-achievements. To meet these objectives at the end of the year the appraisee reflects about his performance and identifies factors that helped him in doing whatever he has done and factors that helped him in doing whatever he has done and factors that prevented him from doing better. He classifies these factors into factors within his control and factors outside his control. In this process he lists the difficulties he is facing. He then gives his analysis to his supervising officer who may add to the list. This addition helps the appraisee in thinking about his own strengths and environmental constraints. A look at the performance analysis form may give an idea to any outsider the complexity of forces operating within the work environment of the appraisee.

- **Performance Discussion**

After performance analysis is done the appraisee should reflect about his own performance and prepare notes of his assessment. He should then fix a time for review discussion. The review discussion is intended to understand each other more, increase mutuality and help each other so that they can jointly do better in future. The form of self-appraisal and analysis submitted by the appraisee serves as an initiator of discussions. The most important dimension of appraisal is the review discussion. People may be able to share a lot of things in mutual discussions which they may not be able to write. The purpose of the review discussion for the appraisee is to know more about the perceptions, expectations, and assessment of his boss and also to communicate his difficulties and ask for support, if needed. For the appraisee it also provides an opportunity to discover more and more of his own strengths and weaknesses. For the appraiser it is an opportunity to understand his subordinate more, help him to understand his own strengths and weaknesses, and help him to identify mechanisms for development and performance improvement.

Much of the success of the appraisal depends on this dimension. If the appraiser does not set a healthy climate and does not attempt to listen to the feelings of his appraisee, the outcome may be continued poor performance and increased tension between the two. If the appraiser uses this opportunity well, recognises and reinforces the strengths of the appraisee and assists him in discovering his own inadequacies through a process of counselling and feedback, the outcome will be good both for them and for the organisation.

- **Identifying Developmental Needs and Action Planning**

The performance analysis and review discussion would generally lead to the identification of developmental needs. Targets not accomplished or KPAs poorly performed may be indicators of inadequate understanding or lack of capabilities, (knowledge, skills, etc.). If it is lack of capabilities, development of capabilities through trainig, on-the-job coaching, etc., becomes the action plan. If poor performance is due to lack of motivation, it should be dealt with during the counselling session. Alternatively, remedial actions like transfer to other jobs, issuing warning letters, etc., may be done in special cases. Developmental needs flow directly from the assessment (self-assessment as well as the assessment by the appraiser) of performance. The appraiser should therefore indicate the developmental needs of the employee and suggest action.

His suggestions are to be attended by the personnel department or the HRD department. the HRD department collects the appraisal forms of all employees, tabulates the training needs of each category of employees and organises the training required (in-house or outside). Wherever change of job, etc., are recommended the HRD department also should initiate action at the appropriate time.

- **Final Assessment**

The final assessment should be given by the appraiser after completing all the steps mentioned above. By this stage he would have a thorough understanding of his subordinates, his accomplishments, strengths and weaknesses, developmental needs, etc., and is in a good position to assess him on a rating scale. Since such ratings are required for administrative purposes, the supervising officer should complete the process for that period by completing his final assessment. This final assessment should be shown to the employee. In case of any strong differences the appraisee should have the scope for communicating his reaction so that the appraiser's boss would have an opportunity to review the appraisal and moderate. This may be rare, but scope should be provided for this.

The ratings thus assigned are the only ones that go to the personnel department along with the developmental needs form, for administrative and other actions by them. It is these ratings that should be used to reward high performers.

Sequential Steps

The following sequences of activities is suggested for using the components outlined so far:

1. In the beginning of the year (or 6-month period) every employee sits with his supervisor and identifies his individual KPAs and sets challenging targets for the next year (or 6 months).
2. At the end of the year the employee appraises his performance on these KPAs and targets as well as pre-identified behaviours included in the appraisal format. He also completes his performance analysis.
3. He then passes on his form to his supervisor. His supervisor reflects about the performance of his appraisee and make his own notes and comments. He then calls the appraisee for a discussion.
4. During the performance discussion they exchange notes, comments, etc., and try to understand and help each other. They also identify the development needs of the appraisee and set goals for the next period.
5. The supervisor then gives his final ratings and recommends about the developmental needs. He shows these to the appraisee and takes his comments if needed and passes these on to the

personnel department through his supervisor.

6. The personnel or HRD department uses these for training, rewards and other activities.

A model format for this purpose is presented in Appendix 1.1.

Investment in human resources is in the interests of the organisation and it can have good pay-offs if certain conditions are ensured. Performance appraisal system described in this book is one such instrument on which investment can give good pay-offs. The investment should be made in terms of making managerial time available for this purpose. Assuming that every manager has, on an average, about 10 employees immediately below him, he is required to spend about 10 x 3 = 30 hours in a year for identifying KPAs, setting targets, and having performance review sessions. This constitutes less than 2 per cent of his office time. If a manager is not willing to spend this small proportion of his time to understand and help his subordinates, he has no right to expect his seniors to take care of his needs. Even such a small investment of managerial time can increase understanding between the employees and their supervisors, and establish a climate of mutuality, openness, trust, and problem-solving orientation. When such a climate is established the work place becomes an enjoyable place and the productivity of that organisation goes up.

Subsequent chapters of this book are devoted to detailed explanations of some of the important components of such a development-oriented performance appraisal system. Use of a development-oriented performance appraisal system should be based on a good understanding of the concept of development, the need for developing employee capabilities, the nature of these capa bilities, some of the mechanisms of developing these capabilities, the conditions under which these capabilities can be developed and so on. In the second chapter these issues are discussed and the role of performance appraisls in Human Resources Development (HRD) is elaborated.

Key Performance Areas, Self-Appraisal, Performance Analysis, Performance Ratings and Counselling are the most important components of a development-oriented performance appraisal system. Each of these components is discussed in some detail in Chapters 3, 4, 5, 6 and 7. Chapter 7, presents various aspects of performance counselling. Chapter 8 presents some of the ways in which appraisal data can be used. Chapters 9 to 15 present case studies of some organisations practising or trying to practice such development-oriented performance appraisal systems. Voltas have evolved a development-oriented appraisal system on the basis of their own experiments and experiences over years. Larsen & Toubro Limited is the first company in India to introduce such a development-oriented performance appraisal system almost a decade ago as a part of an integrated Human Resource Development System. Some details of the system have been given as it exists today in Larsen & Toubro Limited. The State Bank of India (SBI) has recently experimented with a development-oriented appraisal system and is now in the process of introducing the same all through the bank covering several thousands of officers. Chapter 14 presents the details of the SBI experiment. Any organisation interested in changing its appraisal system from control-oriented confidential reports to a development-oriented system is actually initiating a change in its culture. Such a change is slow, and is likely to be resisted even if it is good for the employees and, therefore, should be carefully planned and monitored. The experiences of a public sector industry in introducing such a system are described in Chapter 15.

Chapter 16 and 17 highlight the performance appraisal practices in India and in other Asian countries. Chapter 18 presents some suggestions and considerations for performance appraisal systems to succeed.

Chapters 19, 20 and 21 present the current practices, experiences and thinking in the field.

Appendix 1.1

Performance Appraisal Form*

Form I

This form is to be filled at the end of the performance year first by the employee and then by his reporting officer. This form is the basis of performance and development interview.

Name of the employee ________ Designation ______ Department ______

Name of the reporting officer ________ Designation ________

Section A : Rating

Listed below are the objectives under different Key Performance Areas (KPAs) which you, in consultation with your Reporting Officer, agreed to complete. Against each objective, give a rating indicating to what extent the objective was achieved in time. Use 5-point scale (1, 2, 3, 4, 5).

Key Performance Areas and Objectives	Weightage (A, B, C)	Self-rating	Rating by Reporting Officer	Remarks by Reporting Officer
KPA 1				
KPA 2				
KPA 3				
KPA 4				
Overall achievements of work objectives				

*From Rao and Pareek (1978)

Behavioural Dimensions	Self-rating	Rating by Reporting Officer	Remarks by Reporting Officer
1. Initiative taken in solving difficulties in achieving the objectives			
2. Creativity shown in solving some problems			
3. Contribution to the building of team spirit through working with others			
4. Contribution made to the development of own employees			
5. Any other outstanding behaviour shown (specify)			

Signature of the employee

Comments and Sig..
by the Reviewing Officer:

Signature by the Reporting Officer

Section B : Performance Analysis

Consider your overall performance and achievements in the last year. Write down below what you see as factors that helped you in achieving whatever you achieved, and factors that prevented you from doing better. These factors may relate to you and within your control (personal) or may be outside your control (environmental).

Facilitating and inhibiting factors	What do you intend to do?	What support you expect from your	Comments by the Reporting Officer
Facilitating factors (Personal)			
Facilitating factors (Envirnomental)			
Inhibiting factors (Personal)			
Inhibiting factors (Environmental)			

Developmental needs of the employee (mention specific needs and suggestions for improving these)

Comments by the Reviewing Officer:

Performance Appraisal Summary

Form II

(To be filled by the Reporting Officer for all the employees he nas assessed)

Employees' Names	Achievement of work Objectives	Initiative	Creativity	Collaboration	Contribution to the development of employees	Other behaviours	Remarks

Signature :

Remarks by the Reviewing Officer

Remarks and signatures by others in line through whom the form goes to GM.

1.
2.
3.

Remarks and signature by the GM.

Development Needs

Form III

(To be filled in duplicate by the Reporting Officer for all the employees reporting to him on the basis of Form I and to be sent to HRD Office)

Employees' names	Development needs	Proposal to meet these needs	Remarks

Signature :

Remarks by the Reviewing Officer :

Remarks by others in line through whom the form goes to GM

1.
2.
3.

Remarks by the GM

Chapter 2

HUMAN RESOURCES DEVELOPMENT AND PERFORMANCE APPRAISAL

The strength of any organisation is its people. If people are attended to properly by recognising their talents, developing their capabilities and utilising them appropriately, organisations are likely to be dynamic and grow fast. Ultimately the variety of tasks in any organisation have to be accomplished by the people. Some of them may have capabilities to do certain tasks better than other tasks and some of them may not have capabilities to do the tasks assigned to them. In any case one of the important process goals of any dynamic organisation is to ensure that its people are capable of doing the variety of tasks associated with their roles/positions. Some of these tasks may be prescribed, well understood and defined well, whereas some of them may not be all that clear and the employees themselves may have to identify these. Therefore, achievement of this process goal requires the organisation to be sensitive to the role requirements on the one hand and the employee capabilities on the other hand. This sensitiveness should lead to the identification of developmental needs and creation of opportunities for development.

People may be treated as resources available for the organisation. By nature, unlike other resources, these resources are dynamic. Unlike the physical resources, human resources have the capability of expanding to unlimited extents. This is because with proper investments the human capabilities can be multiplied. When the capabilities of people in any organisation are multiplied, the organisation has wider choices to make for performing different functions. Such an availability of resources also helps the organisation in its growth in terms of diversification, expansion, vitality, dimensions, etc.

Human beings also have a need to grow and develop themselves professionally. Development of their capabilities keeps them to be psychologically vital. This development needs to be monitored in terms of matching it with organisational requirements.

Therefore, any organisation, interested in developing the capabilities of its employees, should understand the nature of capabilities required to perform different functions as well as the dynamics underlying the development of these capabilities in an organisational context. In the subsequent sections of this chapter an attempt is made to provide an understanding of both these aspects.

Capability Requirements of Different Categories of People in an Organisation

People in any organisation are involved in performing a variety of activities. Performing these activities would require a variety of capabilities. These capabilities can be considered to fall under four categories. These include technical capabilities, managerial capabilities, behavioural capabilities and conceptual capabilities [Katz (1970) identified only three types of skills - technical, human and conceptual]. Technical capabilities involve an understanding of, and proficiency in, a specified kind of activity, particularly one involving methods, processes, procedures and technics. Doctors, engineers, musicians, machine operators, stenographers, etc., are loaded with these kinds of capabilities. Most of the professional training of these categories of people is loaded with these capabilities.

Managerial capabilities involve planning, organising, coordinating, monitoring, controlling, evaluating, supervising, etc., of a variety of organisational activities. Professional training of administrators, managers and supervisors is heavily loaded with these skills.

Human capabilities are concerned with the ability of people to deal with other people. In the organisational context, these may include abilities to motivate others, influence others, lead others, generate team spirit, resolve conflicts, etc. Short-term training programmes like Sensitivity Training, Personal Growth Labs, Leadership Training, Motivation Labs, Counselling Workshops, etc., aim at developing these capabilities. Professional training of managers includes this component to a very limited extent and mostly stops at providing cognitive inputs rather than attitude change and skill development. Human skills are demonstrated in the way the individual perceives his superiors, colleagues and subordinates and the way he behaves subsequently. A person with highly developed human skills is aware of his own attitudes, strengths and weaknesses, needs and values, and also assumptions and beliefs about other people (individuals and groups). Besides, he is able to see the usefulness and limitations of his own capabilities and orientations and is able to appreciate the differences in orientations and capabilities others have vis-a-vis his own. While he has positiveness, appreciation and tolerance for others' views, opinions, orientations and capabilities, he is also able to communicate effectively his own intentions and views. Such a person is able to create an atmosphere of appraisal and security in which subordinates feel free to express themselves without fear of censure or ridicule, by encouraging them to take initiative, to act and learn. Thus the following qualities characterise the human skills of a manager.

1. Self-awareness, including awareness of one's own strengths, weaknesses, needs, values, attitudes, styles and beliefs in relation to different individuals, groups, events and situations that relate to various tasks he is involved in.
2. Ability to predict his personal reactions and responses to the stimuli created by other people.
3. Appreciation of the needs, values, beliefs, orientations, and strengths and weaknesses of others who interact with him even if they differ from those of his own.
4. Sensitiveness to the needs, values, beliefs, attitudes, orientations and capabilities of others.
5. Ability to predict the consequences of his behaviour in terms of its impact on others.
6. Ability to control his own emotions and others' behaviours.
7. Certain amount of openness, risk-taking and perceptiveness.
8. An ability to receive and use feedback.

Real skill in working with others should become a part of the individual's system and thus be a continuous activity as human skills are required in almost every activity a manager undertakes. Human skill cannot be developed in a short time. A strong desire on the part of the individual to develop his human skills is essential. Along with this an orientation to continuously experiment and introspect is also required.

Conceptual skills involve the ability to see the enterprise as a whole. It includes recognising how the various functions of the organisation depend on one another and how changes in one part affect all the other parts and it extends to visualising the relationship of the individual business to the industry, the community, and the political, social and economic forces of the nation as a whole. Conceptual skills also include the ability to visualise the future of the organisation and give it a direction in terms of such a vision for the organisational future.

These four categories of capabilities are involved in performing different roles in any organisation. These are required in different combinations for performing effectively different roles. For example, lower level job holders like operators, technicians, skilled workers, stenographers, first level engineers, etc., require a high level of technical capabilities. Once we go to the junior and middle level managers they require managerial capabilities like planning, monitoring, coordinating, etc. As one goes still higher up in the managerial hierarchy, behavioural and conceptual capabilities also become very important. For example, if the head of a department or a general manager does not have leadership and team-building capabilities he may not be able to lead that unit well. It is common experience to find heads of departments who are insensitive to human processes in their own department, and through their behaviour demoralise the entire staff of that department.

EXHIBIT 2-1

Capability Requirements for Different Levels of Jobs

Capabilities / Jobs	Technical	Managerial	Behavioural	Conceptual
1. Operators, Skilled Workers, Clerks Typists, Foremen, etc.	Very much essential	Not needed	Some desirable Some essential	Not needed
2. First Level Supervisors, Junior	Very essential	A few are desirable	Some desirable Some essential	Not needed
3. Junior and Middle Level Managers	Some important Many not essential	Important	Some essential	A few are useful
4. Senior Managers Heads of Departments/sections	A few are desirable	Very essential	Many are needed Some are important	Desirable
5. Unit Heads, General Manager, etc.	A few are desirable	Very essential	Many are essential and important	Essential
6. Chief Executives	Not needed	Important	Very essential	Most essential

As organisations cannot afford to have a large number of people demoralised, the need to ensure that senior managers are equipped with the necessary behavioural capabilities. The top level managers (the corporate management) require a high degree of conceptual capabilities. In order to lead the organisation, they need to be visionaries. The level of capabilities required for performing different categories of employees are presented in Exhibit 2.1. It may be noted that the technical capabilities include knowledge and skills relating to various technologies and processes; managerial capabilities include knowledge of various management systems and techniques as well as skills to develop and use them; behavioural capabilities involve knowledge about behaviour processes, attitudes and skills; and conceptual capabilities include knowledge about interrelationship between the organisation and various social, economic and political sub- systems in the country.

Mechanisms of Developing these Capabilities

There are three behaviour dimensions involved in most of the capabilities. These are cognitive, affective and active. The cognitive dimension of a capability involves gaining of an under standing, knowledge, information, insight, etc., in order to perform the task. The affective dimension deals with gaining the motivation and desire to use the knowledge and understanding one has. The active dimension deals with the skill involved actually in performing the task.

As an example let us take the position of an Assistant Manager - Progress in a heavy engineering company. This is a link role in the production process. The incumbent of this role has to work with various shops where different components are made for a particular product X. Some of the components go to the assembly shop straight away. Some of the components go from one shop to another after completion for further processing. The components involved run into a few hundreds and there are 12 shops where the components are being made. The Assistant Manager - Progress has to keep track of the status of these components in each shop and ensure speeding up of work processes, better utilisation of men and machines, and reduce build-up of in-process inventories. The most important function of this position is follow-up and knowl edge of the status of process-components. His role involves monitoring the production processes of various components, planning of the work, preparation of job cards, etc. The following capabilities are required to perform this function:

1.0 Technical Capabilities

1.1 Knowledge of various inputs (components), their status and their physical location (cognitive).

1.2 Knowledge of status of inspection (cognitive).

1.3 Knowledge of working of various departments (cognitive).

1.4 Knowledge of machine capabilities and loads (cognitive)

2.0 Managerial Capabilities

2.1 System development capabilities (cognitive and active).

2.2 Ability to forsee problems and plan (cognitive, affective and active).

2.3 Ability to organise men and allocate responsibilities (affective and active).

2.4 Ability to take decisions at a short notice (cognitive, affective and active).

3.0 Behavioural

3.1 Assertive - should not yield to deviations unless supported by genuine reasons (effective, active).

3.2 Sociability - should have good poise for meeting people both on task and non-task matters (affective, active).

3.3 Memory - (cognitive).

3.4 Practicality - should not sit on procedural matter but take pragmatic approach (affective).

In the above example, it may be noted that the technical capabilities required are mostly at cognitive level. Thus a mere under standing is enough. Whereas, the managerial capabilities require understanding, attitudes and action. For example, to develop systems he needs to have knowledge of techniques and systems (e.g. computerised information systems as hundreds of components are involved, monitoring systems, scheduling techniques, etc.) and should have skills in developing and using these systems. Behavioural capabilities may involve mostly affective (attitudinal) and active (skill) dimensions. For other roles the combinations may be different. For example, a Design Engineer should have not only technical capabilities at cognitive level but more importantly at the active (skill) level.

It is relatively easier to develop cognitive abilities as compared to attitudinal and action capabilities. Reading books and other literature and attending lectures and lecture-based courses help acquiring these abilities. Skills can be developed only through actual participation by doing the tasks in real life settings, simulated setting and laboratory settings. For example, one cannot be a good surgeon by listening to lectures on surgery. Practice is needed. The more the practice one gets the better would be the developments of these skills. The more guided the practice and the more one has opportunities to assimilate the experience of practical training through a process of review, reflection and integration with cognitive learning (theory) the higher the level of skill development. Professional education in an engineering college or a management institute equips people mostly with cognitive abilities but not necessarily with skills. Engineering colleges through the use of laboratories, workshops and field experiences attempt to prove a few technical skills. Management schools normally dont go beyond the development of cognitive abilities. Those institutions that use case method, organisational experience through summer training, project methods, etc., attempt to develop a small component of managerial skills. However, such attempts are limited only to a few institutions and even these institutions mostly use practical experience to increase cognitive abilities rather than to develop skills. For example, case method is a very useful tool for developing analytical abilities of managers, but analytical abilities developed through this still remain at cognitive level, although it may facilitate acquisition of action capabilities subsequently.

Development of capabilities under the affective domain is mostly neglected in all educational institutions. People acquire motives, attitudes and values in a completely unplanned way by observing others (elders in the family, seniors in the society and the school, the faculty in educational institutions, superiors in the organisations, etc.).

From this discussion the following conclusions may be drawn :

Educational institutions at present mostly focus on cognitive development and therefore a major responsibility of attitudinal and skill development particularly in relation to managerial and behavioural capabilities lies with the employing organisation itself.*

**It is not the intention here to take away the responsibility of attitudinal and skill development from the educational institutions and give it to organisations. This is only reflective of the existing state of affairs in educational institutions. There are instances where employing organisations had to put in efforts to make their new recruits unlearn some of the attitudes and orientations they acquired in educational institutions. In fact these institutions should thoroughly examine their role and put in more efforts in a planned way to develop particularly the affective dimensions (attitudes, values, motivations, etc.)*

Thus the responsibility of developing employee capabilities to suit its own requirements lies with the organisation. This responsibiity is likely to remain even if educational institutions do an extremely good job of thoroughly preparing students on all the three dimensions because organisationally suited development can take place better in organisational settings. If this is imperative, it is necessary to understand the dynamics of development. For this purpose we need to understand the concept of development, the conditions under which development takes place, climate required for development. These are discussed below and it is in this context an attempt is made to show that performance appraisal systems can be an effective instrument for developing employee capabilities (particularly managerial and human).

Concept and Conditions of Development

Development involves acquisition of new capabilities (cognitive, affective and active). In the organisational context it involves, acquisition of capabilities (technical, managerial, behavioural and conceptual) that would enable a person to perform well the different functions associated with the role he is performing at a given point of time or the role he is likely to perform subsequently.

For developing the capabilities, the following conditions must be met:

1. The individual should himself be interested in developing his own capabilities. Development cannot be forced on any one. If the person is not interested, he is not likely to learn. Therefore, it is necessary to ensure that the person is himself interested in development. Periodic appraisal of performance is one of the mechanisms of development. Knowledge of the effects of one's own behaviour or performance feedback has some motivational value. When an employee knows that his performance is being appraised, he would have a desire to maintain it high because every individual has the need to maintain his self-respect and proper self-image. As he is being compared with others, the moment he recognises any inadequacy in his capabilities, he would try to acquire these capabilities. So organisations have the responsibility to create a climate that motivates people to acquire more and more capabilities. This can be done through linking performance with rewards and creation of learning opportunities.

2. The individual would develop his capabilities faster and better when he is aware of the direction in which he could develop.

Development is faster when it is directed. The individual should know the directions in which he can develop and the directions in which he needs development. Directions in which he can develop can be decided by an assessment of his basic abilities, aptitudes and potential. His development needs are decided by the nature of jobs he is performin and those he would be required to perform in future. In relation to jobs he is already performing the individual shuld be helped to become clear about his develepent needs. In relation to jobs he is likely to perform in future also, he should be helped to understand the same. Both these can be done by those who are his supervising officers by virtue of their knowledge about him and the organisation. Understanding of one's potential should come from early school days when those who observe the individual in action, his interests, his accomplishments provide him a feedback and the individual also collects such feedback about himself.

3. The individual should make clear choices about the directions in which he would like to grow and develop.

People normally have a lot more potential than they use. Once recognised, the individual should decide the direction in which he would like to grow. For example, an engineer might recognise that he is good at designing, production, industrial engineering, research and development and so on. At some point of time in his career he has to make a choice about the line he would like to pursue (unless he makes a decision to be in each of these for some time not mastering any of them even in this case if he makes a conscious choice he is likely to do well).

4. He must be aware of his strengths and weaknesses that help him move in that direction.

Awareness of strengths and weaknesses helps the individual to continue to retain his strengths and also make efforts to develop in weak areas so that he becomes effective. Feedback from superiors helps in becoming more and more aware of one's strengths and weaknesses.

5. The individual should identify the opportunities within and outside the organisation for his development with the help of his supervisors and others with whom he interacts.

Supervising officers have the responsibility of helping an individual identify these opportunities as well as to create mechanisms for using these opportunities. They have this responsibility because when the individual develops, it is very much for the benefit of the organisation.

6. The individual should then make efforts to develop.

These efforts may be in terms of learning new skills, reading books, experimenting, trying out new methods, new systems, applying what he learns in a training, etc. Unless he makes efforts, learning is likely to be limited.

7. He should then review the consequences of his learning and application of learning periodically with the help of his boss.

The boss here works as a trainer, motivator, feedback giver as well as a coach and guide. Such coaching plays an immensely useful rule. This is most crucial phase of development. The supervising officer therefore should provide a positive emotional and professional climate for the development of his employees. Open and supportive feedback, a climate of trust, empathy and mutuality facilitate development.

Thus promoting employee development is the function of both the employee as well as his supervising officer. Periodic review of performance, feedback and planned experimentation become important factors in development.

In the example of the Assistant Manager - Progress, let us imagine that a particular manager M is not doing well. M may have made his mark in the production department earlier as an excellent assistant manager of production. As he has aspirations to become eventually a factory manager, he would like to perform a few different roles and test himself out. In their plan for job rotation, the top management has now put him in the progress department. Now how does he develop?

According to the conditions stated above, the following should happen for M to develop as a good manager of the progress function:

1. He should first know that he is not doing well. This can be done through a systematic performance review and feedback by his supervising officer. He should therefore get interested in developing his capabilities as a progress manager.

2. He should know what exactly he is lacking to do well as a progress manager. He discovers this with the help of his supervisor. He may list various functions he is expected to perform and may then review with his boss the functions on which he is not doing well. He may discover that he has been failing on one critical function - system development - because he has not acquired these capabilities.
3. He may therefore decide with the help of his boss that he should develop his system development capabilities. They may jointly also identify an appropriate training programme M should attend to develop his system development capabilities. Meanwhile he may also try to learn some of these by reading books suggested by his boss, by discussing with his boss and those who performed that job well in the past. He may also attempt to develop simple systems to monitor the movement of critical components.
4. After attending a training programme he may work hard and develop a new system (one that was not tried out so far in that company). Initially he runs into problems. He discusses this problem with his boss who encourages him to consult some experts and also provides support for his travel to visit an expert.
5. After all the efforts the system may be established and may prove to be a fairly good system.

Thus the organisation has a better system and the individual has new capabilities which are useful to the organisation as well as the individual for the present and for the future. Thus development involves systematic review of performance on different functions and assessment of capabilities, identification of development needs, creation of development opportunities and supportive climate for improvement and experimentation.

In the subsequent year M and his boss may identify "assertiveness" as a new area for development of M's capabilities. Thus the development process continues for the good for the individual as well as the organisation. In this process the employee as well as his supervising officers have joint responsibility - the individual's responsibility is to desire and make efforts for development whereas that of his boss is to create conditions.

Development of managerial and human capabilities requires continuous feedback, review, reflection and action. It is relatively a little more difficult to develop behaviour capabilities in adults as compared to the development of managerial capabilities. This is because behaviour capabilities require development of certain attitudes and orientations and often these have already been formed through a process of early socialisation. Developing these capabilities requires more support, review and feedback from the supervising officers as well as high involvement on the part of the individual. For example, a supervising officer may discover that one of his subordinates is very creative but lacks initiative. Whenever he is asked for suggestions, he gives any ideas and he is incapable of any self-initiated independent action. Realising the capabilities, his boss may want to help him develop initiative-taking abilities. Now how does he develop this? First the employee should understand his ohter capabilities. He should also be helped to understand how his lack of initiative is hampering the expression of other abilities. The individual should be helped to understand opportunities for his to take initiative in his work-life and also motivated to take initiative. This requires supportive feedback and continuous help through discussions. Whenever opportunities for taking initiative comes, it can be pointed out to him. Whenever he takes initiative, feedback and encouragement could be given. The individual may not take the initiative on his own in the first few occasions. He may require coaching and encourage ment andeven detailed discussion (counselling) to help him understand the dynamics of his behaviour. Thus helping him to move step by step his initiative-taking behaviour could be im proved. Some employees respond very fast to feedback and others take more time. Behaviour capabilities can also be developed through feedback, review, reflection and experimentation.

Chapter 3

PLANNING PERFORMANCE FOR ROLE CLARITY ACCOUNTABILITY AND EFFECTIVENESS

Indian managers are excellent in managing crisis situations. They are equally good in creating such crisis situations. While each executive emerges out as competent in handling the crisis created by others, little does he realise the role he plays in creating crisis for others.

Organisational life is full of interdependencies. Effective performance of tasks of one manager may depend on the task performance of another manager. Managers waste a lot of time negotiating with each other, managing each other, sorting out their ego problems and so on. Crisis management also keeps the manager constantly powerful as the manager can break all rules, use up organisational resources, cut the chain of command, take away the autonomy of subordinates and show to the top that he is doing a lot of work. Crisis management is a good way to cover up ones own inefficiencies and postpone less enjoyable and non-tangible things like planning and development. So powerful is the crisis management competence of Indian managers by habit and attitude that it is very difficult to get them to plan their performance or the performance of their subordinates.

Performance planning fixes accountability, sets role boundaries, helps better time management and requires time at least once a year. It also helps the manager to understand and analyse his contributions and increases his responsibility for continuous performance.

Performance planning may be defined as a systematic outlining of the activities the manager is expected to undertake during a specified period so that he is able to make his best contributions to the developmental and organisational outcomes. The activities thus outlined are indicative of the nature of contributions the manager as an individual in his role is expected to make to the departmental goals. They also provide a framework for performing the role. They indicate how the manager is likely to be spending his time during the year. They also indicate the quality, magnitude and variety of contributions he is expected to make.

They set directions for time management. They indicate what could be expected by all those whose contributions are to be based on his contributions and what is expected from those whose contributions become inputs for this manager's work. Performance planning also indicates the relative emphasis to be placed by the individual on different activities he undertakes during the year.

Whose Performance is to be Planned

Often it is said that individuals performance cannot be planned and it is the department or organisation's performance that can be planned. I would like to argue that it is easier to plan an individual's performance rather than that of an organisation's. This may be true for several reasons. Every individual manager understand the reality and circumstances under which he is expected to perform. Individual performance is subject to much lesser uncertainties than that of an organisation. The organisational uncertainties are a sum of the uncertainties faced by each employee and those from the external environment. Not all managers are required to deal with external environment. Most individuals can plan their performance with some understanding of internal uncertainties in the organisation. Unfortunately managers seem to imagine too many uncertainties facing the organisation and feel as though each one of them is going to affect the role he as an individual is likely to perform. Hence they argue that performance cannot be planned. This is a good escape mechanism.

Organisational plans at best can be goals to strive for. Individuals plans should be the actions expected to be undertaken by the individual manager with the hope of achieving the organisational goals. Organisational goals, corporate plans, mission statements, annual operating plans, budget statements, performance guidelines etc., issued from the CEOs office from time to time provide the perspective and framework required for thinking out the departmental goals and thus provide the context for an individual performance plan. However, individual performance plans need not wait every year for such context as the context exists most often and only marginal changes are expected from year to year with some exceptions.

It is ideal of these guidelines are available before the individual plans his performance. But in the absence of such guidelines every group of managers can sit together and set new goals for their department in the context of their previous years performance and their knowledge of the current situation by asking a few questions like:

How have we done last year?
What influenced our performance?
How can we improve over it?
What new challenges can we undertake?
How is the situation going to be different this year?
How do we intend to improve our quality and quality of outputs?

What new process, technology, systems etc., do we want to introduce this year? Organisations should set their goals and plan their strategies. Departments and other sub-systems should delineate their roles and plan their contributions. Individuals should plan their performance. Ideally the sequence should be from organisation to department to individual. It helps in many ways. However, one should not wait for the other indefinitely. Lack of information on organisational plans and strategies should not prevent departments and other sub-units from planning their improvements and individuals from planning their performance.

Often it is argued that the organisational plans should follow individual plans. This is against the reality in Indian organisations. First of all it does not make sense to consolidate individual plans to make departmental goals and then determine organisational goals. It is difficult to do so. Secondly participative management cannot be stretched to such an extent.

Planning Individual Performance

Annual Performance Appraisal exercises provide good opportunities for performance planning. There are many ways in which individual performance can be planned. Some of these include:

1. Task Analysis and/or Activity Analysis
2. Key Performance Areas
3. Key Result Areas
4. Task and Target Identification
5. Activity Plans/Action Plans
6. Goal Setting Exercises.

All these are different methods of planning an individuals performance on a given job annually. There are only subtle differences in these six methods mentioned above. All these methods emphasise to some extent the key tasks the individual is expected to perform as a part of his role during the year. Some of them emphasise a detailed analysis and listing of all activities (Task Analysis or Activity Analysis), others emphasise the outcomes or results expected or targeted by the individual KRAs, Goal Setting Exercises), a few others emphasise the planning part of the work (Activity Plans etc.) and some others emphasise the performance or what the individual is expected to do (KPAs).

The distinctions are smaller if we treat each of these as different ways of planning performance. Any of these could be used. There is no standard technology available for each of these methods. What is important is that the individual should be able to plan his work and as a result of that should have more clarity of the activities on which he should put his effort.

The author feels that the Key Performance Area approach is best suited for the purpose of planning as it emphasises individual performance and also gives scope for quantification. This approach is explained in detail in this Chapter.

KPAs and Performance Planning

Identifying KPAs and setting quantifiable targets wherever possible is only one way of planning ones performance. Some organisations stress on increasing objectivity in ratings through KPAs. The author is of the view that "increasing objectivity" depends on a number of factors. KPAs help reducing subjectivity but sometimes not in very visible ways. Objectivity in appraisals is difficult to achieve and ratings will always have limitations as explained in subsequent chapters. Hence organisations would do better in aiming at inculcating a planning orientation and role clarity through KPAs than improving objectivity.

A lot of managerial time gets wasted in goal-setting process if it aims at objectivity and some ill-feelings also may be associated with it. On the other hand if KPAs or target setting are viewed as performance planning, role clarity and direction setting mechanisms the numbers assigned to weightages etc., take a different meaning.

There is no well tested out technology of identifying Key Performance Area. If the following questions can be answered positively after the KPA exercise one could say that KPAs have been well identified.

1. Do the KPAs and targets emphasise/indicate what the manager (appraisee) is expected to do by himself (rather than what his department, subordinates etc., are expected to do?).
2. Together do they cover a large part of his job and include all significant contributions expected from his role?
3. Do they indicate the priority areas of work for the appraisee during the year?
4. If all KPAs are well done can the appraisee to be labelled as a good performer?
5. Are the targets set challenging and stretch the capabilities of the appraisee moderately rather than being routine?
6. Are they comprehensive?
7. Do they specify the standards of performance expected from the appraisee?
8. Do they take into consideration realistically the conditions under which the appraisee is expected to function during the year?
9. Are they satisfying both to the appraisee and appraiser?
10. Has adequate time been spent on the process of identifying KPAs and gaining role clarity?

All these questions cannot be answered by looking at the written KPAs on a piece of paper. The appraisee and appraiser are the best judges about these.

The Need for Clarity of Roles and Functions in Modern Organisations

Any organisation interested in its growth has to be dynamic. Dynamic organisations are continuously on alert looking for growth opportunities, creating challenges for themselves and making an impact on their environment. Such an organisation has to have certain amount of flexibility in its own internal organisational structure, roles and role relationships. Thus dynamic organisations are continuously in the progress of change either in response to its own needs and growth plans or in response to the environmental changes. These changes have impact on the roles - particularly the managerial roles in any organisation. For example, in the banking system the role of the banks today is substantially different from the role they were playing about 20 years ago. With the taking up of agricultural development and lead bank roles, working with government agencies, supporting small-scale industries and participation in the industrial development of backward areas, etc., the role of branch managers and other officers of the bank today has become much more complex and demanding than it used to be in the past. The rising expectations of a variety of clients and the changing scene of industrial relations have imposed additional demands on the role of branch managers and other officers. This change in roles is true with many organisation. For example, the role of personnel managers in most of the organisations has been changing as new demands are being created on them due to changes in the environment as well as growth of organisations.

The nature of managerial roles is such that it is not possible nor is it desirable to rigidly define all the tasks and functions associated with it. In fact effective managers are constantly creating new tasks and functions for themselves around the roles assigned to them and top management of organisations would do well in encouraging such dynamism among managers.

In the previous chapter we have examined the need for developing capabilities among managers to perform different functions. We have also stated that the first step in development is the creation of a desire to develop. We have also seen that development is faster when the individual sees the need as well as the direction for development. These conditions require a thorough under standing of his role and the functions associated with it. This also requires an understanding of the capabilities required to perform different functions. For example, in the case of the assistant manager of progress, it was easy to identify that he lacks system development capabilities because we were aware of the different functions associated with his role. Similarly, we could identify the need to develop his assertiveness because we were aware of the capability requirements of his role. Thus in order to help people to develop various capabilities, a clear understanding of the different functions associated with their roles and the capability requirements need to be clearly understood. Performance review along these dimensions is likely to be more meaningful and helpful for development. The concept of key performance areas explained below intends to serve this purpose.

KPAs as Mechanisms of Role Clarity and Development

Key performance areas may be defined as the important, or critical categories of functions to be performed by any role incumbent, over a given period of time. These categories of functions should be so defined that the performance of any employee can be assessed meaningfully for any given period of time. In addition these functions should specify what the employee would be doing rather than what results are expected from him. Some examples of KPAs are:

For a Sales Officer
1. Contacting potential customers
2. Market survey for new products
3. Attending to customer complaints, etc

For a R & D Manager
1. Identifying product improvements
2. Development of new products
3. Testing out samples, etc.

For an Accounts Manager
1. Budget preparation
2. Payment of bills to suppliers
3. Developing a system of computerisation

For a Branch Manager of a Bank
1. Balancing of ledgers
2. Public relations
3. Recovery of sick accounts
4. Mobilising new deposits, etc.

As the above samples of KPAs indicate, KPAs are broad categories of functions to be performed by any employee in relation to his job. Normally KPAs can be obtained from job descriptions if such job descriptions are elaborate and extensive. However, most often the job descriptions maintained by most organisations are very broad and sketchy. Even if they are supplied to new incumbents of any job, they may not be able to get a complete picture. Also for the reasons mentioned earlier in this chapter the nature of jobs may be changing. Hence it is desirable to have periodic exercises in identifying performance areas for each role and KPAs for each person in relation to his role.

The following is the process recommended for identifying key performance areas in the context of the appraisal system suggested in this book.

Identifying Performance Areas for a Given Role (Existing)

1. A small group consisting of 4 or 5 persons may be involved in this process. This is because once identified these PAs may form a bais for any role incumbent to identify his own KPAs in that role. This group

should consist of mainly two categories of people - those who are performing that role at present and those who performed that role in the past and are new supervising those performing that role now. This group is constituted to list all the tasks associated with that role and then to classify them into meaningful categories. Hence those who are currently involved in performing the role are likely to give exhaustive information about the tasks they are handling. Those who are supervising them will be able to provide guidance and in the process may sharpen their own clarity about their subordinate's role, its relationships with them and their obligations to the role incumbent.

In some cases the same role (or designation) may have dif ferent functions associated with it. For example, in a divisionalised organisation, each divisional manager may have different set of function to perform depending upon the nature of the division they handle - its size, its location, its history in the organisation. Similarly, in a marketing organisation with different branches or zones, the branch/zonal managers located in different geographic regions may have different functions to perform (although their designations are the same). In such cases it may be useful to constitute separate groups for each role. If it is not feasible to have such groups for any reason, the role incumbent and his supervising officer may jointly work and identify the performance areas. In this case the same pair can also identify the KPAs using the procedure described below.

2. The group should then sit together and make an exhaustive list of all the tasks the role incumbent is expected to undertake. In making such a list of tasks the following questions may be useful:

– What are the main activities in which the role incumbent is involved?
– What exactly does he do in these activities?
– How much of his time goes for each of these activities?
– What can be considered to be his unique contributions by virtue of occupying this position?
– If his performance is to be rated as excellent in the next 6 months/one year what would he have done as this role incumbent? etc.

Answers to these questions may provide a set of tasks/activities to be undertaken by the role incumbent. An exhaustive list needs to be prepared.

3. In the next step all these activities may be grouped into meaningful categories of functions. All activities/tasks that can be classified under one category should be classified into it. If any activity/task by itself is considered critical and deserves special attention it could be spearately listed as a performance area without grouping it into any area. While there is no hard and fast rules about the number of performance areas for any role, normally these are around 10 (in some cases it is possible to have as many as 20).

4. After the performance areas are identified they could be given weightages for their relation importance to that role. Thus a weightage of 3 could indicate that the particular PA is very central and important to that role. A rating of 2 may indicate that the PA is quite important but is not as central. A weightage of 1 may indicate that the performance area is important. There may be few performance areas which may not be considered as important contributions of the role incumbent. These are the ones on which the employee need not be appraised separately as they do not need that much attention. Thus the group could make their suggestions on the weightages to be assigned to the performance areas. These weightages are only suggestive and may change from time to time or from one role incumbent to another. The group only gives their suggestions.

5. After such an exercise is done the PAs for different roles could be listed and made available to employees in the form of a directory of performance areas. This directory helps as a basic guideline to set the thinking of every employee in planning his work for any given period.

6. For performance appraisal purposes, in the beginning of the year (exact period to be decided by each organisation), every employee discusses with his boss, and considering the plans of the organisation or his department and the nature of demands that he has to meet for the coming year, he selects or identifies the performance areas. The areas selected or identified should be the areas which the appraisee and the appraiser consider as significant dimensions on which the appraisee's contributions should be assessed for that year. The appraiser and the appraisee may also determine the weightages of each of these areas. (Discussion on weightages may be useful irrespective of whether these weightages are used or not for final assessment.)

In the steps outlined above, steps 2, 3 and 4 are to be done by groups wherever feasible, step 5 could be undertaken by the personal/HRD/Industrial Engineering departments. Step 6 is very important as the process by which the appraiser-appraisee pair before the beginning of every year. Step 6 is very important as the process by which the appraiser-appraisee pairs discuss and come to an understanding about the KPAs is very critical for achieving the objectives of appraisal outlined in Chapter 1.

Steps 2, 3 and 4 are a non-time task as once the basic performance areas for each role are worked out, they only need marginal changes once in a while. In organisations where separate group for doing this task are not feasible (or are not needed), the appraiser-appraisee pairs can sit together and complete steps 2, 3 and 4 before they come to step 6. Thus it is a matter of one or two sittings and may involve only about 2 to 3 hours of time. This time however is worth investing.

In the process of agreeing on the KPAs fr the assessment period (i.e. in Step 6.) both the appraiser and the appraisee should aim at the following:

a) Have a clear and common understanding of the various activities to be performed under each KPA by the appraisee.

b) Have a clear understanding of the importance of each of these activities and what exactly is expected to be done by the appraisee i.e., the nature of effort we should put in, the possible outcome expected as a result of his efforts, etc.

c) Have an understanding of the expected problems and support required by the appraisee from the appraiser as well as others in the organisation and the support the appraiser can give to the appraisee.

d) Have an understanding of the level of performance expected in relation to each of the KPAs and the possible ratings associated with different performance levels. (Quite often it is difficult to be specific. However, some discussions may establish a common understanding.)

This requires therefore a thorough discussion between the appraiser and the appraisee. A climate of openness, mutuality and trust facilitates this process. The purpose should be kept in mind by both of them. The appraiser and the appraisee should be concerned more about increasing their understanding each other in relation to their roles and strengthening their relationships as well as facilitating the development of the appraisee in relation to his role.

KPAs prepare the groupd for employees to understand in a systematic way the capabilities they have and the capabilities they lack. This understanding may take place as the employee is performing various tasks and experiences, success and failures. It gets organised through a process of review and reflection at the end of the year when the employee realises consistency in his own successes and failures. This is the beginning of development. Thus KPAs serve as anchors with the help of which the individual employee may gain insights into his own capabilities and development needs. In addition, they also offer opportunities for him to decide on his own work patterns, experiment with them and learn wherever such possibilities exist. When a manager feels that he has not done a good job in his role, and is not able to identify where he has failed, it is difficult for him to do better next time. But, when a manager knows that he has failed only in relation to one critical function (KPA) and that he failed because that function involved proper scheduling of cer tain activities and he did a poor job of it, he may recognise the need to develop his scheduling capabilities. The second manager is in a better position to improve his performance because he knows what he lacks and he may make efforts to develop these. KPAs help in this process, and clarify thinking of managers.

In addition, due to common understanding existing between the boss and the subordinate, the appraisee may concentrate his efforts on the right kind of things. Due to clarity of understanding of the various areas of performance, the appraisee gets assessed on a number of performance areas and therefore the subjectivity of the appraiser is likely to be less.

Performance Targets

To add more objectivity to the exercise, it is possible to identify performance targets under each KPA. These performance targets may be qualitative or quantitative, but shuld be time bound and should specify level of acceptable performance for getting high performance ratings. The targets should focus more on the nature of efforts to be made by the appraisee in relation to each of the KPAs. Here is an example.

1. Role. Marketing Manager
   KPA. Introducing a new product X in the region assigned to him (weightage-2).

Performance Targets

1. Complete training programme for all district representatives and ensure readiness for distribution of the product X within the next 3 months.

2. To personally contact a random group of 10 major customers from each district and get their feedback on the products.

3. Evolve a marketing strategy by the end of the year for increasing the sales of this product in consultation with district representatives.

2. Role. Manager (Finance)
   KPA. Cost-reduction (weightage-3).

Performance Targets

1. Complete write-up and acceptance of company cost-reduction manual and distribute to all managers by the year end.

2. Collect ten suggested-cost reduction ideas per month from each of six operating managers.

3. Role. Manager (Research and Development)
   KPA. Development of New Production (weightage-2).

Performance Targets

1. Complete literature and patent search by the end of the year for five patentable ideas useful in entering new markets.

2. Complete design and development of new prototype in 12 months within the cost of Rs.1,40,000 without farm-out work to vendors.

4. Role. Junior Manager - Production
KPA. Work-simplification in machine shop (weightage-1).

Performance Targets

Master ten techniques in work simplification as related to machine-shop operations through monthly cost-reduction meetings for machine-shop supervisors.

5. Role. Manager HRD
KPA. Introducing a new system of Development-oriented performance appraisal (weightage-3).

Performance Targets

1. Collect information about the development-oriented appraisal systems in use from ten different organisations in the city and suggest a system for use in our organisation on the basis of these experiences.

6. Role. Branch Manager (State Bank of ....)
KPA. Deposit mobilisation

Performance Targets

1. To institute a system of deposit mobilisation through collective efforts of all officers in the branch by holding monthly meetings and reviewing progress.

2. To personally contact at least ten potential clients in the town every month and try to get them to open accounts.

It may be noted that these objectives emphasise the effort to be put in by the appraisee than the results. For example, in the case of Branch Manager (No. 6) above the target could be stated as "To mobilise deposits worth Rs.50,00,000 in the next 1 year." Similarly for Manager-Finance (Role No.2 above) the target could be "to bring about cost-reduction by 10% in the next one year". In both these the focus is on results rather than on effort. Results of this kind depend on a number of factors. In appraising performance the focus should be on efforts rather than results. This is because it is the performance of an entire group or department or an entire function in any organisation. Hence the need for emphasis on efforts rather than results. Of course, in this process it is hoped that the results are also obtained. If every employee puts in high effort and if still results are not accomplished, it may be indicative of something wrong womewhere in the organisation. If efforts do not lead to results in most cases, the organisational processes need to be examined. If efforts do not lead to results in any individual case, the nature of efforts may need to be changed, or other constraints may need to be identified and dealt with and this again may involve joint responsibility of the appraisee and the appraiser. Performance appraisal could thus become an instrument to enhance the collaborative capabilities of boss-subordinate dyads to make things happen in the organisation and thus contribute to its growth.

Some Examples of Key Performance Areas

Example 1

Branch Manager of a Bank. The Performance Areas are presented below. A list of activities to be performed by the branch managers are presented under each PA.

KPA 1. Deposit mobilisation

Activities. Ensuring prompt service to customers
Periodic meetings with the staff
Contacting prospective depositors
Developing strategies collectively
Maintaining liaison with government authorities, etc.

Possible Objectives. Result objective is to increase deposits by atleast 10 per cent. Effort goals could be:

(a) To contact at least about 200 potential customers; and
(b) To hold discussions with staff and involve them in improving customer service.

KPA 2. Advances to clients

Activities Checking proposals for advance
Periodic inspection of advances
Identifying priority sectors for advances
Lodging of claims DICGC

Attending to audit irregularities and steps for recovery of advances.
Actions for disposing wilful default cases

Objectives. Effort goals

(a) To establish a system of processing all loan requests within 15 days of receiving the request.
(b) To initiate action against all non-receivables by the end of the year.
(c) To contact major clients for outstandings and recover at least 50 per cent.

KPA 3. House Keeping

Activities. Periodic checking of records and stationery
Ensuring stocks of stationery
Spot-checking for balancing of books
Follow-up action on audit reports and prompt rectification
Monitoring timely submission of returns and statements

Objective. Result goal. To ensure balancing of all books.

Effort goals

(a) To check all important records once a month
(b) To develop a system of monitoring returns and statements and implement the same.

KPA 4. Customer Services

Activities Attending to customer complaints
Giving advice to customers
Correspondence with customers
Contacting customers and asking for their difficulties.

Objectives. Result goal. To ensure a high level of customer satisfaction.

Effort goals

(a) To personally attend to customer complaints
(b) To install a suggestion box and use the suggestion box.

(c) To reply to all letters/enquiries from customers within a week of receiving them.

KPA 5. Staff Management

Activities. Sanctioning leaves
Work allotment
Attending to staff grievances
Ensuring facilities and work conditions for staff
Counselling
Identifying development needs and providing opportunities.
Job rotation
Planning for staff requirements

Objectives

(a) To have a meeting with every staff member once a month and ensure their satisfaction.
(b) To initiate a system of informal get- togethers every quarter.
(c) To experiment with a system of job-rotation given by HRD unit.

Example 2

In this example the performance areas and their weightages for a number of roles, taken from a large engineering company manufacturing heavy equipment, are presented. The roles are selected from different departments to give an idea of KPAs. This organisation is a multi-product, multi-unit company employing about 15,000 employees. Targets are also given in some cases:

Role 1. Assistant Accounts Officer (Reports to Accounts Officer)

Key Performance Areas	**Weightage**
1. To to get people from other units/sections to work in place of absentees to pull up areas of attendance work so as to feed the input to EDP as per schedule for computation of wages/salaries.	3

2. To compare the wage bill of each month with that of the previous month to check violent variations, if any, arising from possible computer errors. 2

3. To verify whether all early payments, court attachments and other recoveries to be effected subsequent to the receipt of computer statements have been reduced from the net amount payable to the concerned employees before preparation of the Teller Statement for drawal of cash for disbursement of wages/salaries. 3

4. To ascertain whether the work of statutory remittances such as, ESI contribution, professional tax, CTD, etc., are progressing as per programme and to facilitate such remittances to be made before due dates so as to avoid penalty and other consequences, if necessary, by drafting people from other units. 2

5. To take stock of pending claims in respect of LTC, Expense Reports & Termination settlements at monthly intervals and to get them cleared wherever such claims are more than a fortnight old. 2

6. To attend to enquiries of employees and ex-employees in respect of their personal matters connected with pay-roll, which cannot be solved at the staff-level. 1

Role 2. Assistant Account Manager (Reports to Accounts Manager)

Key Performance Areas and Targets **Weightage**

1. To review the system of audit, the procedure followed and the extent of audit checks exercised to ensure adequacy of audit. 3
(Target. To complete one unit per quarter)

2. To review adequacy of various other internal controls in operation for effectiveness in the department. 2
(Target. To complete one unit per quarter)

3. Coordinate and ensure completion of monthly audit and issue of report and take up follow-up action. 3

(Target. Audit up to June 1982 to be completed by September 1982; report for the first quarter to be issued.)

4. General review of procedure and system followed in the internal audit, its policy and suggest improvements wherever there is scope. 2
(Target. Complete this item at least in respect of two areas. One regarding selection of vouchers in accordance with drill and another regarding follow-up action on observation made.)

Role 3. Assistant Manager, Stores (Reports to Materials Manager)

Key Performance Areas and Targets **Weightage**

1. Seeing all incoming daks pertaining to Stores Department and attending to important papers. 3
(Target. To ensure that delay in correspondence is avoided)

2. To keep a watch over critical items (production and non-production including standard stock items) for receipt with regular follow-up till finalisation. 3
(Target. To avoid hold-up of production)

3. Clearance of materials received in receiving 2
(Target. To avoid demurrage/inconvenience to carriers)

4. Departmental verification of stores. 3
(Target. To ensure no loss of material warranting write-off action.)

5. Review of (a) R.R. finalisation; (b) rejected stores items; (c) repairable items; (d) critical standard stock items having stocks less than 2 months; (e) shop rejection; and (f) claims on carriers/insurance. 3
(Target. To ensure that functions detailed to officers are carried out promptly.)

6. To ensure that all the stores and tool cribs function without disruption. 3
(Target. To avoid dislocation in the stores function)

7. To inspect all stores to ensure maintenance of proper storage — 3
(Target. To avoid spoilage and deterioration of materials.)

8. To ensure that appropriate action is taken for disposal of scrap arisings — 3
(Target. To ensure that periodical clearance is done without accumulation.)

9. To exercise proper control on inventory holdings — 3
(Target. (a) To coordinate with Departments for review of excess inventory
(b) To identify non-moving stocks and take appropriate action for disposal thereof.)

10. General Administration — 3
(Target. To ensure smooth functioning of stores) .

Role 4. Design Manager (Reporting to General Manager)

Key Performance Areas	Weightage
1. Coordination with Research Designs and Standards Organisation with regard to the development of new designs for...	3
2. Guide in the development of new designs for export of the products.	3
3. Coordination with shops and other departments with regard to the prototype building and productionising the drawings	2
4. Guide in the preparation of specifications, testing procedures, etc.	2
5. To provide modern and latest facilities for the design and drawing office, laboratory, library and blue printing sections.	2
6. Guide in the development of different types of product variations	3

7. Overall supervision of the department, viz., aboratory, library and blue printing sections — 1

8. Guide in the preparation of quotation for quoting against vendors. Scrutiny of offers received and offering technical comments — 2

Role 5. Assistant Manager - Progress (Reports to Manager, Planning)

Key Performance Areas — **Weightage**

1. Ensuring availability of right number of cylinders in all the shops when required economically. — 3

   Targets:
   (a) Assessment of shopwise requirement before end July.
   (b) Update the loading report every day.
   (c) Stock-outs not more than twice a month
   (d) Ensure collection of empty cylinders within three days of completion

2. Initiating and monitoring the progress of spares work orders — 2

   Targets
   (a) Coordinate with shops and keeps Planning Manager posted of all relevant information.
   (b) Develop a good record-keeping system for monitoring the progress of spares by mid-August.
   (c) Ensure loading of spares JC's, material to meet the committed delivery dates and subsequent follow-up with shop verbal/IOM'S.
   (d) Monthly status of spares W.O. to be prepared.

3. Initiating and monitoring the progress of various stock-work orders. — 3

   Targets
   (a) Develop a good record-keeping system by mid-August.
   (b) Maintain reliable records on stock work orders.
   (c) Initiate closure of stock W.O.'s promptly
   (d) Prepare monthly status report.

4. Making heat-treated items available to assemply shops 3
   (a) Weekly review of the progress at various points and make a report.
   (b) Arrange to send fortnightly/status report to concerned departments within 2 days of the succeeding fortnight.
   (c) Efficient follow-up with various departments in connection with heat-treatment and keep Manager Planning posted of relevant information.
   (d) Record of W.O.'s of heat-treatment opening/closure

5. Arrange to despatch/store credit excess, rejected items, loaned items, subcontracted items. 1

   Targets:
   (a) Action to be taken within 6 days of receipts of communication in the normal course.
   (b) Efficient follow-up with parties concerned.

6. Attending to administrative, personal problems of employees in the department 1

   Targets
   (a) Sanctioning leave letters within one day
   (b) To bring to the notice of the manager, grievances, problems of employees in time to take suitable action.

Role 6. Superintendent-Maintenance (Reporting to Factory Manager)

Key Performance Areas	**Weightage**
1. Ensure uninterrupted major plant facilities like sanitation, water supply and power in the plant	3
2. Ensure transport services for progress department, senior officers, purchase and medical section, etc.	3
3. Ensure minimum breakdown on shot blast machines, sheet metal machinery, machine shop and furnaces	
4. House-keeping of the plant in general and positive improvement in illumination level	3

5.	Timely erection of new machines, progress on old machinery breakdown and developments, including preventive maintenance procedure	3
6.	To bring down reportable accident rate insisting on suitable safety measures and bringing about inter-departmental safety competitions	2
7.	Maintaining cordial relations with outside agencies for achieving the above	3

Role 7. Engineer-Manufacturing (Reports to Superintendent, Production)

	Key Performance Areas	**Weightage**
1.	Entering the shop in time to mark attendance; confirm full shop attendance	2
2.	Checking breakdowns of machinery taking immediate action when needed	2
3.	Going through the log for safeguarding the priority of jobs	2
4.	Coordination with other departments to solve daily problems	2
5	Planning targets in advance and ensuring the availability of necessary tools for projects	3
6.	Supervision and regular contact with subordinates for identifying their work requirements.	2
7.	Attending meetings and ensuring implementation of decisions	3
8.	Leaving the necessary reports for the follow-up shifts and confirming the same.	2
9.	Discussion with reporting officer about advance plan and priority jobs and other information	2
10.	Attending to all inter-office memos	2

Chapter 4

INCREASING SELF-AWARENESS AND UNDERSTANDING : SELF APPRAISAL

The experience with performance appraisals so far indicates that appraisals are for the benefit of the organisations and that they are the responsibility of appraisers and the HR departments. As long as this perception continues performance appraisals will run into problems.

A large part of performance appraisals are for the appraisees. Performance plans help the appraisee to set directions for his work, identify areas of his significant contributions and avoid wastage of time. Performance reviews can help in communicating perspectives, difficulties and expectations to the seniors and get more support for improving ones performance. Performance appraisals should be seen as instruments of development for every employee. They should be owned much more by the appraisees than by the appraisers and HR departments. To achieve this probably one should move away from "appraisal" culture to "planning", "analysis", "review" and "development" culture. In all these "appraisal" is involved but it is not the focal point, it is only a part of the process. If this spirit is inculcated the systems may be owned by the appraisee. When the system is owned by the appraisee the meaning of self-appraisal changes.

Self-appraisal is not meant to be a ritualistic form filling exercise. It is a significant initial step for performance development. A lot should happen in self-appraisal which may not be reflected in the forms filled by the appraisee. In fact a good self appraisal need not result in good form filling although it results in increased self awareness through a process of review and reflection on the part of the appraisee.

Self appraisal has an important role to play in employee development. As we have seen in the previous chapters, development is self-directed. The individual is not likely to learn and develop himself unless he is interested in his own learning and development and makes conscious efforts to develop. Such efforts would include identifying possible directions of growth, choosing the directions in which one wants to grow, identifying the growth, experiencing growth through action, review and reflection to continuously monitor the growth. Thus for any employee to develop his capabilities to perform a particular function associated with his role, he must know the importance of that function to his role and the links between learning to perform that function and his future growth in (or outside) the organisation. Then he must know how well he is performing this function, the capabilities he has and those he lacks to perform that function well. He can discover these by actually trying out performing this function and receiving feedback from others about his performance levels and his capability indicators. He may use this feedback and reflect it along with his own experience to finally identify the capabilities he has and the capabilities he lacks. He may then make plans for developing these capabilities with the assistance of his supervisors and others in the organisation. Thus the "individual" is always a focal point and determiner of his development and performance improvement. The organisation provides a supporting environment and other facilities required for his development. It is in this context self-appraisal becomes an important step in performance improvement and development.

Self-appraisal should be a continuous process. More than his reporting officer, the employee should himself take steps to continuously assess his own performance, identify his strengths and weaknesses and continuously keep a record of efforts made as well as his own success and failure experiences while performing different functions. He should also analyse the causes for his successes and failures. While this process should go on continuously, the individual should take time for himself once in a while and review all his efforts, success and failure experiences to assimilate and identify consistencies in his successes or failures and to prepare his development plans. Performance appraisal period provides one such formal opportunity for every individual to review his performance and growth over the entire year.

The following can be considered as the purposes of self-appraisal:

1. To provide an opportunity for the employee to recapitulate:

    a) the various activities he has undertaken in relation to different functions associated with his role;

    b) his achievements and failures with regard to these;
    c) the capabilities he demonstrated and capabilities he felt as lacking in carrying out these activities and the various

managerial and behavioural dimensions he demonstrated over the year.

2. To identify his own development needs and plan for his development in the organisation by identifying the support he requires from his reporting officer and others in the organisation.

3. To communicate to his reporting officer his contributions, accomplishments, and reflections to enable him to view his (appraisee's) performance in the right perspective and assess more objectively. This is a necessary preparation for performance review discussions and performance improvement plans.

4. To initiate an organisation-wide process of annual review and reflection to strengthen self-initiated development for managerial effectiveness.

Self-appraisal should start at the end of the performance period just before the performance review discussion takes place. Self-appraisal should start with the appraisee taking up his KPAs and objectives for the period that was over and reflecting about his achievements and failures. He should have with him the notes he maintained about any events, critical incidents, and reflections he had during the period and use them to recapitulate his contributions and success and failure experiences. He may analyse his performance using the guidelines suggested in the next chapter, "Performance Analysis". He may then assess himself using the rating scales, if any, decided by the organisation. He should make brief notes of his reflections in the appraisal form to communicate to his appraiser.

The appraisee should follow this process also for behavioural and managerial dimensions. He should also make his suggestions about developmental needs identified, if any. Self-appraisal form completed in this process should then be passed on to the reporting officer for his assessment and planning for performance review and counselling discussions.

Appraisers should treat such self-appraisal reports received from the appraisee seriously. Appraisers normally do not get enough time to observe each of their subordinates closely. Most often appraisers tend to form impressions about their subordinates on the basis of one or two of their failures which may be striking to the appraisers. Sometimes one or two success experiences may also leave highly positive marks. It is necessary for the appraiser to review each and every aspect of performance and behavioural and managerial qualities shown by the appraisee if he has to understand the appraisee and contribute to his development. The only way an appraiser can get a good deal of information about the appraisee and his performance is by asking him. Data provided by the appraisee through self-appraisal shows this purpose well. Some appraisers get worried that their subordinates like to highlight only their accomplishments and strengths but not their failures and weaknesses. This perception is often wrong. Even when it is true, there is no need to worry because the appraisee has every right to highlight his accomplishments and the appraiser has the obligation to take cognizance of these in his appraisal. If there are failures and weaknesses the appraiser perceives, these could be pointed out during appraisal discussions. It should also be remembered that when an appraisee points out only his strengths and accomplishments, he is raising the expectations of his boss from him for the subsequent period. More challenging goals can be set the next period.

Thus self-appraisal can be a very useful component of a development-oriented performance appraisal system, if viewed seriously by the appraisee as well as the appraiser and used appropriately for generating more understanding about the appraisee.

Self-Appraisals for Managerial Effectiveness

There are organisations where "self-appraisal" does not find place in the performance appraisal system. Or often a small space is provided for the appraisee to write down his accomplishments or tasks assigned and results achieved. This cannot be called as self-appraisal. In such cases often executives ask about what should be done.

The author would like to take the stand that self-appraisals can be done independent of the performance appraisal systems. Every manager should develop a discipline of reviewing his own performance as a manager at least once a year. Such review should be systematic and truthful. As no one else is involved in this process the manager can say to himself things that he may not like to share with others. Such self-appraisal process may focus on the following questions.

1. What have I accomplished in the last one year?
2. How do I rate my accomplishments or contributions as against last year, and as against what all was possible this year?

3. What contributed to my performance? What factors helped me and what factors prevented me from doing better?

4. What are my own competencies and attitudes that helped me to do better and that prevented me from giving my best?

5. How are my own attitudes affecting my growth and development as a competent manager?

6. What opportunities have I missed during the last year and how do I propose to use them this year if I face similar situations?

7. What support do I need from my seniors and from the organisation to be able to make better contributions?

8. What support do I need to develop my own potential and capabilities for future?

9. What are my action plans for next year to become more effective manager?

10. What do I want to communicate to my superiors to help them understand me better and also to help them to empower me for better performance?

Chapter 5

PERFORMANCE ANALYSIS

PERFORMANCE analysis is an important component of appraisal. Any ratings to appraisees should be given only after a thorough analysis of performance.

If subjectivity in appraisals has to be reduced the appraiser should not only assess the level of performance achieved by the appraisee but also understand and assess the conditions under which the appraisee has accomplished whatever he has accom plished. The appraiser should know if the appraisee could have done better with more effort or with some more control over certain things he has done. The appraiser should also know the nature and extent of effort put in by the appraisee. He should know the difficulties faced by the appraisee. He should also know the extent to which the appraisee is aware of his own strengths and weaknesses in relation to his performance different tasks. The appraiser should then use this understanding and knowledge to reinforce the strengths of the appraisee, to help him recognise his weak points, to determine the support to be given, to identify developmental needs as well as to help the appraisee in identifying KPAs and targets for the next period. Thus performance analysis can be considered as the heart of the appraisal system. This becomes clear when we see how performance analysis forms the basis for appraisal ratings, counselling discussions, identification of developmental needs and action plans.

Objectives

Performance analysis should lead to the following:

1. Identification of factors that have helped the appraisee to reach the level of performance he achieved in relation to various KPAs, targets and various other functions associated with his job. These may be called "facilitating factors".

2. Identification of factors that have prevented the appraisee from doing better or those that hindered his performance. These may be called "hindering factors".

3. Identification of factors (from those above) about which the appraisee can do something (to retain if they are facilitators or reduce and eliminate if they are hindering) those about which the reviewing officer or somebody else in the organisation can do something, and those for which not much can be done. Such an identification would suggest action plans for the appraisee as well as for the appraiser.

4. Identifying developmental needs for better performance on critical functions associated with the present role.

5. To gain a better understanding about the appraisee, his role requirements and the situation in which he is working and also to share with him the expectations and understanding of the appraiser so that the communication between both of them is increased.

Methodology

For doing performance analysis the following steps should be followed:

1. After discussions on KPAs, objectives and other dimensions with the reporting officer, the appraisee should periodically keep reflecting about how well he is progressing in his work and in relation to KPAs and other dimensions.

2. During the performance period whenever the employee comes across success experiences or feels helped in his performance, he should note the same on a piece of paper (or diary). In noting this focus should be on the factors that are helping him do well and how these are facilitating his performance. A brief mention is enough as reminders for him in the final performance analysis.

3. Similarly, whenever he experiences failure or runs into difficulties or feels prevented from doing better, he should note the factors that are causing this. (It is a part of the managerial role to continuously keep communicating such factors to one's reporting officer and take his help to overcome them. However, these should be noted somewhere for annual review.

4. At the end of the performance period the appraisee considers his own performance on each of the KPAs and other dimensions. Taking into consideration the effort he had put in, difficulties he

experienced, the results he achieved and the context in which these were achieved he rates himself on a rating scale (or at least categorises his performance as excellent, good, average, poor, etc.)

5. After assigning himself such ratings, he should now start listing down all the factors in detail that have helped him in accomplishing whatever he accomplished. Similarly he should list down all the factors that have prevented him from doing better or that have become constraints on his better performance. In listing these factors he should take the help of the notes he maintained during the year (steps 2 and 3 above). He may also go through item by item in his KPAs to make the list exhaustive. (While KPAs are helpful for performance analysis, the appraisee should go beyond KPAs and look at each and every aspect of his work and list the facilitating and inhibiting factors.)

6. After listing down the facilitating and hindering factors exhaustively the appraisee should then classify these factors into following categories:

Facilitating Factors

(a) *Personal or individual facilitating factors (FIS).* All those factors that are attributable to the performer, his abilities, effort, etc. (e.g. job knowledge, interpersonal competence, previous experience, initiative, hard work, etc.).

(b) *Facilitating factors attributable to the reporting officer (FROs).* All those factors that are attributable to the reporting officer (e.g. fast decision-making, staff support, delegation, guidance, approachability, etc.)

(c) *Facilitating factors attributable to the organisation and its systems (FOS).* All those factors which are part of the organisation, its structure, policies, procedures, systems, etc. (e.g. flexible policies, good work conditions, good control systems, open climate, accountability, collaboration from other departments, support from reviewing officers, etc.).

(d) *Facilitating factors attributable to the subordinate (FS).* Those factors attributable to the appraisees own subordi nates (e.g. hard work by them, motivation, cooperation, not taking leaves, punctuality, high ability, etc.).

(e) *Facilitating factors attributable to external environment (FE).* Those that are not a part of the above 4 and that are attributable to the larger socio-economic politico and other conditions of the environment external to the organisation (e.g. liberalisation of some policies by government, support given by newspapers, cooperative officials of the government, improved economic situation, poor image of competitors etc.).

Inhibiting Factors

The same categorisation as given earlier:

(a) *Inhibiting factors attributable to the individual (II)* e.g., poor memory, family problems, need to devote attention to children's education, poor health, problems of expression and language etc.

(b) *Inhibiting factors attributable to the reporting officer (IROs).* Delays in decision-making, lack of guidance and direction, busy boss, ambiguous goals, allotment of tasks on adhoc basis, not providing adequate facilities.

(c) *Inhibiting factors attributable to subordinate staff (IS).* Lack of cooperation, union problems, absenteeism, slow work, poor capabilities, close supervision required by them, etc.

(d) *Inhibiting factors attributable to the environment (IEs).* Sudden changes in the economic, social or political climate, delays in supplies, unexpected events affecting work, strikes, etc.

(e) *Inhibiting factors attributable to the organisation and its system (IOs).* Policies like that of unplanned transfers, etc., changes in top management, introduction of new technologies that demand time, etc.

7. After such an analysis, individual (appraisee) may reflect about individual facilitating factors he would like to maintain or further strengthen and the inhibiting factors that he would like to overcome in future. He should think about the mechanisms he would like to adopt for improving his strengths and overcoming his weaknesses. He may also think about the support he requires from his reporting officer to implement his plans.

8. In addition the individual should also reflect about the support that could be extended by his reporting officer to maintain the external facilitating factors and to reduce or weaken the inhibiting factors.
9. He then should pass on his performance analysis to his reporting officer for his comments, additions to the factors identified and performance review and counselling discussions. The performance analysis projects the achievements/contributions of the appraisee, his failures and factors contributing to both these. This analysis also communicates to the reporting officer the difficulties experienced by him during the process of carrying out various activities (PAs) during the year.

Using Performance Analysis for Counselling and Identification of Development Needs

Performance analysis done in the manner outlined above helps in counselling, identifying development needs as well as in planning action for improving the performance situation by removing blocks being experienced by the appraisee.

By adding to the factors identified by the appraisee, the appraiser communicates the attention he has been paying to the appraisee and his role. In adding to the individual facilitators and inhibitors the appraiser is contributing to increase the self-awareness of the appraisee through a process of feedback. Recognition of strengths not identified by the appraisee gives positive strokes when the appraiser communicates the same. Agreeing with strengths already identified by the appraisee also strengthens the awareness of one's strong points on the part of the appraisee. Disagreements should lead to discussion during counselling sessions in which the appraiser is likely to change his perceptions of the appraisee or the appraisee himself may get new insights. Adding to the weak points through a process of feedback may help the appraisee to explore areas he needs to improve. Disagreements with some of the personal inhibiting factors also helps the employee to develop better self-awareness.

The appraiser need not write everything on the form itself, just as the appraisee need not write everything. Only brief points are written as guides for discussion. These forms should remain with the appraisee and the appraiser only, and need not go to the reviewing office and should not go to personnel department.

During counselling the appraiser and the appraisee try to understand each others' expectations, difficulties and perceptions, and move close to each other in the process of planning for improving their performance. In this process they may also identify development needs of the appraisee wherever the appraisee needs to acquire capabilities. Some of these development needs may have to be attended to by the training division or the HRD department through training programme, job rotation, etc. Other development needs may require action on the part of the appraiser in the form of more guidance, on the job training and discussions with the appraisee. A few of these may require self-study and development by the individual himself. Performance analysis should provide the basis for all these.

An example, of how performance analysis data provide information about the facilitating and inhibiting factors for a variety of actions at appraisee, appraiser and organisational levels, is given in the following case.

Example
Performance Analysis of Branch Managers of a Bank

The following is an example of how tabulated performance analysis data of employees of a given unit can be utilised for organisation development purposes. The following are the facilitating and hindering factors identified by different branch managers (n = 22) in a region. All of them were reporting to a regional manager. The facilitating and hindering factors identified by them were tabulated from their appraisal forms. The factors were categorised under the following:

FI	=	Facilitating factors attributable to the individual
FRO	=	Facilitating factors attributable to the Reporting Officer
FOS	=	Facilitating factors attributable to the Organisation and Systems
FS	=	Facilitating factors attributable to Subordinate Staff
FE	=	Facilitating factors attributable to the External Environment
II	=	Inhibiting factors attributable to the Individual
IRO	=	Inhibiting factors attributable to the Reporting Officer
IS	=	Inhibiting factors attributable to Subordinate Staff
IE	=	Inhibiting factors attributable to the Environment
IOS	=	Inhibiting factors attributable to the Organisation and its Systems.

Category	Sr. No.	Facilitating Factors
FI	1	Patience and willingness to listen to all the problems of the staff and customers first and then work out a solution for the problem (7)*
FI	2	Perseverance (5)
FI	3	Soberness and tact (4)
FI	5	Goodwill and fellow-feeling towards others (3)
FI	6	Keen desire to help customers by giving them one's personal attention (3)
FI	7	Aggressive nature/ability to convince customers (2)
FI	8	Ability for intelligent communication and public relations (2)
FI	9	Interest in Bank's work (2)
FI	10	Ability to motivate staff (2)
FI	11	Sensitivity to the feelings of others and hence success in inter-personal dealings (2)
FI	12	Application of democratic methods while dealing with staff and customers (2)
FI	13	Willingness to respect all staff members and to solve their personal problems, whenever possible (1)
FI	14	Asking for feedback from staff and customers to identify many weaknesses (1)
FI	15	An inherent liking and sympathy for people (1)
FI	16	Specialisation in advances at academic level and entire career till date (1)
FI	17	Inherent desire to exceed targets (even self-imposed targets) and stretch one's ability to the fullest (1)
FI	18	Quick decision-making (1)
FI	19	Adequate delegation (1)
FI	20	Analytical and imaginative bent of mind; ability to perceive new ideas and initiate new actions (1)

* The number of Branch Managers mentioning each factor in their analysis is given in brackets.

Category	Sr. No.	Facilitating Factors
FI	21	A willing learner (1)
FI	22	Good health (1)
FI	23	Bachelor status (1)
FI	24	Ability to control one's ego and hence less ego clashes (1)
FI	25	Judicious use of discretionary powers (1)
FI	26	Punctuality (1)
FI	27	Good acceptance with staff, having previously worked with them (1)
FRO	28	Good and timely support from controlling authority and his office (11)
FS	29	Sincere and hard working branch clerical staff(8)
FOS	30	Good premises (6)
FS	31	Good support from supervisory staff at the branch (6)
FRO	32	An RM who is really appreciative of good work done (5)
FE	33	Good potential for business in area of operation (2)
FS	34	Efficient and competent 2nd line (1)
FS	35	Experienced staff (1)
FE	36	Good assistance from other local BMs (1)
FS	37	Good team of field officers (1)
FE	38	Cooperation extended by units for for visit of branch staff (1)
FE	39	Cooperation extended by units for visit of branch staff (1)
FS	40	Highly motivated staff, with good moral and team spirit (1)
FOS	41	Good network of SBI branches (1)

Category	Sr. No.	Inhibiting Factors
II	1	Mild/good nature which is sometimes taken to be a weakness (4)
II	2	Oversensitive/overemotional - get upset easily (2)
II	3	Indifferent health (2)
II	4	Inadequate job knowledge, particularly relating to SSI advances (2)
II	5	Lack of confidence while dealing with aggressive staff (1)
II	6	Short tempered - lack of patience to appreciate the limitations of staff (1)
II	7	Heavy social obligations (1)
II	8	Disregard for minor rules and regulations (1)
II	9	Amenable to accept authority only from RM and none else (1)
II	10	Limited power of expression inEnglish - unable to put across ideas (1)
II	11	Inherent faith in goodness of human nature, which often leads to disillusionment (1)
II	12	Difficulty in motivating staff (1)
IOS	13	Absence from branch due to leave/deputation/training (2)
II	14	Lack of command over Gujarati (1)
II	15	Inability to scold subordinates, as one realises their limitations in respect of initiative and job knowledge (1)
II	16	Inertia in the absence of pressure (1)
II	17	Lack of adequate training (1)
IOS	18	Shortage of clerical staff (4)
IOS	19	Congested/badly situated/inadequate branch premises (4)
IOS	20	Shortage of supervisory staff (3)

Category	Sr. No.	Inhibiting Factors
IE	21	Long distance of the branch from most residential areas (3)
IS	22	Non-cooperation of clerical staff (3)
IS	23	High degree of absenteeism among staff (2)
IE	24	Competitors (companies, cooperative banks, etc.) offering more interest (2)
IE	25	Intense competition (2)
IE	26	Inadequate potential for business in the area of operation (2)
IE	27	Borrowers belonging to a cross-section who lack integrity or who do not appreciate the value of financial data (2)
IS	28	Permanent conflict between certain members of the staff, not easily resolved (1)
IS	29	Head cashier not taking interest - keen to leave early (1)
IS	30	Shortage of subordinate staff (1)
II	31	Absence of any promotion opportunities in the Bank (1)
IE	32	Political influence at the branch/LHO level (1)
IOS	33	Lack of time to carry out all the duties (1)
IOS	34	Delay in decision-making at LHO (1)
IOS	35	Heavy government work upsets branch routine (1)
IS	36	Limitations of clerical staff promoted from the subordinate cadre (1)
IE	37	Interference by outside consultants in our decision to call up advances (1)
IS	38	Limitations in respect of job knowledge, initiative, etc., in the second line at the branch (1)

Category	Sr. No.	Inhibiting Factors
IOS	39	Stoppage of overtime (1)
IE	40	Area prone to frequent civil disturbances (1)

NOTE: All factors categorised as IOS and IRO deserve attention by the Reporting Officer to reduce. Factors marked IS may indicate areas where guidance is required by the appraisee to handle his subordinates. Some of the factors marked as II may be reduced or eliminated through training. In using performance analysis data of the entire unit focus should be on IRO and IOS factors to receive feedback and to change systems. Similarly focus on FRO and FOS factors may help in identifying strength areas to continue the same. A sensitive reporting officer would find these data extremely useful.

Chapter 6

PERFORMANCE RATINGS

AN important component of any performance appraisal system is the performance assessment through ratings. The assessment may be made using categories like "excellent" or "outstanding", "good", "above average", "average", "below average", "poor", etc. A five-point, seven-point or a nine-point scale can be used to assess performance. If categories are used they need to be defined and points may be assigned to them (e.g. outstanding = 7, very good performance = 6, above average or fairly good = 5, average = 4, below average = 3, poor performance = 2 and very poor = 1, etc.).

In the appraisal system described here, at the end of the year after the appraisee completes self-appraisal and gives his appraisal and analysis report to his reporting officer, the appraiser is expected to study the report and make his own observations on each of the KPAs, objectives, managerial dimensions, behaviour dimensions, and facilitating and inhibiting factors identified in performance analysis. He then has a performance review and counselling discussion with the appraisee on a day planned for this purpose. Prior to such discussion the appraiser may make provisional assessment and rate the performance of the appraisee on each of the KPAs/objectives and behaviours (manage rial and behavioural dimensions). If in the self-appraisal the appraisee rates his performance on different dimensions, it is useful for the appraiser also to give provisional ratings. Whether the self-ratings of the appraisee do or do not differ from those assigned by the appraiser, the discussion should take place and should focus on how each of them arrived at the ratings they gave for each dimension. In this process they are likely to exchange views and communicate with each other on a number of issues. The appraisee may share more information. The appraiser may give feedback or share his expectations with the appraisee. A number of processes that should take place and the purposes of this discussion are explained in the chapter on "Performance Counselling".

If self-appraisal requires the appraisee to give ratings also for his performance and the appraiser also gives ratings they could become starting points of the appraisal discussion process. However, to be effective, this process requires the appraiser to share his ratings (even if they are provisional) with the appraisee. This requires a complete openness and trust between the appraiser and the appraisee. This also requires a good degree of emotional climate of acceptance existing between them so that they are not taken away by the ratings and the ratings per se do not become more important than sharing of experience and giving and receiving feedback. If such an openness and healthy atmosphere does not exist in any organisation, it is better to start with a system in which the ratings assigned or to be assigned by the appraiser are not shared with the employee but the review discussion and counselling take place and described in the next chapter. The appraiser may finally assign his ratings confidentially, although he should give some indications about his as sessment during review discussions. This should be done only till such a time more openness and trust is built up and continued practice of confidentiality may hinder developing more trusting relationships.

The following eight combinations of self-assessment, reporting officer's assessment and confidentiality or openness of final assessment are possible. The self-appraisal may include only analysis (accomplish-

Model No.	Nature of Self-appraisal	Reporting Officer's apprasial	Openness
1.	Only analysis, no ratings	Only analysis, no ratings	Confidential
2.	Only analysis, no ratings	Only analysis, no ratings	Open
3.	Only analysis, no ratings	Analysis and ratings	Confidential
4.	Only analysis, no ratings	Analysis and ratings	Open
5.	Analysis and ratings	Only analysis, no ratings	Confidential
6.	Analysis and ratings	Only analysis, no ratings	Open
7.	Analysis and ratings	Analysis and ratings	Confidential
8.	Analysis and ratings	Analysis and ratings	Open

ments, strengths, weakness, etc.) or may include analysis and ratings. Appraiser may also do analysis only and assign no ratings or may also assign ratings after analysis. The most desirable model is number 8 where both of them assign ratings and share (provisional and final) with each other. This is what should be aimed at. Equally effective is model number 4 in which only the appraiser gives ratings and shares them (provisional and final). The next best are model numbers 6 and 2 where the appraiser does not give ratings but analyse the appraisee's performance and share with each other their perception of the appraisee's accomplishments, contributions, strengths, weaknesses, etc. The appraiser may give his final ratings confidentially but he shares his analysis prior to that and looks at the appraisee's performance. The other models (Nos. 1, 3, 5 and 7) are not suitable for development-oriented appraisal systems.

The Need for Performance Ratings

Whatever may be the model used, final assessment, in the form of ratings or assignment of points, becomes very useful for development as well as administrative decisions. If appraisals do not result in such ratings or points being assigned to appraisees on different KPAs (or objectives) and behavioural and managerial dimensions, it is difficult to know subsequently how well the individual is progressing. It is also difficult to maintain and process information about the capabilities of employees to handle different functions. The qualitative analysis done by each appraisee and the appraiser is difficult to be used for training rotation, placement, transfer, promotion, decisions, etc. Whereas, once the ratings are available, it is easy to identify individuals who can perform certain functions well or those who have demonstrated certain managerial and human capabilities. In view of this need appraisals should result in performance ratings on different functions as well as different dimensions of behaviour. It is for this reason, there has been a good deal of research conducted in the West on improving the quality (more objectivity and less errors and biases) of ratings. In the subsequent sections of this chapter we will examine the factors that contribute to poor quality of ratings and then see some ways in which the quality of performance ratings could be improved.

Factors Affecting Ratings in Performance Appraisals

The most commonly expressed dissatisfaction about performance appraisals is in relation to the subjectivity in performance ratings. Employees are very much concerned about this because performance ratings entered in personnel records are likely to have a lot of impact on subsequent promotion, placement, transfer and development decisions to be taken by the organisation affecting his career. Because of this importance, performance ratings have attracted a lot of attention of psychologists and other Behavioural Scientists who have been making efforts to discover the various factors affecting rating and rating behaviour and decreasing the quality of appraisals. A variety of rating scales have been developed and experimental studies conducted to control various biases and errors in performance ratings. Various hypotheses have also been proposed on the basis of theories and findings available from person perception, interpersonal attraction, attribution, information processing and such other areas of social psychology. Most of this work has been done in Western settings and quite often with varying results obtained by different researchers on the same issue. Experimental research having implications for appraisal ratings on Indian subjects is rather recent in India and is actively being pursued only at one or two places. Western researches are plenty on this topic. Journals like the Journal of Applied Psychology, Personnel Psychology, Organisational Behaviour and Human Performance, Public Personnel Management, Journal of Personality and Social Psychology, Academy of Management Review, etc., carry such research articles quite frequently. However, these researches are largely unsystematic and subject to fads and fashions. They focussed too much on formats rather than process es (Decotiis and Petit, 1978). In view of the relevance of some of these researches to our understanding of the dynamics of appraisal ratings, a few of the recent studies and theoretical propositions are presented below. It is hoped that the reader will appreciate the complexity of the issue of appraisal ratings and continue to strive for improving the quality of ratings.

Subjectivity and Errors in Ratings

As long as human beings are involved in assessing other human beings there is bound to be certain amount of subjectivity. Subjectivity or biases occur when the ratings assigned by any appraiser to any appraisee are determined more by factors other than the performance or actual behaviours shown by the appraisee on the dimension under assessment. The following are some of the commonly observed phenomena that contribute to errors and biases in appraisals increasing the subjectivity.

1. Sometimes appraisers like or dislike one or two actions or qualities of the appraisee immensely and therefore tend to rate him positively or negatively on all other dimensions (also called "Halo effect").
2. Some appraisers tend to believe that they should be "nice" to their subordinates and therefore tend to assign then lenient ratings

(leniency effect). Some other appraisers have an opposite philosophy and view of their subordinates and tend to rate them too strictly (severity effect).

3. Some raters do not want to give too high or too low ratings to their subordinates. Due to their overconsciousness they tend to rate most of their appraisees around the average (central tendency or averaging).
4. Some raters tend to like the ratees who are like them and therefore assign them higher ratings than to those who are perceived by them as different from them. Some other raters tend to like those who have characteristics which they do not have but would like to have (called "assimilation" or "differential effects").
5. Quite a few raters make judgements about others on the basis of their first contacts and tend to carry these impressions over a long time (first impression errors).
6. Sometimes raters assign ratings on the basis of the recent behaviours they have seen in their appraisees forgetting about the past behaviours over a period ("recency effect").
7. Some appraisers tend to assess their appraisees on the basis of their expectations and perceptions about how their own bosses are going to appraise them.

Behaviourally Anchored Rating Scales

Smith and Kendall (1963) have evolved a procedure for developing evaluative rating scales anchored by examples of expected behaviours. The format proposed for these rating scales is a series of continuous graphic rating scales, arranged vertically. Behavioural descriptions, exemplifying various degrees of each dimension, are printed beside the line at different heights according to their scale positions as determined by judgements of those who are expected to use scales. The examples (or behaviour descriptions) are intended as anchors to define levels of the characteristic, and as operational definitions of the dimension being rated. Ratings are to be made by checking at any position along the line. The anchors are defined in terms of behaviours expected to be shown by the rate relating to that dimension. For example, while assessing behaviour of nurses, the anchor could be stated in the form of an expectation such as "If this nurse were admitting a patient who talks rapidly and continuously of her symptoms and past medical history, could be expected to look interested and listen", instead of statements such as "shows interest in patients' description of symptoms."

The use of expected behaviours is intended to encourage such conscientiousness by making the predictions (a) so concrete that, in view of previous agreement by the peer group, central tendency or hedging effects will be minimised; and (b) so verifiable that the insight, judgement, values, etc., of the rater are potential ly challenged if later behaviour of the ratee should fail to confirm the prediction.

Based on the procedure used by Smith and Kendall (1963) any organisation interested in developing such scales (known as Behaviourally Anchored Rating Scales or BARS) may follow these steps:

1. Identify the roles or the categories of roles for which such rating system has to be developed. The category of roles should require some common capabilities (managerial and behavioural) for effective performance. These categories could be broad. For example, all secretaries in one category, or branch managers, or middle level managers, or senior managers, marketing managers, etc.
2. Constitute peer groups of appraisers of these roles - as many as possible. These groups may be called for a short- workshop or they could work through periodic meetings. There may be several groups for one category of roles.
3. Ask each group to first identify and list the qualities or characteristics that are important for that role category.
4. Select the most frequently mentioned dimensions. If necessary representatives of the groups can get together and finalise the list for each category of roles. Critical incidents could be talked about for more clarity.
5. Each group formulates general statements representing definitions of high, low, and acceptable performance for each quality.
6. The groups should then prepare examples of behaviour in each quality and these should be edited in the form of expectations (e.g. when faced with staff shortages, examines the work and reallocates staff to handle critical functions).
7. Some of the groups may act as judges and they should attempt independently to reclassify each of the behaviour descriptions into one of the dimensions measured.
8. Where there is no agreement with the original classification either the dimension or the behaviour example is to be eliminated.
9. Use some of the groups to describe outstanding and poor performer in each role category. Use these descriptions to see if the

dimensions identified in steps 2 and 3 are critical to the role category.

10. Present the finally selected behaviours in vertical scale formats. Since the time BARS was developed, a large number of research studies were conducted to examine the effectiveness in reducing errors and increasing the quality of ratings.

Thus, in the Smith and Kendall (1963) format of BARS.... raters were to be given a set of vertical graphic scales and instructed to record the behaviour observed on each applicable scale throughout the appraisal period. The instructions were to observe the behaviour, decide to which dimension it belonged, and then indicate on the scale the date and details of the incident. The notation of the incident was to be made at the effectiveness level on the scale that was considered to be the most appropriate for that incident on that behavioural dimension. The scaling of the effectiveness level of the observation, i.e., the place on the page at which the observer recorded the incident, was to be aided by a comparison with a series of illustrative behavioural "anchors" and "genetic descriptions". (Bernardin and Smith, 1981, p.159.)

After observing and recording such incidents over a period the appraiser may make a summary rating. Thus in this format the sequence is observation-inference-scaling-recording and summary rating.

Rosinger et al. (1982) described the development of Mixed Standard Scale to assess the performance. The following steps are involved:

Step 1. Task analysis that results in behavioural descriptions of major activity areas and tasks.

Step 2. Assignment of importance scores to each task through systematic collection of data on frequency of performance and criticality of the task.

Step 3. Development and refinement of behavioural statements regarding different proficiency levels.

Step 4. Establishing validity and reliability.

The appraisal format they suggest is criterion-referenced rather than norm-referenced and it includes three anchors (average, excellent, poor) for a number of dimensions.

The Mixed Standard Scales are somewhat similar to BARS. There have been a number of such modifications and developments of new scales and also a number of researches on them. Comparisons between BARS and other rating formats have not shown BARS to offer psychometrically superior or more accurate performance ratings (Bernardin, 1977; Dunnette and Borman, 1979; Borman, 1979; Jacobs et al. 1980; Kingstrom and Bass, 1981; and Landy and Farr, 1980). It is however acknowledged that numerous methodological weaknesses exist in these researches comparing BARS with other scales.

Although BARS may not produce error-free or accurate ratings there is some research evidence (though largely inconclusive) available to indicate their potential use for more effective feedback (Home et al., 1982). "Accuracy of the recipient's perception of performance feedback should be enhanced because BARS define scale dimensions and anchors in concrete, behavioural terms, making them more interpretable to the recipient than those dimensions and anchors found in traditional formats. Although BARS are designed to maximise interpretability for raters (to facilitate valid ratings), the same may also be true for ratees receiving feedback from this instrument. Feedback from BARS may also be more accurately perceived if the numerical ratings are documented by specific behavioural examples; thus preventing distortion or denial of feedback" (Hom et al., 1982 p. 569).

Research with formats of much greater sophistication than the traditional graphic, trait approach show fancy scales such as behaviourally anchored rating scales do essentially no better at the game of inhibiting rating inflation (Landy and Farr, 1980). Numerous other studies have compared different types of rating formats such as Mixed Standard Scales, Behaviourally Anchored Rating Scales or Simple Graphic Scales. In general these studies have revealed relatively little differences in the extent of rating error as a function of the format (Bernardin and Cardy, 1982). In fact, there is a strong indication that ratings are as much or more a function of the idiosyncracies of the rater who made them than that of the actual behaviour of the ratees.

Assessment by Peers

Some literature is available on the performance assessments by peers (members of the same level in the organisational hierarchy having working relations with the appraisee). Peer assessments are made through nominations, ratings or rankings. In a recent study Love (1981) compared the reliability, validity, friendship bias and user reaction using nominations, rating and ranking formats. His study was conducted on 145 police officers using a 9-point behaviourally anchored scale for ratings. Criterion rankings and ratings were provided by their squad supervisors. In this study all peer-based methods showed significant reliability and validity and the validity coefficients were not significantly biased by the friendship between peer assessors and assessee. Rankings and nominations displayed significantly greater reliability and validity than ratings. However, user reactions were negative to all methods. They indicated that peer assessment was not fair, not accurate, not liked by them and did not suggest them for promotion decisions.

Some Theoretical Considerations on Factors Affecting Appraisals

"Some of the most important conclusions to be drawn from research on human information processing are that our processing capabilities are limited and that perception and recall frequently do not match reality. The limitation on our processing capacity is handled nicely by cognitive representations called "Schemata" (Neisser, 1976). A schemata directs our attention and aids in categorisation and recall of information. However, schemata can also lead to systematic inaccuracies. Biased ratings may result when a rater relies on an irrelevant, over simplistic, or otherwise faulty schema. For instance, the gender of the ratee may be irrelevant to job performance but yet may set up a schema (in this case a sex stereotype) that may bias perception and recall of the ratee's performance. Ratee sex, race, age, and even a single instance of behaviour may elicit a schema which the rater employs to process and recall ratee performance. Research indicates that once a ratee is categorised, further perception and recall of that ratee's performance is biased toward that category (or schema) (Cantor and Mischel, 1977). There will be a bias to attend to information that is consistent with the schema (Snyder and Swann, 1978). When recalling information concerning the ratee's performance, the rater will be biased toward recalling information that is made most available by the schema. That is, ratings will be biased toward those dimension values which best fit with (most closely resemble) the schema for the ratee (Tversky and Kahneman, 1974). "It also appears that humans are typically unaware of these biasing processes and will deny the operation of such a bias even when it is clearly present" (Nis bertt and Wilson, 1977, p. 353). Bernardin and Cardy (1982) proposed that the accurating as a performance on the part of the rater is a function of the rater's ability and motivation to rate accurately. Level of trust the rater has in the appraisal system affects his motivation to rate accurately. Bernardin and cardy (1982) also suggest that rater motivation and ability to rate accurately are dynamically interrelated. For example, when there is low trust in the appraisal system, the rater may rely heavily on the information provided by his stereotypic schemata rather than searching for information. When there is high trust, the rater may actively search for ratee performance information rather than to rely on his schemata.

There are numerous parameters that can affect accuracy of appraisals. The greater the number of these considered the better off the practitioner will be. On the basis of review of several researches on performance appraisal Decotiis and Petit (1978) have developed a model of performance appraisal process. The model is based on the premise that "the accuracy of performance appraisals can be viewed as a function of: (a) rater's motivation to appraise accurately; (b) job-relevance of the rating standards used by the rater; and (c) rater's ability to evaluate ratee job behaviour." On the basis of their model and their survey of several researches relating to this they propose the following:

Rater Motivation

1. Rater motivation to assign accurate performance ratings is higher when the purpose of appraisal is personnel research than when the purpose is either employ development or administration of organisational rewards.
2. Rater motivation to assign accurate performance ratings is higher when the purpose of appraisal is employee development than when the purpose is administration of organisational rewards.
3. Regardless of purpose, rater motivation to assign accurate performance ratings is higher when the results of the appraisal are confidential from the ratee.
4. When the purpose of appraisal is either employee development or administration of organisational rewards and the rater is required to discuss the result of appraisal with the ratee, rater motivation to assign accurate performance ratings is higher when the rater perceives feedback as a legitimate aspect of his or her role.
5. When feedback of the results of appraisal is required, rater motivation to assign accurate performance ratings is higher if the

rater perceives that he or she has the necessary insights into ratee job behaviour.

6. The easier a performance appraisal instrument is to understand, the more likely raters are to perceive it as being adequate for the purpose at hand.
7. A performance appraisal instrument that is based on systematically gathered job information will be perceived by a rater as more adequate for the purpose of appraisal than an instrument developed on ad hoc basis.
8. A performance appraisal instrument that is based on job information, easy to understand, and perceived as adequate for the purpose of appraisal will lead to increased rater motivation to assign accurate performance ratings.

Rater Ability

1. The more opportunities to observe ratee job behaviour the rater takes advantage of, the higher his or her ability to assign accurate performance ratings.
2. The more correct the behaviour observed by the rater, the higher his or her ability to assign accurate performance ratings.
3. All else being equal, the closer the rater's organisational level is to the ratee's organisational level, the higher the rater's ability to assign accurate performance ratings.
4. Raters from different organisational levels sample different aspects of ratee behaviour. Therefore, the higher the correspondence between the content of the rating instrument used and the rater's sample of ratee behaviour the higher the rater's ability to assign accurate performance ratings.
5. Rater ability is higher when the rater understands the linkage between ratee job behaviour and organisational outcomes than when he or she does not understand the link ages.
6. Rater ability is higher when the rater's personal style stresses goal attainment for ratees rather than consideration of ratees as individuals.
7. Raters trained in the principles and problems of performance appraisal have higher ability to assign accurate performance ratings than untrained raters.
8. Rater training methods that stress active learning result in higher rater ability to rate performance accurately than training methods that stress passive learning.

Availability of Appropriate Rating Standards

1. The higher the correspondence between job context and the rating standard used by the rater, the more accurate the performance rating obtained.
2. The more the differences in patterns of ratee job behaviour are incorporated into the rating standards used by a rater, the more accurate the performance ratings assigned by the rater.
3. Regardless of rater's sex, females tend to be rated lower than males performing similar tasks.
4. When rater and ratee are of the same race, the ratee will be assigned higher ratings than when the rater and the ratee are from different races.
5. The higher the correspondence between the content of appraisal and job content, the higher the likelihood that accurate performance rating would result.
6. The higher the correspondence between performance appraisal procedures and the dominant organisational philosophy the more likely performance will be appraised accurately.
7. The more likely it is that the rater will be held accountable for the ratings he or she assigns the more accurate will be the appraisal ratings.

Feldman (1981) has described in detail the various cognitive processes that influence the appraisal processes. Person perception, the basis of performance evaluation, is conceptualised as a dual-process system. Persons assign persons to categories. "These categories are fuzzy sets, defined by family resemblances among their members and exemplified by category prototypes or images. Stimulus persons may be assigned to categories automatically, by virtue of their possession of obvious or salient at tributes; the specific categories to which they are assigned is a function of perceiver and situational factors (e.g., personal constructs and contextual salience)" (p. 134). This automatic process may be superseded by a controlled, or consciously monitored process, when no salient category provides a satisfactory fit or information discrepant with initial categorisation is obtained. "Categorisation affects performance evaluation by limiting and selecting information about the employee when memory-based judgements are made and by influencing stimulus-based judgements through the operation of attributional bias" (p. 135). When employees are evaluated information has to be retrieved from memory. "Recent research has shown that memories about people (except for their very recent behaviour) are biased toward the prototypes representing the categories to which they have been assigned. Dispositional factors in the perceiver and situational influences render certain categories more salient than others and certain memories (and prototype generated false memories) more available than others. Via the operation of representativeness and availability heuristics in judgement, these further bias the prediction of future behaviour. Seeking further information to improve evaluation is an inherently biased process, for people's information-gathering strategies selectively attend to supportive information and elicit hypothesis-confirming behaviour" (p. 138).

On the basis of his analysis of cognitive processes and information processing effects on performance assessment Feldman (1981) suggests the following implications for users of appraisals.

1. BARS and behaviour observation scales may be seen as an attempt to define a more valid prototype of the successful-unsuccessful employee. Training in the use of such scale is an attempt to teach common prototypes to a set of raters to improve validity.
2. Multiple evaluations of appraisees may help overcome idiosyncratic biases of any one person's category system, although common prototypes may still retain some biases.
3. The use of hard criteria should be encouraged in performance assessment (absenteeism, punctuality, job samples, etc., wherever appropriate).
4. Evaluators should be trained to make behaviour sampling a routine part of their job to circumvent memory-biases.
5. The use of trait ratings should be discouraged.

Cognitive complexity is another variable that has been proposed as affecting accuracy of appraisal ratings. Cognitive complexity was defined by Schneier (1977) as "the degree to which a person possesses the ability to perceive behaviour in a multidimensional manner" (p.541). Cognitively complex people have a highly differentiated system of dimensions for perceiving the behaviour of others as compared to cognitively simple people. Schneier's (1977) study supported a cognitive compatibility theory of performance appraisal that compatiability of rater cognitive structure with the cognitive demands made by the rating format is crucial for quality ratings. Schneier (1977) found that cognitively complex raters were more confident in their ratings with BARS, made less leniency and restriction of range errors, and showed less halo effect as compared to cognitively simple raters. Subsequently five empirical investigations were carried out and no support has been found to this cognitively appealing theory of cognitive compatibility (Bernardin et al. 1982). Four experiments conducted recently by Bernardin et al. (1982) also failed to support this theory. There are some interesting re search findings from attribution research that seem to have implications for performance analysis and through it for rating behaviour.

When a supervisor attributes poor performance of his subordinate to individual factors (internal) rather than to external (environmental or task related) factors, he is likely to give poor ratings or show a higher punitive response to his subordinate. A supervisor is more likely to blame a subordinate for the poor performance than the environment because an environmental attribution might suggest that poor supervision was involved. Kipnis (1972) demonstrated that supervisors gave more internal attributions for subordinate failure than for subordinate success. Studies show that external attributions are more likely when the environment is made more salient than when the environment is not salient (McArthur and Post, 1977). Mitchell and Kalb (1982) in an experimental study supported subsequently a field study demonstrated that experience on the task may make the supervisors more aware of the external causes of poor performance such as a disruptive environment. The implication is that inexperienced supervisors should pay more attention and check their tendencies to attribute failure of their subordinates only to internal factors and thereby improve the quality of their ratings.

Another factor that influences rater's biases is his own inability to differentiate performance inputs of the appraisee (effort) from the performance outcomes (results). While effort and ability are attributable to the appraisee results or outcomes are a consequence of interactions between individual and environmental factors. Most often appraisers tend to assess their subordinates on the basis of outcomes and particularly when the outcomes are poor they tend to rate the "inputs" also as poor. In an experimental study by Mitchell and Klab (1982), supervisors with and without knowledge of outcomes of their subordinates' behaviour were studied for their attribution tendencies. Those with outcome knowledge tended to attribute negative outcomes more to their subordinates. Appraisers therefore should become aware of these tendencies and focus more on the behaviour of their subordinates rather than outcomes of their actions.

Reducing Rater Biases

The above theoretical considerations bring but the complexity of appraisal process. As stated earlier, as long as human beings are going to assess other human beings there is bound to be certain amount of subjectivity. One way of reducing these is by making the assessors more and more aware of the dynamic factors affecting their perceptions and evaluations of their subordinates. This can be done through rater training, rater participation in the construction of rating scales and the use of some statistical methods. Some research evidence is available on these aspects.

Rater Training

For example, rater training has generally been shown to be effective in reducing errors, especially if the training is extensive and allows practice (Landy and Farr, 1980; Kearney, 1978; and Decotiis and Petit, 1978).

Hyde and Smith (1982) have pointed out very well what training can do and what it cannot to remedy the various problems associated with performance appraisal. They hypothesise that "training" can have very minimal impact on the motivation among raters and ratees as this is a behavioural problem and not skill deficiency. Training of appraisers also has very little impact on "time delays in feedback" as this is essentially a system problem. Training also has very little impact on solving appraisal problems arising due to task-interdependence, observability or task performance, structure of authority system, power differentials and nature of communicated appraisals because these are all complex interrelated organisational problems that must be confronted before any appraisal can be developed. Training has some impact on helping appraisers to comprehend the conflicting objectives of appraisals (e.g., development and control at the same time) and meet the requirements. Training has the highest potential for effective change in reducing subjective errors in evaluation like halo effect, polarity, central tendency, etc.

Hyde and Smith (1982) suggested four-phased-training for effective introduction of appraisal system.

Phase 1. Knowledge presentation
Phase 2. Analysis and evaluation methods and errors
Phase 3. Practice evaluating performance
Phase 4. Evaluation of training.

Rater Participation in Scale Construction

Another method used in reducing rating errors is by participation of the raters in scale construction. Empirical studies indicate that when raters participate totally in constructing the scales they use, it is likely to reduce rating errors (Friedman and Cornelius, 1976; and Warmke and Billings, 1979). Friedman and Cornelius (1976) found that full participation in scale construction significantly reduced halo and increased convergent validity among Reserve Officer Training Corps Cadet's ratings of instructors. This study showed that the effect held across scale for mats (BARS and graphic scales) and that construction of one scale also reduced errors on another unfamiliar scale. Warmke and Billings (1979) indicate from their study that even a short 2- hour time investment required four scale development can increase scale acceptance and reduce rating errors.

Statistical Control of Rating Errors

With inconsistencies in research findings on the effectiveness of BARS in reducing rating errors, attempts have been made by some researchers to statistically control "halo effect" and such other errors. Holzbach (1980) presented a logical basis for using partial correlations as methods of reducing halo errors. His suggestion is based on the assumption that raters are unable to make ratings on individual performance dimensions that are independent of their overall evaluation of the ratee. Therefore it is possible to remove the halo component from the dimension ratings by statistically eliminating the variance in common between the dimensions and overall ratings. Holzbach (1978) reported striking reductions in the mean dimensional intercorrelations after removing the effect of overall rating. Landy et al. (1980) found support for the effectiveness of partialing. Harvey (1982) examined this practice by questioning the lack of empirical base for the causal assumptions made on halo effect as well by empirically demonstrating that a re-analysis of data used by Landy et al. (1980) indicates that the effectiveness partialing out may be an artifact.

Researchers in this area do not seem to have tried out statistical feedback to raters as a mechanism of reducing rater biases. If biases take place in the minds of raters it is futile to look for corrections through statistical controls. Statistical controls can at the most give temporary reductions and that too to a questionable degree as indicated above. Statistical feedback to raters can be a potential way to reduce errors and bring about some common frames of reference among different raters. Such a rater feedback involves the following analysis to be done by the personnel and HRD departments and fed back to the raters:

1. Trends of appraisal ratings of every appraiser over a period of time. Data like the following ones have to be compiled, analysed and fed back.
   (a) Number of ratees rated by the appraiser in the last few years (a 3-year period is minimum).
   (b) Dimension-wise analysis of performance rating assigned by him to all the appraisees rated by him (e.g., fre quency and percentage of times the rating of "5" was assigned on "initiative" or frequency and percentage of times a rating of '3" was assigned on "initiative", etc.). These may be further analysed for each category of ratees (secretarial staff, supervisors, assistant managers, etc.) if the rater is the reporting officer for a variety of them. Since KPAs may not be common to all the appraisees all KPAs may be treated as equal and combined for such calculations.
   (c) Dimension-wise average (or per KPA average) and stand ard deviation of the ratings assigned to all the appraisees rated by him.

2. Trends of appraisal ratings given by peer appraisers (similar rank, position, role incumbency, etc.) to their subordinates (with or without mentioning their names). Similar analysis like in step 1 above should be presented to enable the rater to compare if he has been a lenient rater or a strict rater.
3. Company-wise trends (frequencies, percentages, means and standard deviations) of appraisal ratings over the last few years on each dimension.

Finding back these data helps the appraiser to see his own rating behaviour vis-a-vis others in the company and accordingly modify, if needed, Discussions can be organised between the raters and the ratees around these data so that they may benefit from each other.

Performance Ratings for Development vs Administrative Decisions

As suggested in the first chapter, the performance appraisal system should have the assessment of managerial and behavioural capabilities as an integral part of it. In a development- oriented appraisal system performance ratings are not ends in themselves. They are one of the instruments that aid the process of development. Hence these dimensions should be identified and incorporated in the appraisal form with a view to generate data for development purposes. A list of such dimensions taken from the appraisal formats used by different organisations in India are presented in Appendix 6.1.

Subjectivity is very much a part of development and executives need not be over concerned about the ambitious task of generating objective data. The concern should be more on generating and including the most appropriate dimensions that are important for performing well the existing jobs as well as for developing their potential for future roles. Rating scales like BARS are useful to the extent they provide clarity on the behaviours associated with the different dimensions. If such scales can be developed complimenting the development objectives, it should be encouraged. Involving the executives in developing such scales, making the appraisers share their expectations with appraisees in the year-beginning, training them and giving periodic statistical feedback about their rating behaviour may take care of some biases.

It is necessary to separate appraisal ratings for development purposes from those for reward purposes. In development-oriented appraisal the performance standards are decided between the appraiser and the appraisee in the beginning of the year and may differ from appraisee to appraisee. For reward administration, promotions and other administrative purposes appraisal ratings based on common performance standards (common at least to appraisees of the same level in the managerial hierarchy) are required. Here the appraiser compares (and even unconsciously ranks) the subordinates he is appraising and then rates them. Objectivity becomes much more important for such purposes and given our culture we may not be able to do away with confidentiality for some more time. Even if the employees are confidentially rated on a few dimensions for administrative decisions, biases are likely to be less if such ratings are given after assessment is made for development purposes. Using development-oriented appraisal systems is likely to make available to the appraiser a lot of performance information and thus reduce his biases. Participation in a development-oriented appraisal system may improve the cognitive complexity of the appraisers as well as appraisees and may help reduce biases. It may also help executives develop cognitive flexibility in categorising employees by making available a large number of schemata on the basis of information available to the appraiser. Since the counselling process (discussed in the next chapter) strengthens the dyadic relationship between the appraiser and the appraisee and generates trust, biases may be further reduced.

However, when two different appraisal formats are used separately for development and administrative purposes, there is a possibility of appraisers assigning different ratings for the same individual in the two forms. Appraisees should be helped to comprehend this difference due to varying performance standards being used for the two appraisals.

Appendix 6.1

List of Managerial and Behavioural Dimensions being used by Different Organisations in their Performance Appraisal

1. Planning ability
2. Organising ability
3. Coordination
4. Supervision
5. Leadership and dynamism
6. Initiative
7. Resourcefulness
8. Creativity and imaginativeness
9. Development of subordinates
10. Contribution to team spirit
11. Analytical abilities
12. Delegation
13. Public relations
14. Sociability
15. Self-confidence
16. Decision-making
17. Cooperativeness
18. Flexibility
19. Problem-solving
20. Risk-taking
21. Ability to motivate subordinates
22. Conflict management
23. Communication skills (oral and written)
24. Perseverance
25. Hardwork
26. Integrity
27. Drive
28. Empathy
29. Assertiveness
30. Originality
31. Data management

(For a detailed description of some of these dimensions identified through a systematic study of critical attributes in Larsen & Toubro Limited, see U. Pareek and T.V. Rao, Designing and Managing Human Resource Systems, New Delhi, Oxford & IBH, 1981, pp 63-73).

Chapter 7

PERFORMANCE COUNSELLING*

PERFORMANCE COUNSELLING is quite often misunderstood. It is wrongly interpreted as a process of correcting or controlling the employee behaviour by giving him negative feedback in an assertive manner by his boss. When employees make mistakes or become unmanageable or non-cooperative, executives often state that they need counselling. Some managers also are known to make statements like "I called him for counselling and gave him a bit of my mind" or "I called him for counselling and told him clearly that I am not going to tolerate his behaviour any more" or "I called him for counselling and finished him off", etc. Unfortunately, due to such misuse of the term "counselling" it has acquired some negative connotations in the minds of some managers. They confuse "verbal threats", "criticism" and "negative feedback" to be counselling. Actually such behaviours prevent counselling.

A second reason why counselling has acquired a negative image in the minds of some executives is because of equating it with clinical counselling and psychotherepy which are more often associated with problem cases. In fact, a major difference between clinical counselling and performance counselling is precisely this. Performance counselling is normally done in regular course of performance when there are no problems. When there are problems, executives should resort to appropriate methods of solving them rather than to counselling. Because exclusive focus on a particular problem or issue may prevent performance counselling. Performance counselling focuses on the entire performance (tasks and behaviours) during a particular period rather than on a specific problem. However, specific problems may be discussed during counselling as a part of analysing and understanding performance patterns.

In clinical counselling the client goes to a therapist for help on his own initiative and therefore has a high motivation to solve his problems and improve his capabilities to deal with his environment. In performance counselling the counsellor initiates the discussion as a part of an

---

*This chapter is a slightly revised version of "Performance Counselling" by U.Pareek and T.V.Rao, CR Reading 18, Learning Systems, New Delhi.

appraisal system or as a part of some processes that take place in the organisation. The onus of making the counselling successful is jointly with the counsellor and the counsellee, although the counsellor has a major responsibility by virtue of his position in the organisational hierarchy. It is this, that makes performance counselling complex. The counsellor who is at a higher status level has to carry on the task of helping his subordinate by creating an atmosphere of acceptance. Thus, unlike clinical counselling, in performance counselling the counsellor has an additional task of motivating the counsellee to participate effectively in the counselling process. In addition while continuing to exercise his authority as a boss outside the counselling session he should generate a climate of acceptance, mutuality, trust and openness during counselling. Recognition of this complexity is essential for the successful implementation of counselling. Failure to recognise this often leads managers to point out inconsistencies in their bosses by statments like - "He was nice during counselling and out of it he is very hard on me." Counselling is a separate event and certainly should lead to more understanding but need not result in "lenience" or "softness" in dealing with people.

While performance counselling should take place at least once in a year as an integral part of the appraisal system outlined in this book, it could be carried out more frequently by managers. It is advisable to have performance counselling discussions quite frequently depending upon the needs of each appraisee and the time availability of the counsellor. In fact, the more attention a manager pays to counselling his subordinates, the more time he is likely to gain in the long run as a result of improved capabilities of his subordinates.

Any organisation interested in using a good performance appraisal and review system that aims at developing employees has to practice and pay enough attention to performance counselling. Performance appraisal does not serve the purpose of developing employees unless an effective system of performance counselling is introduced and practised in the organisation. Performance counselling can be defined as the help provided by a manager to his subordinates in analysing their performance and other job behaviours in order to increase their job effectiveness. Performance counselling essentially focuses on the analysis of performance on the job, and identification of training needs for further improvement.

Counselling is a dyadic process. It is based on the relation between two persons, a manager who is providing help or who is counselling and an employee to whom such help is given or who is a counsellee. It differs from training mainly in its intensity of dyadic relationship and its focus on establishing mutuality and confidentiality. Managers provide such help or counselling at various stages. For example, an employee may be provided such personal help soon after his selection or when he is facing difficulties or problems. The focus of performance counselling is the employee's performance on the task assigned to him.

Performance counselling sometimes is also called "coaching" mainly because the purpose of counselling is to improve the performance of the employee. Although the word "coaching" is widely used for this purpose, the word "counselling" is a much wider and appropriate term for such a process.

Objectives of Counselling

Counselling aims at development of the counsellee. It involves the following:

1. Helping him to realise his potential as a manager.
2. Helping him to understand himself - his strengths and his weaknesses.
3. Providing him an opportunity to acquire more insight into his behaviour and analyse the dynamics of such behaviour.
4. Helping him to have better understanding of the environment.
5. Increasing his personal and inter-personal effectiveness by giving him feedback about his behaviour and assisting him in analysing his inter-personal competence.
6. Encouraging him to set goals for further improvement.
7. Encouraging him to generate alternatives for dealing with various problems.
8. Providing him empathic atmosphere for his sharing and discussing his tensions, conflicts, concerns and problems.
9. Helping him to develop various action plans for further improvement.
10. Helping him to review in a non-threatening way his progress in achieving various objectives.

Conditions for Effective Counselling

Counselling is a means and not an end in itself. Development does not occur just because there is counselling. Counselling could be an effective instrument in helping people integrate with their organisation and have a sense of involvement and satisfac tion. The following conditions are necessary for counselling to be effective.

1. General Climate of Openness and Mutuality :

If the organisation or department in which the employee is working is full of tension, and people do not trust each other, counselling cannot be effective. A climate of minimum trust and openness is essential for effective counselling.

2. General Helpful and Empathic Attitude of Management :

Counselling involves effective helping which is not possible unless the counsellor has general helping attitude and has empathy for the counsellee.

3. Sense of Uninhibited Participation by the Subordinates in the Performance Review Process :

Unless the subordinates in a department or organisation feel free enough to participate without inhibition in the process of review and feedback, counselling cannot be effective. Counselling is not a one- way process of communicating to the employee what he should or should not do. It is a process of developing dialogue which eventually contributes to better understanding on the part of counsellee.

4. Dialogic Relationship in Goal Setting and Performance Review :

Performance counselling focuses on the counsellee's achievement of the performance goals he had set in consultation with his manager. Joint participation by the employee and his reporting officer are necessary both in goal setting as well as in the performance review. Without such collaboration effort, counselling does not achieve its purpose.

5. Focus on Work-oriented Behaviour :

The main purpose of performance counselling is to help the employee in improving his performance. Counselling can be effective if the focus is kept on the work-related goals rather than diffusing attention into various other areas. While doing so, discussion may involve other related and personal issues, but these are used to refocus on improvement of organisational roles rather than on personal or general personality problems.

6. Focus on Work-related Problems and Difficulties :

Performance counselling is not related only to the achievement of goals, but also to the contextual problems in achieving or not achieving the goals. Analysis of performance therefore becomes the basis of counselling. Details of performance review and analysis are discussed in Rao and Pareek (1978).

7. Avoidance of Discussion of Salary and Other Rewards :

Perfor mance counselling may not serve its purpose if it includes discussion about salary raise, rewards, etc. The main purpose of performance counselling is to use performance appraisal in planning and improvement of the employee, rather than understanding relationship between performance and reward like salary, etc. Bringing such discussion in the performance counselling may vitiate the main purpose of counselling.

What Constitutes Counselling?

Counselling is given by one who is senior to the other person - in competence, or in knowledge, or in psychological expertise, or in the hierarchical position in the organisation. There are three main processes involved in counselling - communication, influencing, and helping. The counsellor essentially communicates with the counsellee. Communication involves both receiving messages (listening), giving messages (responding), and giving feedback. The person who provides counselling does all the three things. Counselling also involves influencing the counsellee in several ways. The manager cannot escape the fact that he is influencing his employee in such a way that the latter is able to move in some direction. However, this influence is of a special type, enabling the other person to exercise more autonomy, providing positive reinforcement so that desirable behaviour is further strengthened, and creating conditions in which the person is able to learn from the behaviour of the counsellor through the process of identification.

The third element in the process, i.e., helping also functions in a similar way. It involves three different elements. Helping behaviour is based on concern and empathy the counsellor has for his counsellee. It is also based on mutuality of relationship; counsellee responds as much to the counsellor's needs as the former does to the latter's. And finally, helping primarily involves identification of developmental needs of the counsellee so that he may be able to develop and increase his effectiveness. This dynamic process of counselling is shown in Exhibit 7.1. The various elements of the process will be explained in more detail.

EXHIBIT 7.1

The Process of Counselling

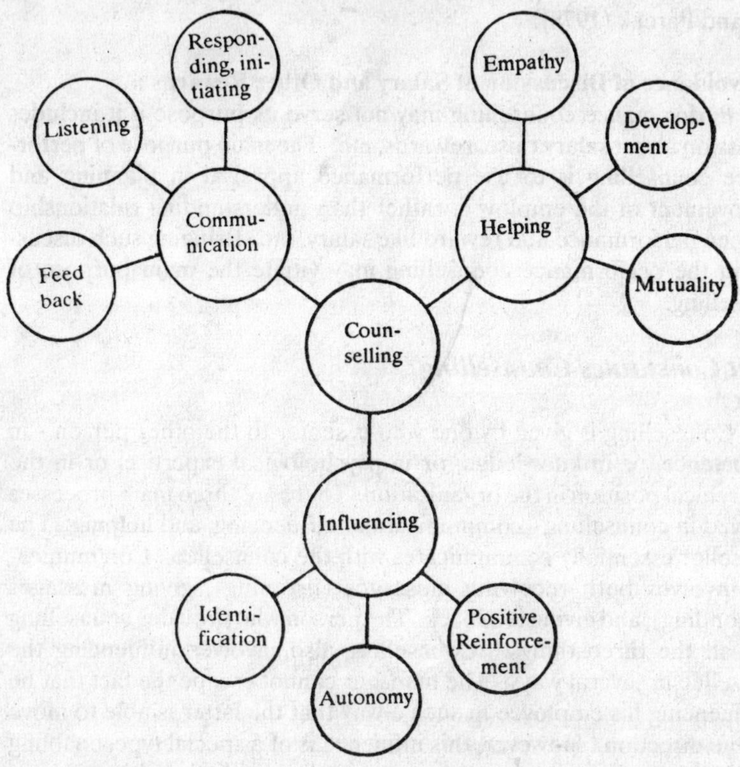

1. Communication

Interpersonal communication is the basis of performance review in which both the employee and his reporting officer are involved. The general climate of such conversation in performance review should be congenial which may help the employee to be in a receptive mood. It is important to keep in mind that communication is greatly influenced by how problems and issues are perceived by the two persons in volved in the conversation. Communication may get distorted if people are not empathic to each other and do not try to understand each others' point of view. Non-verbal communication is as important as verbal communication. People speak much more through their gestures and postures than through words. The tone and manner of speaking is also important. There are three main elements in communication.

Listening

Listening is the first effective step in communication. Listening involves paying attention to the various messages being sent by the other person. The obvious message is the ideas being communicated (cognitive message). But more hidden may be the feelings and the concerns the other person may not be able to put clearly in words. Listening to feelings and concerns is very important for effective counselling. This involves skills which can be practised. Some exercises can be used to improve listening of such hidden messages (see Rao and Pareek, 1978a).

Asking Questions and Responding

Questions can facilitate or hinder the process of communication. Questions can serve several purposes: they can help in getting more information, establishing mutuality, clarifying matters, stimulating thinking. In a counselling situation questions play a very important role. Some questions can shut off the counsellee, or make him dependent on the counsellor. Another set of questions can build autonomy of the counsellee. Obviously the latter will be helpful, and not the former.

Questions that do not Help

The following types of questions are not only not helpful, they hinder the process of effective counselling.

Critical questions: Questions which are used to criticise, reprimand or doubt the counsellee create a gap between him and the counsellor. The way the question is asked (tone or sarcasm) may indicate that the question is a critical one. The choice of words may also indicate the critical nature of the question. "Why did you fail to achieve your targets?" communicates criticism, whereas "Why could you not attain your targets?" would normally communicate invitation to examine hindering factors. "How did you again fall short of your target?" is a reprimanding question. "How can you achieve this target you failed last time?" indicates doubt in the ability of the counsellee. All such critical questions either shut off the counsellee, or make him diffident.

Testing questions: Questions which are asked to find out whether a person is right or wrong or how much he knows are evaluating or testing questions. Such questions may tend to make the other person defensive. In a testing question the person who is asking the question takes a superior attitude, and the other person is put in a kind of witness box. Such questions may also take the form of cross-examination. A reporting officer who proposes to find out why his employee was not able to meet his target can easily slip into a cross-examination, testing or evaluating posture. Again, the tone of the interviewer may determine whether the question is asked as a testing question. Such questions are sometimes similar to critical questions.

Resenting questions: A person may ask questions to indicate his resentment for the behaviour of the other person. When an employee in a counselling situation asks: "How should I attain a higher target?" it may indicate his resentment depending on the tone in which such a question is asked.

Leading questions: Quite often unknowingly we ask questions which indicate what kind of answers we want and we may get such answers in return. Such a question may be asked after making a statement. For example, a reporting officer may say to his employee: "You could not attain the target be cause Maintenance Department did not cooperate. Is that true?", or it may be put in the question form "Were you not able to attain the target because the Maintenance Department did not cooperate?" Both are leading questions. A leading question almost seduces the other person to go along the line of thinking of one who puts the question. This tends to stop further exploration and is not helpful.

Questions that are Helpful

The following types of questions may be helpful in developing more healthy relationship and in increasing the effectiveness of the other person.

Testing questions: Questions which are asked to indicate that the questioner is seeking help or suggestions may inicate the trust he has in the other person. The question "How do you think I can deal with the problem I am facing?" is seeking help from the other person. Such questions may be asked both by the employee and the supervisor.

Clarifying questions: Questions may be asked to collect information, more facts and figures. Such questions are very helpful. If a counsellor asks his employee several questions to help him to get more information about various aspects he would help him in having relevant information to understand his problems. After listening to a person for some time the counsellor may paraphrase the counsellee's statement (also called "mirroring"), then may ask a question to confirm whether his understanding is correct. For example, the question "You are worried about your lack of knowledge of the new system. Is that so?" is a clarifying question. Clarifying question helps the manager and the employee to remain at the same level throughout the conversation.

Open questions: The most useful questions are those which stimulate reflection and thinking on the part of the counsellee. "Why do you think we have not achieved the targets this year while the other company has done so?" is an open question inviting the other person to explore the various possible dimensions, and to share these with the person who is asking such a question. Open questions encourage creativity, a tendency to explore several directions which might have been neglected so far. Such questions are very useful.

Responding to Questions

Counsellors sometimes use responses some of which are useful and some other dysfunctional. Some counsellors may be using more often certain types of responses than others. It is necessary to be aware of these. Responses that alienate the employee, criticise him or order him are more likely to be dysfunctional. Empathetic, supportive, and exploring responses are more functional. Various verbal behaviours in counselling situation that characterise these responses are shown in Exhibit 7.2.

Feedback

Interpersonal feedback is an important input for increasing self-awareness. It helps in reducing the blind area of a person, helping him to become more aware about his strengths and weaknesses. If properly used, it results in higher mutuality between two persons. The process of interpersonal feedback and conditions which make it effective have been discussed in detail elsewhere (Pareek, 1976). The following hints are reproduced from that source.

Feedback will be effective if the person who gives the feedback (counsellor) makes sure that it is:

i) descriptive and not evaluative;
ii) focused on the behaviour of the person and not on the person himself;
iii) data based and specific and not impressionistic;
iv) reinforces positive new behaviour;
v) suggestive and not prescriptive;

vi) continuous;
vii) mostly personal, giving data from one's own experience;
viii) need-based and solicited;
ix) intended to help;
x) focused on modifiable behaviour;
xi) satisfies needs of both the feedback given and one who receives feedback;
xii) checked and verified;
xiii) well timed; and
xiv) contributes to mutuality and building up relationship.

Exhibit 7.2

Counsellor Responses

Unhelpful	Effective and helpful
Alienating	Empathic
Continuous stress on conformity	Levelling
Not encouraging creative acts	Rapport building
Passive listening	Identifying feelings
Lack of verbal response	Supportive
Critical	Recognising
Criticising	Communicating availability
Pointing inconsistencies	Committing support
Repeated mention of weaknesses	Trusting
Belittling	Exploring
Reprimanding	Questions
Directive	Reflecting
Prescribing	Sharing
Ordering	Probing
Threatening	Closing
Giving no options	Summarising
Pointing out only one acceptable way	Concluding
Quoting rules and regulations	Contracting for follow-up and help

From the point of view of one who receives feedback it is necessary that the reaction to feedback is more in terms of exploring ways of improving behaviour rather than in terms of defensive behaviour. The following defensive behaviour might not help in using feedback properly, and the behaviours which are opposite of these may be helpful.

i) Denying feedback as opposed to owning up responsibility for behaviour.
ii) Rationalisation (explaining away feedback by giving reasons) as opposed to self-analysis to find why such behaviour was shown.
iii) Projection (contributing negative feelings to the other person) as opposed to empathy (trying to under stand the point of view of the other person).
iv) Displacement (expressing negative feelings to one who may not fight back) as opposed to exploration (taking help of the other person in knowing more about the feedback which has been given).
v) Quick acceptance without exploration as opposed to collecting more information and data to understand the behaviour.
vi) Aggression towards the person giving feedback as opposed to seeking his help in understanding the feedback.
vii) Humour and wit as opposed to concern for improvement.
viii) Counterdependence (rejecting the authority) as opposed to listening carefully to the person giving feedback.
ix) Cynicism (generally strong skepticism that things cannot improve) as opposed to positive critical atti tude to accept some feedback and question some other.
x) Generalisation (explaining things in a general way) as opposed to experimenting.

2. Influencing

Influencing would mean making an impact on the person in relationship. Such impact need not necessarily be of restrictive type. Influencing in effective counselling would involve the following three aspects.

Increasing Autonomy of the Person

Usually, influencing is understood in the only sense of restricting the autonomy of the person and directing him into channels which are predetermined by the person who is exerting influence. Positive influencing is the opposite of it; the autonomy of the other person is increased and he has larger scope of making his own choice. Even this is influencing. But this is a different kind of influencing. Flanders (1970) makes distinction between two modes of influence, one called direct mode of influence (which restricts the freedom of the other person), and the other indirect mode of influence (which increases the freedom of the other person). Flanders has developed some categories to indicate the two modes. He classifies criticism and punishment in the first category, and encouraging a person in the second category of influence. The reason is obvious. When a person is criticised or punished, some actions for which he is criticised or punished are inhibited and the person avoids doing those in future. This restricts his freedom. On the other hand, if a person is praised or recognised, he feels encouraged to take more initiative in exploring new directions. This results in an increase in the field of his autonomy. Pareek and Rao (1971) have discussed this in details, how teacher education and training strategies can be remodelled based on some research findings about these two kinds of behaviour. In counselling much more use is made of indirect mode of influence, by recognising feelings; expressing feelings, acknowledging and praising good ideas given by the counsellee and raising questions which promote thinking and exploration.

Positive Reinforcement

It has been established by Skinner (1971) that change in behaviour cannot be brought about in human beings through punishment or negative reinforcement, but only through positive reinforcement. Influencing would involve providing encouragement and reinforcing success so that the person takes more initiative and is able to experiment with new ideas. Change cannot take place without experiment and risk taking. And these are encouraged through positive reinforcement.

Identification

Levinson (1962) has stressed the importance of the process of identification of the employee with his manager. One major influence which helps an employee to develop is the opportunity for him to identify with individuals having more experience, skill and influence. This according to McClel land (1975) is the first stage in the development of psychological maturity or power motivation. This legitimate need should be fulfilled. Levinson (1975) is the first stage in the development of psychosocial maturity or power motivation. This legitimate need should be fulfilled. Levinson (1962) states several barriers which may come in the way of such legitimate process of identification; lack of time, intolerance for mistakes, complete rejection of dependency needs, repression of rivalry, and unexamined relationship. Levinson suggests that to help the development of the process of identification it is necessary that the manager also examines his own process and needs of interacting with the subordinates.

3. Helping

Counselling is essentially helping. Helping involves several processes but the following three are mainly important.

Concern and Empathy

Without manager's concern for his employee, effective helping cannot be provided in the counselling session. Such concern is shown when the counsellor is able to feel for his subordinate and is able to empathise with him. These would be reflected in the kinds of questions asked and the tone in which conversation takes place. Managers may constantly ask themselves how much concern and genuine empathy they have for the employees whom they are counselling. Without such genuine concern, counselling may only degenerate into a ritual and cannot achieve its goals.

Mutuality of Relationship

Counselling should not be regarded as merely giving help. It is also receiving help on various aspects. Unless such a relationship is established - i.e., both persons involved in the relationship feeling free to ask for and provide help to each other counselling cannot be effective. Mutuality is based on trust and genuine perception that each person has enough to contribute. Although the counsellor is in a superior position, he continues to learn and to receive help from the counsellee.

Identifying Development Needs

The main purpose of performance counselling is to identify development needs of the employee which can be met through various ways. It is necessary that counselling results in clear and systematic identification of such needs and subsequent plans as to how these needs will be fulfilled.

Sperry and Hess (1974) have advocated the use of contact counselling which they defined as ".... the process by which the manager aids the employee effectively in the techniques of keying, responding and problem-solving and development, using guiding". Contact counselling is based on a transactional analysis approach and makes use of several skills discussed above. Keying refers to reading people. The supervisor uses an appropriate frame of reference to perceive what the employee means by his verbal and non-verbal responses. Responding concerns what the supervisor communicates back to the employee. What was learnt from keying is replayed in a manner which adds to, subtracts from, interchanges with the meaning the employee communicates. Guiding is the technique the supervisor used to motivate or help the employee to change his behaviour. The supervisor as motivator can function to increase the employee's drive to direct his drive that it better accomplishes the objectives.

Morrisey (1972) has suggested a few other techniques like a **you-we** technique, second hand compliment, advice-request and summary. In the **you-we** technique, one uses **you** to compliment and **we** to criticise ("**you** are doing a great job, **we** have a problem"). The **second hand** compliment is communicat ing to the subordinate a compliment for him received from a third party (Mr. Raman says that you have done an excellent job for him). The **advise-request** is asking the employee for suggestions and advice. Summarising at the end helps clarifying the decisions taken and fixing the responsibilities and integrating the whole discussion.

Sequential Process of Performance Counselling

Counselling is helping the employee to grow and develop in the organisation. Every manager is counselling his employee knowingly or unknowingly in his day-to-day work-life. An effective counsellor-manager is one who helps his employees to become more aware of their strengths and weaknesses and helps them grow to improve further on the strong points and overcome weaknesses. By the process of mutuality and support he helps the employee to develop, providing the proper emotional climate. Mutuality involves working together with the employee and developing future plans of action for employees growth and contribution to the organisation. Support involves acceptance of the employee as a total person with his strengths and weaknesses and encouraging him with warmth.

Counselling requires certain interpersonal skills which can be acquired easily if a manager is genuinely interested in developing his subordinates. Counselling skills are important for a manager particularly at time of performance review.

Good managers counsel their employees regularly in their jobs whenever a necessity arises. Annual performance reviews provide formal opportunities for formal counselling. Such a formal counselling process passes through certain stages which are important for the managers to note. The counselling process has the following three phases: rapport building, exploration, and action planning.

In the rapport building phase a good counsellor attempts to establish a climate of acceptance, warmth, support, openness and mutuality. He does this by empathysing with employees and his orientations, by listening to his problems and feelings, by communicating his understanding to the employee, by expressing empathy and genuineness of interest in him.

In the exploration phase the counsellor attempts to help the employee to understand himself and his problem better. He may do this by raising questions to help the employee explore his problems, and helping him to diagnose the problem properly.

In the action planning phase, the counsellor and the employee jointly work out or plan specific action steps for the development of the employee. The manager makes commitment to provide specific support he could offer to contribute to employee development.

Exhibit 7.3 gives the three phases (and the sub-phases) of the counselling process. Against each sub-phase are mentioned counsellor behaviours which are helpful in the counselling process and those which are likely to hinder the process.

Rapport Building

Rapport building is essential for any effective counselling outcome. Rapport building phase involves generating confidence in the employee to open up and frankly share his perceptions, problems, concerns, feelings, etc. The counsellor-manager should level himself with his employee and tune himself to his orientations. This can be done adopting the employee's frame of reference.

Attending

Opening phase of counselling is very important in rapport building.

General opening rituals may communicate messages of attending to the counsellee and give importance to the counselling transaction. Inviting rituals like offer the chair, closing the door to indicate privacy, asking the secretary not to disturb or not to pass on the telephonic calls during the conversation may indicate that the counsellor is attending to the counsellee. However, all such rituals should come out of the genuine concern and attempt for full attention to the employee during the counselling session.

Listening

It has already been discussed that listening is important for effective counselling. As already stated it is important to listen to what the employee says, as well as to his feelings and concerns. Physical posture (e.g. leanig forward) and keeping eye contact with the employee are indicators of listening.

Acceptance

Establishing a climate of acceptance is a necessary part of establishing rapport. The employee must feel that he is wanted and his counsellor is interested in understanding him as a person rather than as a role or a position in an organisation. The counsellor communicates this to the employee by listening to all the problems of the employee and communicating back to the employee that he is listening. The counsellor can communicate back to the employee by paraphrasing, mirroring or reflecting what the employee says. For example, when an employee says, "I am really mad. I have tried to do my best in the past year. I have worked twice as hard as any one else in the office. But I never get promotion", he is expressing his anger. The counsellor may reflect back and say, "You feel that your superiors have not shown proper recognition for your hard work". Such a reflection or mirroring would help the employee feel that he is being under stood and that his counsellor is interested in him. This builds in a climate of acceptance and facilitates the process.

Exploration

Besides accepting the employee, listening to him, and establishing a climate of openness the counsellor should attempt to understand as well as help the employee understand his own situation, strengths, weaknesses, problems and needs. Nobody would like to be directly told his weaknesses. Counselling skill lies in making the employee discover his own weaknesses, and identify his problem. At the most the counsellor may use open and exploring questions.

Exhibit 7.3

Sequential Process of Performance Counselling

Phases	Helpful Behaviour	Hindering Behaviour
Rapport Building		
Attending	Rituals Conversation on personal matters	Discussion of behaviour from the start
Listening (to) feelings concerns problems	Physical attention (posture) Eye contact Response (verbal and non-verbal) Keeping out telephones, noise, disturbances, etc.	Distraction (attention other things, telephones Signing letters, talking to others, etc., during conversation.
Acceptance (empathy)	Communication of feelings and concerns Paraphrasing feelings Sharing own experience	Lack of response Passive listening for a long period
Exploration		
Exploring	Monitoring or paraphrasing Open questions Encouragement to explore	Criticising Avoiding or hedging
Problems Identification	Questions to explore possible problems Encouragement to generate information Identification of a probable problem	Suggestion of a problem
Diagnosis	Exploratory questions Generating several possible causes	Suggesting the cause

Phases	Helpful Behaviour	Hindering Behaviour
Action Planning		
Searching	Questions on possible solutions Generating alternative solutions	Advising
Decision-making	Questions on feasibility, priority pros and cons Discussion of one solution Discussion of an action plan Contingency plan	Directing Making a fixed plan
Supporting	Identification of needed help Monitoring Contract on help	Promise of general help

Exploring

Exploring helps an employee to search various dimensions of the problem, or discover unidentified problems and bring to surface unnoticed issues. Exploring can be done by using questions and suggesting to the employee to talk more on a problem he mentions. A variety of questions may be used as already discussed.

Problem Identification

After general exploring, questions may be asked to help the employee focus on the problem. It is necessary for the counsellor to use questions both to generate information on some concerns and problems, and to narrow down focus to identify a more probable problem. For example, if an employee feels that his problem is that others do not cooperate with him, the counsellor may ask questions to narrow down the problem to the employee's relationship, with a few colleagues; and then questions may be asked to help the employee see what he does that prevents possible cooperation. Eventually the problem may turn out as to how the employee may deal with competitive relationship, and yet collaborate. Identification of a problem is the necessary step in planning for improvement.

Diagnosis

Diagnosis of the problem is the next step in exploration. Explorations should lead to the diagnosis. Without diagnosis there is little scope for solving any problem. Open questions like "Why do you think people are put off when you talk with them?", "Can you recall occasions when you got full cooperation?", "What do you attribute it to?", "What personal limitations mainly bother you?" may help the employee more towards a better diagnosis. The main attempt should be to generate several alternative causes of a problem.

Action Planning

Managers are expected to guide their employees and contribute to their development. Counselling interviews should end with specific plans of action for the development of the employee. Identifying a training need, job rotation, sponsoring for further training, increased responsibility, role clarity, etc., are some of the likely outcomes in such action plans. Three sub-phases can be identified in action planning.

Searching

The main contribution of the counsellor to action planning is the help he provides to the employee in thinking of alternative ways of dealing with a problem. In addition to encouraging the employee in brain storming such alternatives, the counsellor at a later stage can also add to this list of alternatives for further exploration. This should, however, be done only after some time. The employee should primarily take the responsibility of generating alternatives.

Decision-making

After the alternatives have been generated, the counsellor may help the employee assess advantages and disadvantages of each alternative, raise questions on the feasibility of the various alternatives and help finalise a plan to be implemented. This may, however, be regarded as a contingency plan, to be altered in the light of further experience.

Supporting

The final and the crucial stage of counselling is to communicate support and plan for such support in implementing the agreed action plan. Psychological contract of providing help should emerge after considerable exploration and discussion. Support and help in further increasing autonomy of the employee, and not his dependence on the counsellor. Design monitoring the action plan, and needed follow up may also be prepared. This then chooses the counselling interaction.

Making Counselling Effective

In performance counselling or developmental counselling formally organised by the organisation, the employee may not ask for counselling but his superior may organise counselling interviews as an organisational requirement. On such occasions the employee may be forced into a counselling situation. If counselling is given without having sought, it is likely to be of limite value. It may be frustrating both to the counsellor and to the employee. In such situation the counsellor would do well by forgetting about performance counselling and talk to the employee about his interest/lack of interest in growth. The employee is likely to come out if the counsellor establishes an open climate. If the employee has serious emotional blocks in dealing with the superior there is no use in organising a counselling interview. They need a problem solving session before that. Hence make sure before counselling that the employee is willing to learn from this interview.

Some employees are loyal and some superiors so protective, that there is a danger of employees becoming totally dependent on the counsellor. The counsellor should check from time to time through reflection, if he is making the employee too much dependent on him. Allow him to make his own decisions and help him in making decisions but do not take decisions for him as he is going to be the actor.

Make sure that the employee understands the purpose of counselling. If he does not understand or if he has wrong expectations, he may not receive whatever you say in the proper perspective. If you feel that he has some misunderstandings it is better to use the first session to clarify these misunderstandings and then schedule another session.

Minimise arguments. One argument is sufficient to make both of you defensive. Accept everything he says and try to build on it. Acceptance is the best way of bringing about self-realisation in the person.

Good counselling sessions fail to produce effective results due to lack of follow-up. Follow-ups through informal exchanges go a long way in communicating your interest in the employee. Otherwise he may feel that the counselling is only artificial and may lose interest in it eventually.

Chapter 8

USING PERFORMANCE APPRAISAL DATA

EFFECTIVENESS of performance appraisal systems depend to a great degree on how well the data generated by the system are utilised for variety of purposes and to what extent the employees see the data being utilised. Appraisal data can be utilised for development decisions as well as for personnel management pur poses. The following categories of development decisions could be taken on the basis of appraisal data: (i) organising in company training programmes; (ii) sponsoring executives for external training; (iii)job rotation; (iv) career development; (v) potential development; and (vi) delegation. The following personnel decisions could also be made on the basis of appraisal data: (i) performance rewards; (ii) placement and transfers; (iii) promotions; (iv) change of duties.

Development Decisions

The path for development on the job is already carved out for employees through key performance areas, behavioural dimensions, self-appraisal, performance analysis and counselling. At every appraiser-appraisee levels role clarity obtained through mutual discussions of PAs and KPAs, increased understanding and insights generated about managerial capabilities and behavioural qualities required for effectiveness in the organisation, identification of facilitating and inhibiting factors through performance analysis and recognition of factors that one can influence and change, and the discovery of one's own strengths and weaknesses as well as opportunities for development all contribute directly or indirectly to employee development. However the insights gained during performance review and counselling discussions and the development plans prepared by the appraiser and the appraisee should be reinforced and strengthened by supportive administrative decisions by the personnel or HRD departments or by the senior line managers who can take such decisions. For example, an appraising officer can make recommendations to meet the training needs of his appraisee but unless administrative action is taken on them the seriousness of the appraisal system may get lost and its effectiveness may go down. In this section we will look at the various ways in which appraisal data can be used for development decisions.

Identification of Training Needs

Ultimately performance appraisal should result in better performance and a sense of satisfaction on the part of each appraisee about his own performance. Every employee may not have all the capabilities required to perform each and every function associated with his role. Performance appraisal should be able to indicate the capabilities the person has and the capability he lacks to perform each of the functions (or atleast the important functions) associated with his role. The capabilities the employee lacks once identified needs to be developed through appropriate mechanisms.

Capability gaps can be identified in performance appraisals by looking at the ratings given on various KPAs, objectives, and managerial and behaviour dimensions. Low ratings on any area or dimension may indicate capability gaps. Low rating is an indicator of poor performance. Poor performance may be a result of low motivation or low capability. It is therefore necessary to ascertain the reason for poor performance. This should normally be discussed and decided during performance review and counselling discussion by the appraiser. The appraiser should then indicate in the "development needs" section of the appraisal form. Most often appraisers have a tendency to recommend directly the names of training programmes to which the appraisee should be sponsored rather than giving details of the capability requirements. While this may make the HRD department's job easy, there is a danger of the individual being sponsored for training programmes that have little relevance for his capability requirements.

The following processes may be used by the HRD department to identify training needs and create learning opportunities for employees:

i) Collect the appraisal ratings of all the employees.
ii) Categorise the employees into role related or function related categories (e.g. all branch managers, all zonal managers, sales men dealing with a particular set of products, marketing managers, production supervisors, etc.)
iii) Identify common performance areas for each category of employees. These common performance areas should require by and large the same or similar capabilities.
iv) Tabulate the final appraisal ratings by the appraiser against each performance area for all the employees having that performance area. Where there are ratings assigned to different objectives it is useful to tabulate the ratings, objective-wise.

v) The trends in ratings are indicative of the areas that need attention. Those areas where ratings are poor indicate training needs. These need to be probed further to determine whether poor ratings are reflections of capability gaps or motivational issues or rather biases. The HRD manager has to use his insight here. He might interview a few appraisers and appraisees to ascertain the training needs.

vi) On the basis of such analysis, areas where a large group of employees need to be trained could be identified. Wherever there are large groups of people required to be trained in-house programmes could be organised. Wherever only small number of people need to be trained in select capability areas they could be sponsored for outside programmes.

Thus an active pursuit of appraisal ratings to identify trends in capability gaps is very much required on the part of the personnel/HRD departments. Exclusive reliance on the appraiser's recommendations of the training needs may not give a complete picture of the developmental needs. A thorough analysis of the appraisal forms and appraisal ratings is required. Similar tabulations on managerial and behavioural dimensions may indicate areas where the employees may need help. For example, if most people in a unit/department get low ratings on a quality like "initiative" or "creativity" or "team spirit", it indicates the need for the members of that unit/department to be helped in developing that quality. Training programmes may be organised or other forms of developmental processes (like weekly process meetings for improving team spirit), periodic creativity exercises, discussions on initiative taking behaviour etc. could also be initiated.

In large size organisations the appraisal data could be fed to a computer and the computer could be programmed to give print-out lists of those that may need different kinds of training on the basis of consistent low ratings they may be receiving over a period of 3 to 4 years. These lists could then be further processed and employees should be contacted before taking any development decisions.

It must be remembered here that any development decision is not likely to be effective unless the employee himself accepts this and undertakes the task of developing himself by utilising the opportunities created by the organisation.

Performance analysis done by the appraisees is another useful source for identifying development needs. Individual inhibiting factors identified by the appraisees may be indicators of capability gaps. Inhibiting factors attributable to reporting officers and others in the organisation also may indicate some developmental needs for senior officers. The HRD managers who analyse such data should be sensitive to various cues being offered by the appraisees and appraisers in their performance analysis.

On the basis of his own analysis the HRD manager should get back to the departmental heads and give them a feedback of the capability gap trends his analysis reveal and check with them the various hypotheses he may have developed about the training needs. When such an effort is put in by the HRD department the performance appraisal systems are likely to be taken more seriously.

Job rotation is another effective way of developing employee capabilities. Job rotation involves periodical changing of employees from one job to the other with a view to giving them an experience of handling certain minimum variety of jobs in the organisation. Some organisaiion use jobs rotation as a mechanism of identifying and developing the potential of employees. For example, one organisation that manufactures heavy engineering equipment has a norm that all its new entrant engineers recruited at junior managerial levels should be rotated every two years to work in a different department. Thus by 10 years of joining the company the person would have gone through at least 5 different departments. the individual forms better perspectives about the entire organisation and its functioning. As he has seen and worked in different departments, he understands their work, their difficulties, their requirements etc. and therefore will be able to collaborate well with others and work as a team member. In this way seeds have already been sown to prepare every young engineer to be a general manager of that company. In addition, by observing his performance in different departments of the company, individual's suitability for different departments is ascertained and the organisation is able to help him formulate his career paths.

It may not be possible for all organisations to have these kinds of mechanisms. However, performance appraisals may point out the needs for ratation in some cases. At the time of the appraising performance the appraisee himself may ask for a change if he has worked for long years doing the same job; or if he has not been able to perform some of the functions associated with his present job and prefers to try himself out on a different job. Such job-rotation requests and suggestions should be mentioned in the "developmental needs" section of the appraisal form and every year, after collecting all the forms the personnel or HRD department should be able to arrange such changes to the extent feasible. Those appraisees or appraisers whose requests for change cannot be accommodated, should be contacted and informed about the reasons and future possibilities.

Potential development and career development related decisions can be taken by the appraisee himself during appraisal discussion. If any set of qualities (strengths) unique to that individual are observed which the appraiser feels may be useful for certain higher level jobs in the organisation, he could give informal feedback about the same and assist him in developing other qualities required to perform those roles. In this way the appraiser is helping the appraisee to prepare for future possible responsibilities through potential development. Career counselling and delegations could also be given to him during appraisal time. Delegation can be used as mechanism of developing employee capabilities in new areas for well performing employees.

Inputs for development needs are given by the appraisee and appraisers through the performance appraisal forms. Development decisions should be taken by the top management. Here the personnel/HRD departments play a very important role. They should go through carefully all the data supplied through the forms. They should review each appraisee's case every year and assist the top management in taking the development decisions. In some cases the final authority to take such decisions is also given to the personnel or HRD departments. In case where no action is required or where the organisation considers it difficult or inappropriate to meet any needs expressed in the forms, the personnel or HRD department staff should get in touch with the appraisee or his reporting officer and explain to him their point of view. If such action is not taken, the employees are likely to feel that they and their needs are not being attended to by the organisation.

Administrative Decisions

The administrative decisions like salary increases and other form of rewards for good performance, transfer and placement decisions are normally taken by the top management or the personnel department. In some organisations committees consisting of personnel managers and line managers at senior levels take such decisions. Largely these decisions are based on performance and performance appraisals play a significant role in this. Most of these administrative decisions fall under performance rewarding. Let us examine here some issues regarding performance rewarding and see how appraisal data can be used for administering performance rewards.

Performance Rewards

Performance rewarding is a very controversial issue in organisational life. Many chief executives do not pay attention to this aspect of management partly because of limited time in their busy schedules of profit maximisation and other things. Particularly in manufacturing and service organisations, productivity depends to a great degree on the effort put in by employees. People are likely to put in more effort if they feel that their effort will be recognised by their superiors and that they will be rewarded for their efforts.

However, performance rewarding is controversial because there are no easy ways of quantifying performance for reward purposes. Some chief executives may feel once an employee is rewarded in financial terms or in other observable ways, it may be demoralising to those other employees who are only marginally inferior to the employee rewarded. An unfortunate consequence of this thinking is that after some time in such organisations the employees, particularly high performing employees, lose motivation because high performing and low performing employees are treated alike.

Rewarding an employee means giving him something more than what is usually given to him or other employees at the same level. If he is rewarded with something as a mark of recognition of some thing he has done, then it is motivating to the employee. This recognition may be in terms of tangible benefits to the employee, or non-tangible ones such as the issuing of certificates.

Performance rewarding is involved only when an employee is rewarded for high performance in his job over a period of time (usually a year or two) and this should be differentiated from other forms of rewards and awards such as those for bravery, social service, best employee, sportsmanship, etc. Performance awards are generally given to individuals for doing consistently outstanding work in their jobs although group performance rewarding is also not uncommon.

Philosophy behind Performance Rewarding

Several research studies in the past have indicated that the need for recognition is a very important need that directs employee behaviour. Every employee desires that his efforts should be recognised and that he should be treated as an important being in the organisation. If the existence of employees is not taken note of, after some time the employee may resort to mechanisms of drawing attention of the top management to their existence. Thus performance rewarding is a way of communicating employees that every individual employee is considered important and his per formance is recognised.

Another purpose served by the rewards is to reinforce desirable behaviours shown by employees so that they continue to contribute to the organisation by exhibiting such behaviours. Rewarding also serves the purpose of creating a healthy competition among employees by encouraging less hard working ones to compete with more hard working ones. Thus it is one of the ways of keeping an organisationalive and dynamic.

Reward Mechanisms

Several mechanisms of rewarding performance are being used by different organisations. These include salary increases, annual performance awards, outstanding performance awards, promotion to higher positions, change of jobs involving higher responsibilities and status, sponsorship to conferences and tours to other countries, appreciation letters and certificates, transfers, advanced training and development opportunities, announcements in newsletters etc.

Salary Increase

The general pattern of salary administration in most organisations is by associating salary grades with different positions. Annually the salary of every employee increases by a fixed amount associated with that grade. In many companies this is a routine matter and there are salary increases as soon as the employee completes a year of service.

In some companies however, the salary increases are not given until the performance appraisal report of that employee is received from his supervisor. In these companies, employees, whose performances are rated higher than most others, are also given additional increments in salary as a mark of recognition of their contribution. Since such additional increments cannot be given to all the employees, generally the company adopts certain criteria such as rewarding the top ten per cent or so every year.

These criteria may also involve certain restrictions on the employees receiving these rewards. For example, no employee may receive the reward consecutively for two years.

A few other companies have very liberal policies and even reward employees by giving more than one additional increment. Some of these companies also have the practice of stopping even the normal increments of an employee whose performance is not satisfactory. This is generally avoided and even in those companies, stopping of increments is a rare phenomenon and is resorted to only in extremely poor performance cases as a measure of warning for improvement.

There are many advantages of using this system of rewards. It is a well understood notion that people see financial incentives as valuable irrespective of the status and personal wealth of the individual. For some people additional money may not have much meaning in terms of its monetary value, but as status symbol value. Salary increments are carried over the years and once the employee is granted an increment he continues to get it all through his career in the organisation. Hence this is an incentive valued by most employees.

Annual Performance Awards

In this system a select percentage of employees is given annual awards which are not linked with their salaries. Thus an organisation may decide to give an annual performance award of a certain amount of money. Or the employee may be presented with some prizes, or extra privileges and benefits may be given to him. These are again based on their appraisal reports.

Outstanding Performance Awards

These are performance awards given to a select few for outstanding performance. Normally, these carry a lumpsum amount of money, a certificate and a memento. Companies can have this in addition to annual salary increments and other forms of rewards.

Promotions

In some companies promotion is treated as a reward. A person is promoted to the next higher grade or next higher position if his performance in the present job is consistently good or excellent. However, this method of rewarding has a serious limitation as promotions can be made only when higher-level jobs exist. If there is no job suitable to the employee he may have to wait until such time a job suitable for him becomes available. This may be quite frustrating to an employee.

Some companies may try to create special jobs for such individuals. However, this results in unnecessary expansion of the company and managerial problems such as role conflicts or lack of coordination may arise. Jobs should be created only when the organisation feels the need for them and particularly when it is expanding and growing.

Another problem of using promotions as performance rewards is that there is no guarantee that past performance is an indicator of future potentia in a new job. For example, a successful production engineer need not be a successful production manager a the skills required to be a manager are different from those required to be an engineer. Similarly an excellent salesman need not turn out to be a good sales manager as selling and managing salesmen and sales operations of an entire region require two different kinds of skills. Thus only those who have aptitude and capabilities for higher-level positions should be promoted. If this is accepted, not all high performers may get promoted.

However, performance appraisal still forms an input for promotions although it is not a critical input. Some companies have the philosophy that good performance in the present job is necessary for promotion but it is not sufficient and good performance alone cannot entitle an employee for promotion. When such mechanisms are used promotion cannot be treated as a reward and hence there is a need for other mechanisms of rewarding good performance.

To overcome this problem, some organisations have resorted to the practice of upgrading the employee status and salary as a reward of good performance. For example, in the Philippines, a teacher in the education department who has been doing well can be promoted to be a master teacher. There are several levels of master teacher and a master teacher working in a school can have the same status and salary as one of his superiors. This takes care of the problem of creating jobs for high performers.

Change of Responsibilities and Status

Some organisations reward their employees by assigning them higher level responsibilities. The head of a department may delegate more powers and authority to a high performing employee. A salesman may get a larger area of coverage or more prestigious areas for his operations or he may be assigned new products that are generally given to a competent salesman. There are many such mechanisms by which the contributions of an employee can be recognised. Such forms of rewarding generally have high motivational value.

However, one pre-condition for this is that both the employee as well as his colleagues in the organisation should clearly perceive such additional assignments as increasing his status and responsibility. It is an opportunity given to him to demonstrate his capabilities and it is in response to his performance. It is not sufficient if only his superiors think so, because the employee may consider it an additional burden.

Sponsorship to Conferences, Tours and Visits to Other Countries

This is another frequently used mechanism by some companies. Outstanding performers are given priorities for attending training, conferences etc. in other countries. Or they may be special ly sponsored to visit industry or other similar organisations in other countries to learn from their experiences. This may be considered as a development reward as it provides opportunity for such employees to develop themselves. Some companies while following this practice never make it explicit, so the employee sponsored may not always realise that his performance contributions are being recognised.

Appreciation Letters and Certificates

This is another mechanism used particularly for employees at lower levels. Such certificates signed by the chief executive or a top level officer may mean a lot. These are distributed at annual functions. When there is a large group of people receiving such certificates, they are handed over to heads of departments for distribution. Some employees value the certificates highly and feel proud to receive them.

Transfers

In organisations having a wide geographic coverage, transfer of employee from one place to another becomes very necessary. Employees normally have their own geographical preferences. For example most employees prefer jobs in well-developed cities and towns or their own home towns if they want to be nearer to their families. Such preferences of employees are met when their performance is good. There are some organisations that give priority to the transfer requests of high performing employees. When such preferences are met the employee concerned may feel happy and motivated.

Advanced Training and Development Opportunities

High performing employees are sponsored to attend training programmes as a preparation for their promotion or higher responsibilities. In some cases, management does not reveal this to an employee and he may get the feeling that there is something lacking in him and this is why he is being sponsored. Thus it may have an opposite effect unless clearly explained.

Announcement in Newsletters, Journals etc.

This is another way of recognising and rewarding good performers. It is not an uncommon sight in some hotels to see pictures of "Employees of the Month" being displayed at lobbies. This form of recognition has also a motivating effect on employees.

This author surveyed the mechanisms of rewarding good performance that are being practised by 45 different companies (Rao, 1982). From this survey it was found that about 73 per cent of companies use salary increments, 40 per cent of them use promotions, 27 per cent of them given cash awards, 24 per cent use foreign travel, 16 per cent given appreciation certificates, 11 per cent use advanced training, 9 per cent use study tours and 7 per cent give higher responsibilities as mechanisms of rewarding good performance. Transfers and announcements in newsletters were also being used in atleast 2 per cent of the companies surveyed and 7 per cent of them reported having no reward system at all.

Whatever is the mechanism used, to make rewards achieve their purposes, the following points should be kept in mind:

1. The employee should know the aspects of his performance that have been judged or assessed as deserving of reward.
2. The employee should know clearly the nature of reward being given to him.
3. The employee as well as his co-employees in the organisation should perceive the rewards as a form of recognition and should attach some value to them.

When these conditions are met, the rewards are likely to be effective.

Reward management, while extremely desirable, is not easy. There are several problems and difficulties. The following are some of the common problems encountered by management.

1. Quantification of performance.
2. Comparison of performance with different types of jobs.
3. Differentiating between the contributions of abilities and efforts to high performance, and giving weightages to the same.
4. Demoralisation among employees who are not rewarded but who consider themselves as high-performing employees.
5. Isolating individual employees' contributions from group contributions.

6. Subjectivity in performance assessment.

There are no easy solutions for these problems. Every organisation should find its own ways of minimising these difficulties as these problems cannot be completely solved. Companies interested in having a reward system may find the following guidelines of some value.

i) *Quantification of performance.* Quantifying performance becomes easier when each job is defined clearly in terms of its functions. Employee performance should be assessed annually on each of these functions using a 7-point, 9-point or 10-point scale. The employees should have a clear idea of the performance expected of them in relation to the different points. The same should be followed if other qualities of the employee are also being assessed.

For a sophisticated user, weightages could be assigned to diffeent functions and behaviours and these weightages may be taken into account for final computation of the perform ance index. Companies may also decide beforehand the weightage they give to behaviour dimensions and to functions. Several problems associated with quantification have already been discussed in earlier chapters.

ii) *Comparison between performance on different jobs.* In every organisation the nature of jobs performed by employees of the same level differ. Some require high technical skills; others require more managerial skills and a few others may be routine. Employees working in a Research and Development Department of a high-technology industry may feel different ly from those working in the personnel or billing department.

There is no way of equating the performance in different categories of jobs. As far as possible in the reward as signment it is better to assign a proportionate number of rewards to each category of jobs (or each department). Thus, in a company with 1,000 employees, if the top management decides to reward the top 10 per cent, the production department may have 25 persons to reward if it has 250 employees, the sales department may have five rewards if it has 50, the finance department may have three if it has 30 employees and so on.

If some departments such as sales needed to be pushed more, the top management can always offer them a few additional rewards. Similarly for rewarding senior managers (heads of departments) different criteria may be used. If managers at this level are generalists rather than specialists, they can be compared more easily across the departments for their contributions.

iii) *Abilities and effort.* Performance is a result of both ability and effort. A highly capable individual may need to put in only marginal effort to give high performance whereas another individual with low ability may need to put in a lot of effort to produce even an average level of output.

If only output is rewarded highly capable employees may be getting a lot of leisure time in addition to rewards whereas those putting in high efforts may be getting consistently low ratings. If for some reason such ability differences exist, reward management becomes somewhat difficult. As this is the case most often than not, the top management should have a clear philosophy on this issue.

It is necessary to reward the combination of both ability and effort. Performance on different functions should be assessed generally in terms of the effort put in by the individual in relation to his capability. Thus if a highly capable employee does not put in effort his performance

Ability	Effort	Suggested Performance Rating
High	High	Highest
Moderate	High	Higher
Low	High	High
High	Moderate	Upper Average
Moderate	Moderate	Average
Low	Moderate	Lower Average
High	Low	Low
Moderate	Low	Lower
Low	Low	Lower

should not be rated high even if his output is good. Similarly if a less capable person puts in more effort and works impressively hard, even if his output is most excellent, he may be given better ratings. This scheme rewards "effort" more than "ability" and "outcome". At the same time, highly capable persons when they work hard, should be given adequate weightage. The above formulae may be useful.

(iv) *Demoralisation among others.* Due to the subjectivity in volved in performance assessment, there are always some employees who feel disappointed that they are not rewarded for their performance. Such numbers may be minimised if there are clear-cut policies of performance rewarding. If the employees are marginal cases, their supervising officer could counsel them and give them a feedback. Alternatively, demoralisation could be ignored as such feelings last only during the reward announcements. If it induces more demoralisation and poor performance, such cases should be counselled.

(v) *Individual vs. group performance.* No tasks can be accomplished by any one individual in organisational life. Tasks are accomplished by team efforts. In performance rewarding so far we have talked about individual performance. In order to promote more collaboration and team work in large organisations, it is useful to reward groups or teams of employees for their joint contributions. When such group rewarding is introduced it may be done on a selective basis using criteria like new innovations, discipline, cost consciousness, etc., besides the output of the department.

(vi) *Subjectivity.* As long as human beings assess other human beings there is bound to be subjectivity. Subjectivity cannot be eliminated completely. It can be reduced substantially by following some of the procedures suggested in the previous chapters. Top management should be sensitive to criticism to avoid morale problems but they need not be unduly overconcerned about its existence as it is natural. Some of these problems discourage top managers from having any form of rewards. In their eagerness to avoid problems, they throw away the baby along with bath water. As a result, organisational performance may go down.

Interpersonal comparisons are a part of human nature. If an organisation does not have any system of rewarding high performers, sooner or later each employee will ask himself the following:

> *I work hard but get the same treatment as the ones who do the least amount of work. I also get the same salary increase and the lowest performer also gets the same. So why should I exert my energies unnecessarily? Why should I not be like him (who is a low performer) and enjoy life?*

This is the beginning of a silent deterioration of human productivity in organisational life. Over a period of time the lowest performing employee becomes the standard for comparison by all employees and every one attempts to be like him. In this process the lowest performing individual starts doing even less and the company is doomed.

So the choice for chief executives is to reward high performers using some form of reward system, and contain or counter the problems associated with it and move forward, or, to have no such system and kill eventually human effectiveness and organisational efficiency by moving towards low standards of performance.

Transfer and Placement Decisions

Performance appraisal inputs could be used for transfer and placement decisions. A transfer decision may be taken essentially to ensure a better matching of the person with the job. Improving the employee-job matching is both helpful to the indiviudal as well as to the organisation. An employee who is not performing well in a particular role because of mismatch could be helped by identifying suitable jobs for him in the organisation where he could do better. For this purpose the appraisal ratings may be used by the personnel department to identify employees needing such help. Those getting consistently low ratings over a period of time (2 years or so) could be contacted and discussions could be held with them and their appraisers. Their strengths should be identified and jobs that require qualities they have as their strengths could be assigned to them. If poor performance is a result of poor interpersonal relations and if there are difficulties in improving them, they could be transferred to work with a different boss.

Another set of placement and transfer decisions may involve employees who are performing well a given role but have more capabilities that are being unutilised. If there are challenging jobs that can use their talents, they could be placed there.

In all such decisions the employee should be consulted as far as possible.

Thus performance appraisal data can serve as inputs for a variety of decisions that may contribute to organisational health and productivity through human resources development.

Chapter 9

MANAGEMENT APPRAISAL SYSTEM IN VOLTAS LIMITED

SINCE its formation in 1954, Voltas has had a system of appraising managerial performance. The performance appraisal system in Voltas has undergone several changes over the years as a result of continuous efforts by Voltas to review its system periodically and ensure that it leads its employees to grow, develop and contribute to organisational excellence. In this chapter the Managerial Appraisal System that has come into operation most recently in Voltas (from the year 1982-83), is described. This system of Voltas has several objectives and components of a development-oriented appraisal system.

The performance appraisal system in Voltas is based on the belief that "the strength of an organisation ultimately depends on its capacity to develop people". In a preamble to the appraisal system, the Vice-President (Personnel) of Voltas* has spelt out the following as objectives of managerial appraisal system:

1. To evaluate performance against established objectives and job accountability.
2. To provide feedback and counselling for self-improvement with supportive training and development programmes.
3. To strengthen working relationship through personal effectiveness and developing an understanding of expectations.
4. To identify people with potential who can be groomed for higher positions.
5. To provide data for organisation development and improved management processes which will sustain a productive and satisfying work culture.

The managerial appraisal system of Voltas focusses on the appraisal of the employee first on job-performance-related areas followed by an assessment on managerial/behavioural dimensions. Performance

---

* The author wishes to thank Mr. K.N. Randeria, Vice-President, Personnel of Voltas Limited for permission to describe the appraisal system and reproduce the guidelines.

on job-related areas is assessed by recording the "Objectives" set for the relevant year, and assessing the achievements in relation to these at the end of the year, and recording the reasons for variations, if any. "The very enumeration of specific targets/tasks along with the actual achievements will be conducive towards greater objectivity. More importantly, it will facilitate a purposeful discussion between the Assessor and the Assessee so that the development process through improved performance is enhanced" (Preamble to the Managerial Appraisal System by the Vice-President, Personnel).

The system also purports to induce an informal, meaningful and trustworthy interaction between the Assessor and the Assessee. "Whilst Assessor-Assessee relationship is an ongoing process which takes place through healthy interaction during day-to-day work life, it must reiterate and strengthen itself through the Appraisal and Counselling Interview by the Assessor, and which is a mandatory part of the System" (Preamble to the Managerial Appraisal System by the Vice-President, Personnel).

Thus appraisal system in Voltas recognises communication and counselling as important aspects of development through self- improvement. Such communication and counselling are also expected to lead to the strengthening of basic role relationships and interpersonal relationships through the process of day-to-day work life and the achievement of results.

The manual of the Management Appraisal System brought out by Voltas is reproduced below. The guidelines and the format explain the system and its components in detail.

Management Performance Review Guidelines

The System

Based on collective experience over the years and the recommendations of the Management Development Committee, the existing Performance Appraisal System has been revised. It is simple and brief, but care has been taken to retain the positive aspects of the earlier system. In line with our policy on Men, the Appraisal System should now be seen as an instrument for improving current performance and the development of the full potential in each human resource.

The salient features are:

1. The appraisal must be based on observed performance and behaviour on the job which requires specific facts to be recorded before arriving at qualitative appraisal of individuals.
2. The new system pre-supposes the practice of goal and target setting as a part of Corporate/Divisional/Unit Plans.
3. Attention is also focussed on the potential and development of each individual. Action taken on the Training & Development Plan for the current year and drawing up the same for the following year are an integral part of each appraisal.
4. Wherever applicable, staff will be appraised by two Assessors. The Assessee must have the opportunity to discuss his/her performance with the Assessor at a formal appraisal interview.

The new Appraisal Form casts a serious responsibility on the part of the Assessor for achieving. Objectivity which alone can ensure the success of the whole appraisal System.

General Explanations

1.Period of Appraisal

It coincides with the financial year of the Organisation, 1 September to 31 August. In the event the Assessee has not held the job (for which he/she is appraised) for the full period of 12 months, the following will apply.

i) If the Assessee is transferred out of the job after February, the immediate superior (first Assessor) from where he/she is transferred will complete the appraisal.

ii) If the Assessee is transferred before February, the immediate superior (the Assessor at the new place of posting) will complete the appraisal as at 31 August.

iii) Where the Assessor is transferred from his/her job after February, he/she will complete the appraisals of those reporting to him/her and proceed on transfer.

iv) Where the Assessor is transferred before February, the appraisals will be done by the new incumbent in the position as at 31 August.

The foregoing will ensure the minimum period of six months which is essential for a meaningful appraisal.

2.Assessment Routes

Some typical assessment routs are given below

	Assesee	First Assessor	Second Assessor	Reviewer
At Branches	Sales Officer	Sales Manager	Branch Manager	GM - Zone, in consultation with the RSM
At Zone	Regional Sales Manager	GM - Zone	Divisional Manager	General Manager (Operations) at Sales HQ.
At Division at SHQ	Product Officer	Sr. Product Officer	Product Manager	Divisional Manager or General Manager (Operations)
At Plants	Production Engineer	Sr. Prodn. Engineer	Production Manager	General Manager (Manufacturing)
Departments in HQ	Asstt. Accountant	Accountant	Accounts Manager	Controller of Accounts

(Approved Organisation Structure should be used as a Guide)

The above examples are illustrative only. The general principles are:

1st Assessor - immediate line Superior of the Assessee.
2nd Assessor - Superior of the 1st Assessor. (not mandatory).

Finalised reports in respect of staff up to grade MMI will be sent to Staff Administration Manager, and of staff in grades SMII and above to Vice-President (Personnel). The whole process should be planned in such a way that completed reports reach Vice-President (Personnel) and Staff Administration Manager by 30 November.

3.Role of Assessors and Reviewers

The first Assessor has the prime role of recording major appraisal details. The second Assessor is mandatory only if he/she is in a position to record comments from personal knowledge of the performance of the Assessee. The role of the Reviewer is more in the nature of monitoring the Appraisal System to ensure uniformity of application (especially standard gradings) than evaluating the Assessee's performance. The Reviewer will ensure that all Sections are filled in, and that evidence is sufficiently complete. He will also check the distribution of ratings, identify with comments, tendencies to over/underrating in Assessors. Any substantial difference between the first and second Assessor must be resolved mutually; in rare cases, the Reviewer's help can be sought. Unresolved cases should be brought to the notice of Vice-President (Personnel).

Your special attention is invited to the Reviewer's role in respect of information under Section VII - "Placement" and Section VIII - "Career Progression". (This is explained on page 156.

Section I : Major Responsibilities/Duties

Job responsibilities/duties should be indicated as precisely as possible - including the Key Result Areas and the Assessee's role in these Areas. It is also necessary to indicate, in the space provided, how long the Assessee has been in his/her present job.

Section II : Performance and its Assessment

In part (a) of this Section, "Objectives" set for the relevant year with specific facts, preferably in quantitative terms, should be recorded. These can be derived, in most cases, from Corporate/Division/Unit Plans which have been mutually agreed between the Assessor and the Assessee. In the next column, "Achievements", the actual results obtained should be recorded, without any attempt at qualitative assessment, thus ensuring factual presentation of observed performance. Similarly, "Reasons for Variance" should be written in an objective manner, taking care that only genuine constraints rather than "excuses" are recorded.

Only on the completion of the factual data, a carefully considered Assessment of Performance should be recorded by the Assessor in II (b), using the grading standards A B C D E as explained under Section V. The Second Assessor writes the comments in the space provided and only then records the assessment in the approximate box.

Section III : Critical Factors and Attributes

A manager's prime role is to "Make Things Happen". To discharge this role successfully he must imbibe, sustain and improve upon a series of critical factors and attributes without which any management process remains incomplete and ineffective. Each of these factors are also defined in the Appraisal Form itself in order to facilitate your assessment and which can be brought out in sharper focus only through the recording of supporting data.

Job Knowledge	Consider the extent and depth of demonstrated technical and professional competence; grasp of the system and procedures; under standing of the product and market place; effectiveness in functional "knowledge leadership".
Planning	Ability to marshal and analyse relevant data; anticipate eventualities and determine strategies with time-bound actions for specific targets.
Organising & Resource Utilisation	Ability to mobilise, allocate and integrate various components of the job and resources of the unit in a harmoniously operating whole for maximising productivity.
Communicating	Consider clarity and precision of verbal and written expression of ideas and feelings; have them understood by others with candour and empathy; desire to share relevant information with appropriate persons and safeguard confidentiality where necessary.
Decision Making	Ability to analyse relevant facts; evaluate various alternatives; indicate unequivocally logical, timely and workable course of action in the interest of the organisation as a whole.
Winning Instinct	Determination to "Make Things Happen", willingness to extend the self towards high aspirations; ability to meet and convert adverse conditions to advantage; inspire others by example; sustain team morale and instil a will to win.

VOLTAS LIMITED

Confidential

MANAGEMENT PERFORMANCE REVIEW - SEPT/AUG. 19__ to 19__

> This is a Vital document for GROWTH & SELF DEVELOPMENT OF PEOPLE. Adherence to the concepts and guidelines given in the Booklet on Management Appraisal System will help you in the task you are about to fulfill.

Name: ______________ Designation: ________ Grade: ________

Divn./Dept ____________ Location ________ Age ___ Service ______

I. MAJOR RESPONSIBILITIES/DUTIES: In present job from :

II. (a) PERFORMANCE

Objectives	Achievements	Reasons for Variance

Comments by 2nd Assessor

II(b) Assessment of Performance

1st Assessor

2nd Assessor

III. CRITICAL FACTORS and ATTRIBUTES (Mark with reference to definitions and ratings to Booklet)

A	B	C	D	E

Support with examples

JOB KNOWLEDGE

Consider the extent and depth of demonstrated technical and professional competence grasp of systems and procedures understanding of the product and market place; effectiveness in providing functional knowledge leadership to subordinates.

PLANNING

Ability to marshal and analyse relevant data, anticipate eventualities and determine strategies with time bound actions for specific targets.

ORGANISING & RESOURCE UTILIZATION

Ability to mobilise, allocate and integrate various components of the job and resources of the unit in a harmoniously operating whole for maximizing Productivity.

COMMUNICATING

Consider clarity and precision of verbal and written expression of ideas and feelings, have them understood by others with candour and empathy, desire to share relevant information with appropriate persons and safeguard confidentiality where neces sary.

DECISION MAKING

Ability to analyse facts evaluate various alternatives indicate unequivocally logical, timely and workable course of action in the interest of the organisation as a whole.

WINNING INSTINCT

Determination to 'Make Things Happen', willingness to extend the self towards high aspirations ability to meet and convert adverse conditions to advantage inspire others by example sustain team morale and instill a will to win.

Comments by 2nd Assessor

IV RELATIONSHIPS - with Superiors, Peers, Subordinates & Business Associates

	Analysis
Strengths	
Areas of Improvements	

Comments by 2nd Assessor :

V. OVERALL ASSESSMENT - Section II, III & IV	1st Assessor ☐ 2nd Assessor ☐

VI RECORDS OF APPRAISAL & COUNSELLING INTERVIEW along with ASSESSEE'S REACTIONS

1st Assessor's Name ____________ Signature ________ Date ________

VII PLACEMENT

(a) Is the Assessee in the right job? Yes ☐ if No, which job will fit the Assesse best and why?

Job: ____________ Divn./Dept: ______________ Reason__________

____

____

(b) Indicate areas of special aptitude where Assess's potential could be harnessed to the maximum e.g.

Marketing ☐ Finance ☐ Personnel ☐ Mfg. ☐

Research ☐ Mg. Services ☐ Purchasing ☐

Any other (Specify): ________________________________

VIII CAREER PROGRESSION & POTENTIAL

(a) Is the Assessee performing a set-up☐ or step down ☐ job?

Reasons :____

(b) Is the Assessee capable of moving to higher positions? Yes Not Ready No
If Yes now as ____________________ in grade__________
If not ready : in ____________ years as________ in grade__________
If No: can be tried out as ____________________________

(c) Any special recommendations for Accelerated Career Progres sion?

____

____

1st Assessor's name : ______________ Signature ________ Date________

IX OVERALL COMMENTS BY 2nd Assessor

Name ______________________ Signature: ________ Date:______

X COMMENTS BY REVIEWER

Name ______________________ Signature: ________ Date:______

Section IV : Relationships and Managerial Style

No manager is an "island unto himself"; indeed successful managers achieve results through people. This section essentially deals with the style of management which will manifest itself from a descriptive analysis of relationships with

(a) subordinates: (b) peers; (c) superiors; and (d) identified publics.

A manager's effectiveness is largely determined by skills in managing relations - both as a member of the team and as a leader.

It must, however, be emphasised that a good manager does not seek popularity. Respect and affection of colleagues, subordinates, and superiors are earned by dint of forthrightness and determination to achieve organisation results along with a genuine concern for those who perform rather than only conform. The descriptive comments must be supported by observed data on relationship at work and should be recorded with a view to helping the Assessee "see himself as others see him". These comments will also form the basis for training and development plans to improve the Assessee's effectiveness with people which, among other things, also includes:

(a) courage of conviction; (b) conflict resolution; (c) influence with rationality; and (d) inspire confidence and trust.

Section V : Overall Assessment

The gradings for Overall Assessment must flow from the total data recorded in Section II, III and IV. The individual gradings of each of these Sections must be systematically considered, although some flexibility in arriving at an overall Assessment is possible. This is an important exercise in the Appraisal System, and due care must be taken by both the first Assessor and the second Assessor.

Please note that the Overall Assessment relates to present job and present performance and not to potential. The following grading standards must be strictly adhered to:

A - Excellent Indicates outstanding performance where exceptional results have been consistently achieved with a high stretch under adverse conditions. The Assessee demonstrates complete mastery of the job and is recognised as a rare professional in the field. Additionally, the Assessee inspires team effort through demonstrated quality of leadership towards achieving Corporate results with entrepreneurial zeal. Few (no more than 3 per cent, will qualify for this prestigious and, by that token) a rare grading.

B - Superior — Indicates very good performance where results surpass high expectations with a good degree of stretch under adverse conditions. The Assessee will have consistently exceeded targets and displayed commendable grasp of the job together with initiative and leadership which requires minimum supervision. The Assessee also shows excellent promise of high return on investment in his/her training and development. No more than 15 per cent will deserve such a high grading.

C - Good — Indicates acceptable performance which means normal expectation where targets have always been met and occasionally exceeded with average stretch under normal conditions. The Assessee is able to meet all the requirements of the job, carries out normal duties with a measure of initiative and occasional supervision. A reliable performer worthy to be retained and encouraged to improve with supportive role from the superior.

D - Fair — Indicates marginal performance with occasional failure to achieve expected results. Requires frequent supervision, is hesitant to take initiative and does not have adequate knowledge of the job and shies away from adverse conditions or stretch in the targets. A below average performer who has reached his/her peak and requires corrective action.

E - Poor — Indicates unacceptable performance with frequent failures to meet expected results. The Assessee lacks adequate knowledge of the job and exerts little to overcome shortfalls and finds excuses around, rather than, within himself/herself. Shows, lack of commitment and is a miscast for the jobs or worse, for the organisation. Such a grading indicates need for vigorous corrective action and failure to respond within 2/3 years would invite severance from service.

Every Excellent (A) and Poor (E) grading must be brought to the notice of the Vice-President (Personnel) and the concerned Vice-President. These appraisals will be discussed by the Corporate Executive Committee.

Section VI : Record of Appraisal and Counselling Interview

This is mandatory. No act of appraisal is complete without:

a) an uninhibited and complete information to the Assessee about his/her performance and assessment thereon;

b) an open discussion and a sympathetic opportunity for the Assessee to express feelings and speak his/her mind with a view to understanding the reasons for the recordings made;

c) a constructive dialogue which aims at:
   i) common understanding of the major duties and responsibilities of the Assessee's job;
   ii) mutually acceptable objectives and tasks;
   iii) training and development plans to enhance the strengths and improve upon the areas of weaknesses. Here, it is advisable to stimulate the Assessee to self-recognition and self-acceptance in the areas of change and from that point lead him her to work out a programme for self-improvement. The Assessee is then far more likely to carry out a plan.

d) A faithful recording of the interview which must incorporate the Assessee's reactions. Signature of the Assessee is no longer necessary.

The counselling role of the Assessor bears repetition. An appraisal must be seen as an opportunity for self-development by the Assessee through the supportive role of the superior. With out soft pedalling, it is possible to create an atmosphere wherein the Assessee will see in the Assessor a leader who in spires, rather than merely demands, ever improving performance.

Section VII : Placement

This section deals with proper placement for harnessing the Assessee's potential as also to meet development needs. The objective should be to take into account the special aptitudes of an individual for his/her placement. Rotational assignment can also be recommended for career development. The reviewer's role in ensuring that deserving managers get appropriate opportunities for job rotation and enlargement is of special significance. It will be his/her responsibility to encourage the Assessors to identify and make available people with potential, and readily agree to release them from the Division/Unit in the interest of improving the quality of managerial inventory for the organisation as a whole.

Section VIII : Career Progression

In VIII (b), promotability of the Assessee should be indicated. Any special recommendation for career progression should be mentioned in VIII (c). Here, the Reviewer will ensure that the evaluation of promotability is objective and realistic.

Sections IX and X

These sections are for overall remarks encompassing all facets of the appraisal by the second Assessor and Reviewer as applicable.

Training and Development Plan

This form has to be prepared in duplicate. The first copy will be retained by the concerned Personnel Manager/Deputy Manager; the second copy will be sent to Manpower Development Manager by 30 November. The first column of this form should be filled by the first Assessor in consultation with the concerned Personnel Manager. The second column should be filled by the Zonal Manager for all staff in Zones, and by GM-Mfg/DM/DpM for Plant/Headquarter based staff.

Current Status

In another revision of the Management Appraisal System carried out by Voltas in 1990 some further changes have been made. The changes are marginal and include the following:

1. Sharper focus on development was brought into the appraisal system. The objectives of the appraisal have been re-stated as follows:

(a) To strengthen the working relationships through establishment of understood and agreed to job objectives/targets;

(b) To evaluate performance and critical attributes against established expectations;

(c) To provide feedback for personal effectiveness and self-improvement through the appraisal interview;

(d) (i) To identify areas requiring improvement and recommend and provide developmental opportunities within the present job,

(ii) to identify people with potential who can be groomed for higher levels of job responsibility with supportive development opportunities;

(e) To serve as an instrument for an objective reward and punishment system;

(f) To provide data for organisation development processes which will evolve and sustain a productive and satisfying work culture.

2. The assessment period was shifted to "April to March" to coincide with the new financial year of the company. Earlier it was September to August.
3. Assessment routes have been modified to suit the changes in the designations and organisational structure of the company.
4. The five-point rating categories have been changed from Excellent, Superior, Good, Fair and Poor to Outstanding (O), Superior (S), Good (G), Fair (F), and Poor (P).
5. Joint target setting by the assessor/assessee pair was made mandatory. This was existing earlier but made more explicit now.
6. Job-rotation opportunities and career plan were given sharper focus in the new format.
7. Recommendations for increments have been introduced in the new format.

Chapter 10

PERFORMANCE APPRAISAL SYSTEM IN LARSEN AND TOUBRO LIMITED*

A DEVELOPMENT-ORIENTED performance appraisal system was introduced in Larsen & Toubro Limited in the year 1976. This system is based on the philosophy of the company the main strength of the company is its human resources and there should be continuous efforts made to develop them and their capabilities. Since the time it was first introduced in 1976 the appraisal system has undergone some changes in the light of the experience gained during its operation. Given below are some details of the appraisal system reproduced from the Performance Appraisal Manual of L & T.

The main purpose of the Appraisal System is to help an employee improve his performance and develop himself. The objectives, the basic features and operational details are given below:

Objectives of the Performance Appraisal System

1) To obtain data, as free from bias as possible, in order to:
   a) identify strengths and weaknesses of the employee so as to contribute to his growth and development by:
      i) self-appraisal;
      ii) feedback and guidance from superior; and
      iii) training
   b) provide inputs for administration of rewards such as salary, promotions, additional responsibilities.

2) To have the employee set objectives for the year in consultation with his superior for the purpose of:
   a) setting realistic goals and improving performance;
   b) helping the employee plan his activities and work for the year; and

---

*The author wishes to express his thanks for Messers Larsen & Toubro Limited for permission to give details of their appraisal system and reproduce a large part of their appraisal manual.

c) enabling the employee to see how his individual goals are derived from, and contribute to overall departmen tal/or-ganisational goals.

Operational Details Objective/Target Setting

1. In the first month of each financial year (i.e., October) every appraisee will set his job related objectives, not more than five to six in number, in consultation with his immediate superior. These objectives will form the basis of his performance appraisal.
2. The purpose of objective setting is to give a sense of direction to one's work efforts so as to contribute towards achievement of departmental/organisational objectives.
3. The objectives for which targets/activities have to be decided, should correspond to the major areas of one's job responsibilities.
4. As far as possible, every appraisee should first determine and write down his objectives along with targets/activities before discussing these with his immediate superior.
5. Before identifying and setting objectives, it is recommended that all appraisees and appraisers study guidelines for setting objectives/targets*.
6. Targets are specific conditions which help in quantifying and measuring the results. These are expressed in terms of "standard of performance" and deadlines. The objectives should preferably be such that quantified targets can be set for their achievement, wherever possible. However, there may be some areas, particularly in service functions, where it may not be feasible to set measurable standards of performance. In such cases, performance can be evaluated by reviewing the accomplishment of specific activities with time schedule for completion as agreed to between the Appraisee and the Appraiser at the time of objective/targets setting. These activities should be such that their accomplishment should logically lead to the achievement of the particular objective. For example, for the objective "Improvement of customer relations", the activities could be:
   a) Calling on customers once in ... (frequency of visit to be mentioned).
   b) Attending to enquiries and order booking within a week (or any time limit that may suit an appraisee).
   c) Quality of after-sales service to be improved by at tending to complaints within... (time limit to be mentioned).

*These are described in the appraisal manual of L & T.

7. Sample objectives for some functions are also given in the manual. Where sample objectives/targets for certain functions are not given, the appraisee is expected to consult his immediate superior or HRD Department.
8. Every departmental head will ensure that the objectives of all the appraisees in his department, i.e., supervisory cadre and above, are set in the month of October and a list of such persons is forwarded to HRD Department by 30 October.

Appraisal Interview

1. **Action by the Appraisee**
By 15 October, each year, the appraisee should fill in Part A and relevant portion of Part B of the form and hand over the form to his immediate superior. Samples of Performance Appraisal as Forms O & M F:2624: HRD and O & M F:2625; HRD are given as Annexures 10.1 and 10.2 at the end of this chapter.

2. The appraisee may find the following check-list helpful in filling the form and preparing himself for the appraisal interview:
   i) Factors which helped performance and those which hindered performance, are to be grouped together and entered in the same column on the right side of Part-A on page 1.
   ii) Prepare a check-list of points you would like to discuss with your immediate superior during the interview.
   iii) Bring out points on which you would require specific action/help from your superiors.
   iv) Use the opportunity to suggest any change in your job which you think will improve the quality/efficiency and effectiveness.
   v) Be relaxed during the interview and try to get the maximum out of it in terms of your own development/improvement of performance for the future.

3. **Action by Immediate Superior**
The immediate superior must ensure that all appraisees under him submit their performance appraisal forms duly filled in by 15 October.
On receipt of the forms from the appraisee/appraisees, the immediate superior will arrange an appraisal interview with the appraisee/appraisees. During the interview, he will discuss the appraisee's performance, strengths, weaknesses and ways of development.

The following checklist may help the immediate superior in preparing himself for the appraisal interview:

A. Pre-Interview Preparation

i) Make certain the appraisee has sufficient notice of the interview to do his own preparation.

ii) Make sure you know that was mutually agreed in terms of job duties, objective standards, performance indicators, etc.

iii) Review appraisee's background, education, training, experience and duration in the present position.

iv) Determine the weaknesses and strengths and development needs to be discussed with the appraisee.

v) For each need you plan to discuss with the appraisee, be prepared with a possible development plan. Ask the appraisee if he has any development plan and what help he would need from you.

vi) Identify key result areas where you would like the appraisee to concentrate during the next review period.

B. During the Interview

i) Be relaxed, friendly and sincere, so as to create a congenial climate for the interview. Ensure that the interview is a two-way communication.

ii) Allot sufficient time and do not rush through the interview. Do not make it mechanical and ritualistic.

iii) Encourage the appraisee to discuss how he views his own performance.

iv) You may decide to talk about strong points first or about the points that will get the interview to a comfortable start. You may intersperse discussion with areas that need improvement. Avoid generalised statements. Cite specific instances/observations you have made.

v) Reach agreement on development plans clearly spelling out what you are going to do and what the appraisee intends to do.

vi) At the end of the interview summarise what has been discussed making it positive and closing the discussion on a friendly note.

vii) Make a record of development plans you and the appraisee have made, particularly points requiring follow-up and specific commitments for action on your part.

viii) Make a self-evaluation of how you handled the discussion - strong and weak points. Also note what additional points you learnt about the appraisee and about yourself.

4. The immediate superior enters his ratings and remarks in Part B, page 2, at the time of interview, after having discussed the ratings and remarks with the appraisee.

5. He will fill in independently his ratings and remarks against overall performance and behavioural attributes in Part C, page3, after the appraisal interview is over. But he will discuss strengths and weaknesses with the appraisee before filling Part C.

6. Any other attributes relevant to the function but not mentioned in the form and your rating of the employee against these attributes may be filled in the two blank spaces provided at the bottom of Part C.

7. The immediate superior will next complete Part D, page 4. He may comment on development and training needs in respect of job/technical knowledge, managerial skills, behavioural attributes and any other area of improvement.

8. Development recommendation other than training programme such as self-study, on-the-job training, job rotation, etc., are to be entered in the second column of Part-D.

9. After completion of all appraisal form, the immediate superior fills the summary of Training Needs form (O & M F:2623: HRD - Chapter Annexure 10.3) for all the appraisees under him.

10. Submits all forms to next superior by 15 December.

11. In case of multiple reporting, the appraisal interview will be carried out by the person to whom the appraisee reports operationally. The person to whom the employee reports administratively will independently do the appraisal on a separate form and send the form to the next superior, who will have the opportunity for checking for incongruency in the two appraisals before forwarding it to the operational superior. We give certain specific cases in the next page :

Note: While the system requires that the performance appraisal interview will be held once a year, the immediate superiors are encouraged to talk to their subordinates more frequently during the year in order to continuously review their performance and provide guidance and counselling wherever necessary.

Appraisee	Operational Immediate Superior	Administrative Superior
Sales Manager	Divisional Manager	Regional Manager
Cost/Works Accountant	Production Manager	DGM Accounts
Regional Accountant	DGM Accounts & MPCS	Regional Manager
Regional Personnel	Regional Manager	DGM Personnel Officer

Action by Next Superior

1. The next superior (the one to whom the immediate superior reports) will review and comment on the ratings and remarks given by the immediate superior against overall performance, behavioural attributes and training and development needs, keeping in mind the following:
   i) Appropriateness of the ratings or a tendency to leniency or strictness.
   ii) Biases and prejudices.
   iii) Discrepancy between current performance ratings and previous year's ratings.
   iv) Suitability of development plans, if any.

2. He will discuss with immediate superior, where necessary, and enter his remarks in Part E, page 4 of the form and return the same to the immediate superior by 30 December.

Action after Completion of Forms

1. The immediate superior will, on receipt of forms, take note of the remarks of next superior. He will retain the pink copy of the Summary of Training Needs form to monitor the progress of training and development of the appraisees under him. He will forward all the forms along with white copy of Summary of Training Needs form in respect of all appraisees under him to HRD Department positively by 15 January.
2. HRD Department, after scrutiny, will forward the performance appraisal forms to Manager, Staff Administration, who will examine the correlation between appraisal and recommendation

for increment or promotions as the case may be. Thereafter, the form will be filed in the employee's file.

3. HRD Department will retain the Summary of Training Needs form and plan the training programmes accordingly.

Performance Appraisal - Secretaries in Supervisory Cadre and Above

1. A separate appraisal form has been designed for the Secretaries in supervisory cadre and above.
2. The immediate superior will hold an appraisal interview with the appraisee in the month of October/November each year. Before conducting the interview, he may refer to the guidelines provided above in Annexure 10.4.
3. During the interview he must discuss with the appraisee his/her performance, strengths and weaknesses and development plans wherever necessary.
4. After the appraisal interview is over, the immediate superior will enter his ratings and remarks against overall performance and behavioural attributes in Part A, page 1, and get the form signed by the appraisee.
5. The immediate superior will also complete Part B, page 2, of the form. He may comment on the development and training needs in respect of job knowledge, other behavioural skills and personal attributes.
6. Rest of the actions on the part of immediate superior and next superior are the same as mentioned earlier.

Performance Appraisal - New Employees and Transferees

1. This performance appraisal system is not intended for use with probationaries, as at present a separate evaluation form is being used for that purpose.
2. An immediate superior will appraise the performance of an appraisee when the appraisee has worked under his supervision for more than 90 days. If the period of working directly under him is less than 90 days and appraisee is a new entrant to the company the performance appraisal exercise will be done at the end of the next appraisal review period (i.e., for 12 months + previous 2 months or so).

Or

3. If the appraisee has been transferred from another Department/Section/Unit after completing 90 days or more in the Department/Section/Unit, the immediate superior of that Department/Section/Unit will appraise the performance and

complete the appraisal form before the individual is transferred to the next Department/Section/Unit.

4. When the appraisee is transferred from one Department to another or from one section to another, he will set fresh objectives in consultation with his new immediate superior. There will be two appraisal interviews for him, one each by immediate superior of the present and the previous section and, therefore, two performance appraisal forms will be filled for him that year.

ANNEXURE 10.4

Suggested Guidelines for Rating Performance Against Objectives

Our Performance Appraisal System makes use of graded scale of ratings from "Inadequate" to "Outstanding". The norms of this rating scale have been developed as an attempt to provide uniformity of understanding and application of the rating scale.

The basic concepts used in developing these norms are as follows:

i) That the appraisal process only applies to the evaluation of performance of a particular appraisee in his specific work sphere.
ii) That objectives and targets are set to match the abilities of the employee. Facilitating and inhibiting factors are expected to be present. The evaluation of performance against these objectives/targets should not be used for comparing achievements of two individuals.
iii) That the objectives/targets that are set will be challenging and will require some stretch out of the employee for achievement.
iv) That the achievement of the set target is normal expectation of the company from its employees.
v) That there will be occasions when achievement of targets will be affected by management decisions or changes in the management policy or other environmental changes which will be beyond the control of the employee.
vi) Lastly, the targets should normally be set under conditions which are mostly "within control" of the person. For example, in case invoicing is largely dependent upon factory production, the person's main emphasis should not be achievement of a certain invoicing figure, but on booking orders or placing a certain number of workable orders on the factory in a particular time frame. It should be appreciated that greater understanding between Appraisee and his Immediate Superior, through face to face discussions, will lead to better problem solving ability and developing such objectives/targets that discussion on "beyond the control" factors is minimised.

Extent to which target is achieved	***Recommended Rating***
i) For achieving 100 per cent Target	
Where the target is achieved with facilitating conditions more favourable than normal, which have appreciably helped the Appraisee in his performance the rating should be	Adequate
Where the target is achieved under normal facilitating and inhibiting factors, because of the stretch element in the target, the rating should be	Good
Where the target is achieved in spite of lack of facilitating and/or severe inhibiting factors, the rating should be	Very Good
ii) Exceeding Target	
Where the achievement exceeds the target with very favourable facilitating conditions, the rating should be as follows.	
Up to 25 per cent of target	Good
Above 25 per cent of target	Very good
Where the achievement exceeds the target with better or favourable facilitating conditions, the rating should be as follows:	
Up to 10 per cent of target	Good
Up to 25 per cent of target	Very Good
Above 25 per cent of target	Outstanding
Where the achievement exceeds the target in spite of severe inhibiting factors or lack of facilitating factors, the rating should be as follows :	
Up to 10 per cent of target	Very Good
Above 10 per cent of target	Outstanding
iii) Achievement below the Target	
With normal facilitating and/or inhibiting factors, achievement of target below 75 percent of the target should be considered as	Inadequate
With normal facilitating and/or inhibiting factors, the achievement of target between 75 per cent and 99 per cent should be considered as	Adequate
Achievement f the target between 75 percent to 99 per cent in spite of severe inhibiting factors or lack of facilitating factors the rating should be .	Good

Note: In as much as targets are set to match the abilities of the employee and facilitating and inhibiting factors are expected to be present, the ratings of performance against these targets should not be used for comparing achievements of two individuals.

Guidelines for Rating Critical Attributes

Job knowledge: Refers to his/her knowledge, grasp, thoroughness of the fundamentals, techniques, policies, procedures and latest development relating to his/her functions and related areas. Ability to apply his/her knowledge to practical situations.

Rating	Indicators for Rating
Outstanding	Possess thorough and latest technical/professional knowledge of his functional area and related fields. Is highly competent in his/her application of knowledge to work situations.
Very Good	Possesses very good latest technical/professional knowledge of his functional area and related fields. Is competent in his application of knowledge of work situations.
Good	Possesses good technical/professional knowledge of his job and related areas. Is fairly up to date with some of the major developments in his field of work. Generally demonstrates good application of his knowledge to work situation.
Adequate	Has adequate technical professional knowledge in his functions. Occasionally updates himself with the latest developments. His application of knowledge to work situations is satisfactory.
Inadequate	Has limited technical/professional knowledge of his area of work. Does not keep himself posted with latest trends. Application of knowledge to work situations is unsatisfactory.

Planning skills: Ability to clearly visualise all aspects of job, to foresee eventualities, and to systematically plan a series of activities and course of action to achieve the goals.

Rating	Indicators for Rating
Outstanding	Can visualise all aspects of the job and plan his job exceptionally well. Foresees all eventuali ties and makes appropriate allowance and plans how to meet them. Can draw effective long-term and short-term plans, which rarely need a change.
Very Good	Does very good systematic planning by visualising clearly most aspects of the job. Foresees obstacles and failures and plans how to meet them. Can draw both short-term and long-term plans, which generally produce very good results and meet the schedules.
Good	Does a good planning of all activities. Foresees interruptions but at times needs guidance to meet them. Good at short-term planning but needs assistance in long-term plans.
Adequate	Plans satisfactorily his job activities in ordinary situations. Needs guidance in complex situations. Cannot foresee all eventualities. Can do immediate planning only.
Inadequate	Frequently fails to plan his work. Needs constant producing.

Organising skills: Ability to mobilise, coordinate and integrate various activities/resources to achieve completion of tasks by appropriate delegation of responsibility and authority.

Rating	Indicators for Rating
Outstanding	Organises, mobilises, coordinates and integrates various components/resources of his job exceptionally well even when under heavy pressure. Clearly states duties of subordinates. Delegates responsibilities to them in an exceptionally fair manner. Utilises his resources consistently to optimum level.
Very Good	Coordinates all activities of his subordinates. Delegates responsibilities to subordinates in a fair manner by defin-

	ing their duties and responsibilities. Generally utilises his resources well.
Good	Generally organises his resources well in ordinary situations. Delegates responsibilities fairly well. But needs assistance in complex situations. Mobilises and utilises resources to achieve good results.
Adequate	Normally organises personnel and other resources. Delegates duties and responsibilities adequately. At times fails to coordinate and integrate various components. Occasionally tries to do things by himself.
Inadequate	Does not define responsibilities and authorities of his subordinates. Allows the subordinates to drift and work haphazardly.

Initiative: Ability to start and complete tasks by solving job- related problems without leaning on others and without waiting for instructions.

Rating	Indicators for Rating
Outstanding	Naturally inclined to take lead in most difficult situations. Operates on his own independently with high confidence.
Very Good	Frequently a self-starter, performs most tasks independently and with confidence. Seeks guidance only in most difficult situations.
Good	A self-starter who takes action on his own in all routine assignments. Require instructions and guidance in difficult assignments.
Adequate	On routine matters generally takes action without instructions, but needs guidance and help when situation or assignment is not of routine nature.
Inadequate	Rarely takes action on his own. Has to be prodded constantly to get the work completed.

Creativity: Ability to come up with new practical ideas for improvement of systems and operations, related to his job.

Rating	Indicators for Rating
Outstanding	Very resourceful in developing new and practical ideas, schemes, programmes with regard to both current operations and future possibilities. Instrumental for many worthwhile changes or developments of major scope and importance.
Very Good	Shows considerable ability to produce new and practical ideas that result in helpful changes or developments on his job. Results are often of significant importance.
Good	Often comes up with new and practical ideas which sometimes produce results of significant importance.
Adequate	Sometimes comes up with a new and practical idea or may have many ideas which are not too practical or helpful.
Inadequate	Practically never contributes an original and workable idea. "Goes by the book" in all situations.

Interpersonal and team relationship: Ability to work harmoniously with superiors, peers and subordinates both individually as well as in teams.

Rating	Indicators for Rating
Outstanding	Is extremely successful at gaining quick and everlasting acceptance and respect from Superiors. Subordinates and Business Associates. Can work harmoniously with all members of the Department/Section, even in difficult situations.
Very Good	Actively establishes very good interpersonal relations with Superiors, Subordinates, Peers and Business Associates and produces effective results on the job.
Good	Generally achieves good acceptance from Superiors, Peers, Subordinates and Business Associates in normal conditions. Shares others' load/responsibility happily.

Adequate	Gains moderate acceptance in due course. Can get along with some and finds difficulty with others.
Inadequate	Often has difficulty in getting along well with others. has low acceptability from others.

Development of subordinates: Ability to identify strengths and weaknesses of his/her subordinates and their growth needs. Effectiveness in training subordinates for improved performance in their present roles as well as preparation for future roles.

Rating	Indicators for Rating
Outstanding	Identifies and assesses the developmental needs of subordinates exceptionally well. Sets up a definite development programme for all subordinates to meet individual and departmental needs for improving performance in their present roles as well as preparation for future roles. Systematically guides his subordinates in setting their personal development objectives. Exceptionally good in appraising and counselling subordinates consistently. Develops back-up people systematically.
Very Good	Is very good in identifying and assessing the subordinate development needs. Draws out specific development plans for every subordinate. Inspires individuals for self growth.
Good	Generally draws out a development plan of subordinates for improving their performance on present roles. Guides and counsels subordinates at periodic intervals with follow-up action for improved performance in their present roles. Sometimes prepares subordinates for future roles also.
Adequate	Occasionally identifies and assesses the development needs of the subordinates. Provides developmental facilities when called upon to do so, but does not draw out a systematic training and development plan.
Inadequate	Cannot identify and assess the development needs of his subordinates. Leaves his subordinates to find their own way for self-development.

Guidelines for Rating Critical Attributes of Secretaries in Supervisory Cadre

Organisation of mail and filing system: Ability to handle routine incoming and outgoing mail, obtain pertinent information and attach it to the respective correspondence. Classify mail into various categories such as most important, urgent, etc., and highlight important points before putting up the mail. Sets up effective system of filing, maintenance of records and retrieval of information.

Rating	**Indicators for Rating**
Outstanding	Can handle routine mail exceptionally well. Always classifies the mail systematically, attaches pertinent information with relevant correspondence, sets up an excellent system of filing and maintenance of records which facilitates retrieval of information without any loss of time and effort.
Very Good	Generally he/she does a very good job of handling routine mail but needs guidance in complex matters. Generally classifies the mail systematically, but at times does not attach pertinent information with correspondence. He/she establishes very good filing system, but retrieval of information takes a little effort.
Good	Normally he/she does a good job of handling routine mail, but at times needs guidance in difficult matters. Classifies mail, but takes more time. Can establish good filing system but takes more effort and time for retrieval of information.
Adequate	At times needs guidance even in handling routine mail. Can classify the mail, but at times does not link up previous/relevant correspondence before putting up the mail. Needs guidance in establishing workable filing system and maintenance of records.
Inadequate	He/she cannot handle even routine mail. Needs guidance and prodding in arranging mail and filing of papers, etc. Finds great difficulty in retrieving information. Generally his/her work is unsatisfactory.

Organisation of material for interviews, meetings and conferences: Extent to which he/she prepares points for interviews, meetings and conferences, sends information to concerned people. Looks into administrative details of meeting/conference room, prepares minutes of meeting/conference, circulates it to concerned people and follows up action required.

Rating	Indicators for Rating
Outstanding	Exceptionally meticulous in working out detailed points and in planning interviews, meetings and conferences. Makes excellent administrative arrangements and consistently follows up action. Always informs concerned people very well in advance.
Very Good	He/she does a very good job of planning and scheduling interviews, meetings and conferences. Generally makes very good administrative arrangements and follows up action. Foresees hindrances and plans to meet them. Has an eye for details.
Good	Does good planning and scheduling of meetings and conferences, but does not look into minutest details. Needs guidance and supervision in administrative details. Not consistent in follow-up action.
Adequate	Needs guidance and assistance in planning and scheduling conferences and meetings. However, makes satisfactory administrative arrangements. Needs prodding in follow up.

InadequateDoes not plan and schedule meetings well. Needs consistent supervision and guidance.

Public relationship: Ability to receive calls, receive and give accurate information, screen calls and visitors. Having pleasing manners, service attitude, courteous behaviour and tactfulness.

Rating	Indicators for Rating
Outstanding	Exceptionally tactful in handling visitors and telephone calls. Is utmost courteous and possess exceptionally pleasing manners. Leaves everlasting impression.

Annexure 10.1

PERFORMANCE APPRAISAL FORM
ASSESSMENT PERIOD : OCTOBER 198 - SEPTEMBER 198

PRIVATE & CONFIDENTIAL

PART A TO BE FILLED IN BY THE APPRAISEE					
MENTION YOUR SIGNIFICANT ACHIEVEMENTS			INDICATE FACTORS THAT INFLUENCED YOUR PERFORMANCE		
APPRAISEE'S NAME	SIGNATURE & DATE	CADRE	P.S. NO.	DEPT.	GROUP REGION

PART - B PERFORMANCE APPRAISAL		DATE OF APPRAISAL INTERVIEW					
TO BE FILLED IN BY THE APPRAISEE		TO BE FILLED IN BY THE IMMEDIATE SUPERIOR AT THE TIME OF INTERVIEW					
AGREED OBJECTIVES AND TARGETS OR ACTIVITIES	RESULTS ACHIEVED	RATING					REMARKS
		OUTSTA-NDING	V. GOOD	GOOD	ADEQUATE	INADE-QUATE	

NOTE : USE ADDITIONAL SHEETS IF REQUIRED.

PART - C APPRAISAL OF OVERALL PERFORMANCE & CRITICAL ATTRIBUTES BY THE IMMEDIATE SUPERIOR

Refer to the guidelines provided in the Performance Appraisal Manual

OVERALL PERFORMANCE & ATTRIBUTES	RATINGS					PLEASE COMMENT ON THE OVERALL PERFORMANCE & ATTRIBUTES OF THE APPRAISEE
	OUTSTA-NDING	V. GOOD	GOOD	ADEQUATE	INADE-QUATE	
OVERALL PERFORMANCE : Based on appraisal of objectives as completed in Part B						
JOB KNOWLEDGE : Refers to his/her knowledge, grasp, thoroughness of the fundamentals, techniques, policies, procedures & latest development relating to his/her functions and related areas. ability to apply his/her knowledge to practical situations.						
PLANNING SKILLS : Ability to clearly visualise all aspects of job, to forsee eventualities, and to systematically plan a series of activities and course of action to achieve the goals.						
ORGANISING SKILLS : Ability to mobilise, coordinate and integrate various activities, resources to achieve completion of tasks by appropriate delegation of responsibility and authority.						
INITIATIVE : Ability to start and complete tasks by solving job- related problems without leaning on others and without waiting for instruction.						
CREATIVITY : Ability to come up with new practical ideas for improvement of systems and operation, related to his job.						
INTERPERSONAL & TEAM RELATIONSHIP : Ability to work harmoniously with Superiors, Peers and Subordinates both individually as well as in teams.						
DEVELOPMENT OF SUBORDINATES : Ability to identify strengths & weaknesses of his/her subordinates and their growth needs. Effectiveness in training subordinates for improved performance in their roles as well as preparation for future roles						
OTHER ATTRIBUTES						
OTHER ATTRIBUTES						

PART - D DEVELOPMENT & TRAINING NEEDS - TO BE FILLED BY THE IMMEDIATE SUPERIOR

AREAS OF INVOLVEMENTS	DEVELOPMENT RECOMMENDATION (OTHER THAN TRAINING PROGRAMME)	RECOMMENDED TRAINING PROGRAMME (REFER TRAINING CODE BOOK OR CONSULT HRD DEPT.)	CODE	PRIO RITY

IMMEDIATE SUPERIOR'S NAME	CADRE	P.S. NO.	DEPT.	IMMEDIATE SUPERIORS SIGNATURE & DATE

PART - E OVERALL COMMENTS BY THE NEXT SUPERIOR

NEXT SUPERIOR'S NAME	CADRE	P.S. NO.	DEPT.	NEXT SUPERIOR'S SIGNATURE & DATE

SEND TO HRD DEPT. POWAI, BEFORE 15 DECEMBER

Annexure 10.2

PERFORMANCE APPRAISAL FORM
ASSESSMENT PERIOD : OCTOBER 198 SEPTEMBER 198

SECRETARIES
PRIVATE & CONFIDENTIAL

PART - A APPRAISAL OF OVERALL PERFORMANCE & CRITICAL ATTRIBUTES BY THE IMMEDIATE SUPERIOR
Refer to the guidelines in the Performance Appraisal Manual

OVERALL PERFORMANCE & ATTRIBUTES	RATINGS					PLEASE COMMENT ON THE OVERALL PERFORMANCE & ATTRIBUTES OF THE APPRAISEE
	OUTSTA-NDING	V. GOOD	GOOD	ADEQUATE	INADE-QUATE	
OVERALL PERFORMANCE : Based on the overall performance of the secretarial duties performed during the year.						
ORGANISATION OF MAIL AND FILING SYSTEM : Ability to handle routine incoming and outgoing mail, obtain pertinent information and attach it to the respective correspondence. Classify mail into various categories such as most important, urgent etc. & highlight important points, before putting up the mail. Sets up effective system of filing maintenance of records and retrieval of information.						
ORGANISATION OF MATERIAL FOR INTERVIEWS, MEETINGS AND CONFERENCES : Extent to which he/she prepares points for interviews, meetings and conferences, sends information to concerned people. Looks into administrative details of meeting conference room, prepares minutes of meeting/conference, circulates it to concerned people and follows up action required.						
PUBLIC RELATIONSHIP : Ability to receive and give accurate infor mation, screen calls and visitors. Having pleasing manners, service attitude, courteous behaviour & tactfulness.						
INITIATIVE : Ability to complete tasks with self-reliance and without waiting for instructions, or a self starter who solves his/her job-related problems without leaning on others.						
INTERPERSONAL RELATIONSHIP : Ability to work with others constructively without causing hard feelings in carrying out his/her job responsibilities. Cooperates willingly with others.						
DEPENDABILITY : Extent to which you can trust him/her in handling secret and confidential mailers/papers. Extent to which he/she can be relied upon to meet schedules.						
OTHER ATTRIBUTES						

APPRAISEE'S NAME	SIGNATURE & DATE	CADRE	P.S. NO.	DEPT.	GROUP/REGION

PART - B DEVELOPMENT & TRAINING NEEDS - TO BE FILLED BY THE IMMEDIATE SUPERIOR

AREAS OF INVOLVEMENTS	DEVELOPMENT RECOMMENDATION (OTHER THAN TRAINING PROGRAMME)	RECOMMENDED TRAINING PROGRAMME (REFER TRAINING CODE BOOK OR CONSULT HRD DEPT.)	CODE	PRIO-RITY

IMMEDIATE SUPERIOR'S NAME	CADRE	P.S. NO.	DEPT.	IMMEDIATE SUPERIORS SIGNATURE & DATE

PART - C OVERALL COMMENTS BY THE NEXT SUPERIOR

NEXT SUPERIOR S NAME	CADRE	P.S. NO.	DEPT.	NEXT SUPERIOR'S SIGNATURE & DATE

SEND TO HRD DEFT. POWAI, BEFORE 15 DECEMBER

Annexure 10.3

To be prepared in DUPLICATE

Period of reVIEW	
FROM OCT. 198	TO SEP.198

SUMMARY OF TRAINING NEEDS
(For all Covenanted/Officers/Supervisory Staff in a Dept.)

APPRAISEE			TRAINING PROGRAMMES RECOMMENDED					
SI. NO.	NAME	CADRE	PRIORITY I		PRIORITY II		PRIORITY III	
			NAME OF PROGRAMME	CODE	NAME OF PROGRAMME	CODE	NAME OF PROGRAMME	CODE

NEXT SUPERIORS'S NAME	CADRE	P.S. NO.	DEPARTMENT	SIGNATURE & DATE

Note : The nomination for the external Training Programmes will be confirmed by HRD Department after getting approval of concerned DGM, RM or GM.

Very Good	Very good in handling visitors and telephone calls. Generally courteous and displays very good pleasing manners. Generally impresses others very well.
Good	Generally good in handling visitors and telephone calls. At times needs guidance. Possesses good etiquette and manners. Conducts herself/himself well. Sometimes tactful, but not always.
Adequate	Handles telephone calls and visitors adequately. Needs guidance. Displays satisfactory manners. Needs supervision and guidance in handling important visitors and telephone calls. At times not tactful enough.
Inadequate	Finds difficulty in handling visitors and telephone calls. Needs constant supervision. His/her manners need substantial improvement.

Initiative: Ability to start and complete tasks by solving job- related problems without leaning on others and without waiting for instructions.

Rating	**Indicators for Rating**
Outstanding	Naturally inclined to take lead in most difficult situations. Operates on his own independently with high confidence.
Very Good	Frequently a self-starter, performs most tasks independently and with confidence. Seeks guidance only in most difficult situations.
Good	A self-starter who takes action on his own in all routine assignments. Require instructions and guidance in difficult assignments.
Adequate	On routine matters generally takes action without instructions, but needs guidance and help when situation or assignment is not of routine nature.
Inadequate	Rarely takes action on his own. Has to be prodded constantly to get the work completed.

Interpersonal relationship: Ability to work with others constructively without causing hard feelings in carrying out his/her job responsibilities. Cooperates willingly with others.

Rating	Indicators for Rating
Outstanding	Is extremely successful at gaining quick and everlasting acceptance and respect from Superiors, Peers, Subordinates and Business Associates. Can work harmoniously even in difficult situations.
Very Good	Actively establishes very good inter-personal relations with Superiors, Subordinates, Peers and Business Associates and produces effective results on the job.
Good	Generally achieves good acceptance from Superiors, Peers, Subordinates and Business Associates in normal conditions.
Adequate	Gains moderate acceptance in due course. Can get along with some and finds difficulty with others.
Inadequate	Often has difficulty in getting along well with others. Has low acceptability from others.

Dependability: Extent to which you can trust him/her in handling secret and confidential matters/papers. Extent to which he/she can be relied upon to meet schedules.

Rating	Indicators for Rating
Outstanding	Exceptionally dependable in handling secret and confidential matters. Consistent in meeting schedules. Can be relied upon to do a given job outstandingly well.
Very Good	He/she can be very well relied upon to handle secret and confidential information. Can do a given job very well. At times needs caution in exceptional circumstances/matters.
Good	Generally reliable to handle secret information, but at times slips. Can be depended upon to do a given job well on time.

Adequate	Can be relied upon to keep ordinary matters secret, but needs caution in sensitive issues. Generally reliable for meeting schedules, but at times needs supervision.
Inadequate	Not reliable to keep sensitive issue secret and confidential. Cannot be entrusted with important tasks, as he/she does not meet schedules.

Current Status

The Performance Appraisal System presented here has undergone some more changes recently. There have been six revisions of the appraisal system between 1976 and 1982. In all these revisions the objectives were not changed but modifications have been made in some of the components and mechanics. The appraisal system presented here is the system that is in practice between 1982 and 1991. In 1991 a series of internal workshops were held to have a relook at the appraisal system. As a result of this internal review some changes have been introduced to make the system (format) simpler and more meaningful. The following are some of the features of the new format.

1. The title has been changed to "Performance Analysis and Review".
2. Form 1 requires the appraisee and appraiser to identify a set of objectives and corresponding targets/activities in the beginning of the year. In addition critical attributes specific to the role also need to be identified.
3. Form 2 requires the appraisee to state the results he achieved in relation to the objectives and targets, his significant contributions (job or profession related and other than the agreed objectives) and also the business, organisational or personal factors that influenced his performance.
4. The critical attributes printed on the form are limited to five (innovativeness, initiative, interpersonal and team relationship, leadership and development of subordinates) and scope is provided to add two more specific to each role which are to be identified in the beginning of the year.
5. A new form (Form 3) has been introduced requiring the appraisee and appraiser to list proposed development actions with target dates. A list of development actions have been prepared for use by the appraisee-appraiser pair. The list includes actions that could be taken by the appraisee, actions by immediate

superior and actions at the group/unit level. This list is reproduced below.

Some Development Actions for the Employee

Self Development Actions

***Knowledge Upgrading**

– Self-study efforts including inter-active packages, correspondence and part-time courses.

– Keeping abreast with latest developments in his area of function through discussions with experts, reading journals and active participation to professional forums.

***Skill Building**

– Hands-on practice for PC working, manufacturing operations, etc.

– Developing good listening habits.

***Behaviour/Attitude Development**

– Learning to work systematically through attention to details, analysis and planning.

– Learning by following superiors and other role models.

– Developing perseverance and habit of hard work.

– Developing attitudes of introspection, learning from mistakes, willingness to change and positive thinking.

Actions by Immediate Superior

***Involvement**

– Involving employee in decision making through participation in meetings and working in teams.

– Asking to make formal presentation.

***Job Enlargement/Rotation**

– Exposure to other functional areas or responsibility within the department.

– Delegating additional responsibilities.

– Special assignments.

– Allowing to officiate in his absence.

***Counselling and Training**

– Clarifying roles, areas of growth and career.

– Regular counselling and coaching sessions.

– Attend/Conduct departmental training programmes.

Actions at Unit/Group Level

***Job Responsibilities**

– Deputation to other departments for short periods.

– Job rotation including transfer across the groups.

– Assignments to task forces and committees formed for special purposes.

***Training**

– Deputations to in-company training programmes.

– Deputations to external training programmes/courses.

– Taking training/teaching assignments.

***General**

– Encouragement for active involvement in professional bodies.

Chapter 11

PERFORMANCE ANALYSIS AND DEVELOPMENT SYSTEM (PADS) IN LARSEN & TOUBRO LIMITED (E.C.C. CONSTRUCTION GROUP)

Although L&T Construction Group is a part of the Larsen & Toubro Limited, before ECC merged with L&T Limited they used to follow the old system of Performance Appraisal (i.e., Confidential Report System). L&T (ECC) Construction Group decided to change its appraisal system as a consequence of a series of Organisation Development discussions the top management had, beginning the year 1983. During the OD exercises several of the members of the top management felt that there is a need to review their system and make it open and development-oriented. A task force was constituted in 1985 to review the existing system and came up with a new system. This task force consisted of members from OD Group. After conducting a structured survey they made some preliminary recommendations and subsequently decided to evolve a system that facilitates various other efforts they are making in their company. This task force interviewed a large number of managers, examined various systems existing in the country in cluding that of the L&T and came up with a system which was considered as an improvement over many other systems operating in the country at that time. This system was titled as "Performance Analysis and Development System". This system was introduced from 1986-87. The system is described here. As may be noted from the description given below in the forms appended while the forms are very simple, the system itself is highly development- oriented. What is reproduced here is the manual used by L&T (ECC) Construction Group Executives.*

Uniqueness of PADS

The use of facilitators is a unique part of the PADS in L&T (ECC). Only competent line managers are used as facilitators. While this inflicts

*The author thanks Mr. C.R. Ramakrishnan of L & T, ECC for permission to include details of their PADS' here.

some constraints on the system the top management felt it essential to have the help of competent line managers to facilitate the implementation of the system. The facilitators have been trained in process competencies and per formance counselling skills. L&T (ECC) has conducted a massive training programme for this purpose and process work through OD is an on-going exercise in L&T (ECC). Along with the introduction of PAD System, L&T (ECC) has also introduced a separate system of rewards and recognition.

Objectives of the System

The objective of the Performance Analysis and Development System (PADS), is to generate relevant data to facilitate action leading to:

* Development and motivation of the employees (through rewards, various forms of recognition, promotion, job-rotation, etc.).

* Improvement of employees' present and future job-related competencies (through training, job-rotation, change of responsibilities etc.) and the generation of a pro-active and development-oriented climate in the group.

In order to achieve these, the system aims at the following PROCESS objectives:

* Generating role clarity on a continuing basis.

* Helping employees recognise their strengths and weaknesses and improve their performance.

* Strengthening Appraiser-Appraisee relationships through increased trust and team spirit.

* Developing self-renewing capabilities in employees through improving their process competencies.

Components and Process of the System

In order to achieve the above mentioned objectives, the Performance Analysis and Development System (PADS) will have the following components:

Task/Target Identification: The appraisee and his appraiser sit together at the beginning of every appraisal year/period and **jointly** identify the tasks required to be performed by the appraisee during that year/period, based on which the appraisal will be made.

The process of task identification should aim at:

- A **clarity of role** for the appraisee through a listing of tasks, by the appraiser and appraisee.

- Establishing the **relative importance** of each of these tasks.

- Describing the **criteria of performance measurement** for each task.

The discussion of tasks and targets between the appraiser and appraisee should result in the listing of tasks (not exceeding 7) on the PADS form.

Self Appraisal

At the end of the performance period, **the appraisal process should start with a self appraisal by the appraisee.**

The appraisee should prepare himself for the self-appraisal by doing the following:

- Identify the factors affecting (facilitating and inhibiting) his performance.

- Identify his development needs.

- Identify the support he needs.

Self appraisal should help the appraisee to prepare himself for a useful final review discussion on his performance, with his appraiser.

The appraisee is encouraged to keep notes (on the blank sheet provided) regarding his thoughts on the above, for use during periodic review discussions, and for his future development.

It is to be noted that the inputs provided by the appraisee during the periodic review discussion, and final review discussion, would help in final assessment by the appraiser.

On the basis of the above self review, the appraisee should **rate himself** on each of the tasks and job attributes, and the form should be returned to the appraiser **before** the final review discussion. The appraisee should also mention any significant aspect of his performance (if any) in the column titled "Remarks by Appraisee".

Final Review Discussion

The Final Performance Review Discussion should take place **after** the appraiser receives the appraisee's self assessment.

The discussion should aim at the following:

* To provide the appraisee an opportunity to communicate and discuss his performance, job attributes, difficulties en countered, support requirements, development needs etc., with his superior.

* To help the appraiser get information for assessing the performance of the appraisee.

* To enable the appraiser to receive feedback about the extent to which he was able to provide support and inputs needed by the appraisee.

* To increase **mutuality, trust and collaboration between appraiser and appraisee**.

The Final Review Discussion is an important part of the Performance Analysis and Development System; the success of PADS depends on the final review discussions. Therefore, the appraisers are requested to ensure that they make a **sufficient time investment** to carry out the appraisal **process**.

Final Rating

Every appraiser, after the final review discussion, is required to give his final rating on each of the tasks and job attributes.

These rating should be given, after taking into consideration the information provided to him during the review discussions, as well as the performance of other staff in similar categories under his supervision.

This final rating may or may not be communicated to the appraisee. In this, the discretion of the appraiser would prevail.

The appraiser may use the space (Remarks by Appraiser) to record any information (e.g., explanation of the variance between self- rating and appraiser's ratings, any significant contributions/ deficiencies of appraisee etc.) that he would like the Reviewing Officer/Personnel Department to know.

It is desirable that these remarks are shown to the appraisee for his awareness and improvement, if needed.

Development Needs

The last page of the PADS form will be used for enlisting the developmental needs of the appraisee.

Every appraisee is expected to express **his perceptions** of his developmental needs of the appraisee.

Every appraisee is expected to express **his perceptions** of his developmental needs here, after his self review, and before he submits the form to his appraiser. These development needs must be related to his job.

The appraiser must comment on the above, based on the review discussions and show his comments to the appraisee.

The P&OD Department will use this information to take Training and Development decisions, in consultation with the Departmental Heads. Every employee may expect to get a feedback from P&OD during the subsequent year.

Review by the Reviewing Officer

The Reviewing Officer is responsible for the development of all the staff in his department. Information from the appraisal forms will serve to sensitize him to the performance of his staff, and their development needs.

Each Reviewing Officer must peruse the PADS forms, to acquaint himself about how the review process is functioning, and to monitor the same. He must further moderate the quality of appraisals, identify varying standards of performances, and ensure equitable rewards.

The Reviewing Officer, after putting his remarks in the space "Remarks by Reviewing Officer", must share this with the appraiser. The form should thereafter be forwarded to P&OD.

Role of Facilitator and Facilitating Process

The four important roles the Facilitator is expected to perform are:

1. As **internal resource persons** in educating and conducting training session on PADS to employees at various levels in different locations.

2. As a **sensor** in perceiving how the PADS is functioning and in identifying the areas of concern and constraints, so that in consultation with other **facilitators** corrective action may be initiated. (At the micro level).

3. As a **Process Facilitator** at Appraiser-Appraisee discussions, to encourage better mutuality and understanding between them.

4. As a **Guide** in helping the Appraiser-Appraisee pair to gain greater role clarity in task/target/weightages/ratings/ development need identification.

The important activities of the Facilitator is expected to under take are:

1. To help in regularly conducting PADS Training Programme.

2. To identify during the course of facilitation those individuals/Appraiser-Appraisee pairs who require more clarity or have had no education on the PADS.

3. To educate (say even informally) those employees (can be even three or four) on the PADS. This can be done wherever needed during Facilitator's visits to regions/sites.

4. To make himself available for facilitating the Appraiser-Appraisee discussions.

5. To periodically get together with other Facilitators to learn from sharing of experiences so as to initiate necessary corrective steps through Departmental Heads/P&OD/Stabilisation Task Force/OD Group.

Chapter 12

SENIOR MANAGEMENT PERSONNEL APPRAISAL : CROMPTON GREAVES LIMITED

The appraisal system in Crompton Greaves Limited (CGL) was evolved and designed after a good deal of debate, discussion and research. The system was designed by the HRD Department. A noteworthy feature of this system is its emphasis on team building and use of peer ratings or internal customers. Reproduced below are the guidelines and forms supplied by the Company to its management staff.*

Philosophy

An organisation is basically an assemblage of hina beings with definite skills, an urge to excel, create and impact as individuals. The organisation therefore, has the responsibility to create a culture where individuals can contribute their best. It is with this recognition that CGL has identified pursuit of excellence and humanism as two major values for the Company. CGL's performance appraisal system, therefore, is governed by this theme and has the following objectives:

1. Objective and fair assessment of performance against performance expectations mutually evolved by boss and subordinates.

2. Strengthening dyadic (boss/subordinate) relationships through open performance appraisal system and thereby contribute to individual development and improved team performance.

3. Helping the employee recognise his strengths and weaknesses and set goals for developing his capabilities necessary for effective performance, individual growth and organisational effectiveness.

4. Defining norms and nuances that distinguish excellent and other levels of performance.

---

*The author thanks Shri K.K. Nohria, President and MD, CGL and Ms. Susan Varaghese for permission to include their appraisal system here.

Introduction

This Performance Appraisal System attempts to assess three values:

1. Assessment of performance in Key Performance Areas

2. a) Leadership and team building

   b) Contribution to team spirit

3. Innovation, risk-taking and venturism.

Part I : Objective Setting Against Key Performance Areas

Goal Setting

Role analysis has helped identify key areas of contribution or KPAs for short. Performance appraisal linked to role expectations requires this to be carried further to include objectives related to these KPAs. The objectives relate to what, how much and expected time of accomplishment and wherever possible at what cost.

The objectives must be derived from overall strategic plan of the division. Related functional performance must then be derived from this. Out of this will emerge the objectives against KPAs for each functional role.

Goal setting should be guided by quantum improvement as well as qualitative improvement in areas of performance.

1. Goal setting for every performer must be within the resources available at the disposal of the division. These resources refer to finance, human, material and structural.

2. The scanning of opportunities is another area of focus - Areas of opportunity a unit can exploit.

3. Goal setting must also include change from old to new. This process can include research and development, application or implementation of an idea already explored in the organisation/outside.

Emphasis should be on setting as high a target as achievable. Divisional requirement will be the primary deciding factor. The level of performance budgeted for one individual must be comparable to that of his peer group. It is possible that objectives/performance targets set in areas such as managing change may vary depending on the inclination and calibre of the individual substantially from that of other areas of performance. Therefore, wherever objectives are scaled down particular mention must be made of this fact. This would be necessary as assessment against performance must reflect quantum achievement as well as the nature of the objectives agreed to between boss and subordinate.

Goal setting must begin with a boss initiating the discussion. He must appreciate his subordinate's positive contribution in the previous year and boss's expectation of continued performance. He may also refer to his areas of improvement, if any. This must be reflected in his objectives for the year. Boss may then request subordinate to identify objectives related to each KPA within the framework of the divisional plans.

A boss will then have to carefully consider subordinate's response in the light of peer expectation, potential to contribute and stretch in performance and resource availability.

Goal setting should be followed by a weighted allocation of points for assessment amongst the KPAs after a prioritisation of importance of each KPA.

Self Appraisal

Appraisees will assess own performance at the end of June of every year against his budgeted areas of performance. He will also complete the Performance Analysis and highlight exceptional facilitating and inhibiting factors. The boss will assign the points. Appraisal interview must precede the rating.

Part II(A) : Leadership and Team Building

CGL considers team building as an important aspect of managerial life. While every individual may contribute his individual best, quality of total performance of a unit/division is dependent on collaboration and team spirit present in the unit/division. Team building, as visualised by CGL executives in a survey on mechanisms that contribute to team effectiveness, consists of six dimensions - Vision/Planing and Clarity of objectives, Operating responsibility/Delegation, Interaction process, Empowering, Responsibility for failure and Personal example. However, only three of these dimensions - Vision, Empowering and Delegation are used for appraisal purposes.

Part II (B)

Internal Customers approved by HRD Task Force for each managerial position will assess the role incumbent on Peer Assessment Form designed for the purpose. The average score will determine a role incumbent's position vis-a-vis his peers.

Idea Generation

Appraisees will be assessed for their personal contribution as well as encouragement given to subordinates, nurturing creative contribution and recognition of it.

Risk Taking and Venturism

Appraisee can be assessed for his venturism and entrepreneurial flair in commercialising a venture or contributing to higher margins or improvement in market share.

Critical Attributes

Appraisee should be evaluated for his level of competence with regard to critical attributes specific to each job. This assessment will be useful for training and development purposes.

Training and Development Needs

The immediate superior will fill Training and Development needs after the appraisal interview. He will also carry forward the critical attributes' assessment for listing development needs.

Overall Rating

Scores of each part of the appraisal should be entered in the overall rating.

Reviewer's Comments

Appraisee's Boss will give his comments in this column.

Annexure "A"

Rating

85 and above	Outstanding
70 - 84	Above Average
50 - 69	Average
Less than 50	Below Average

Who can be deemed outstanding

1. Objectives accomplished with exceptional inhibiting factors and the following/but not all and in equal measure.
2. Performing an element of Boss's role.
3. Performance that is unique and rare.
4. Performance qualified by high risk-taking and creative contribution or influencing creative contribution.

Performance that can be rated as:

Above Average Performance

1. Objectives accomplished in toto.
2. Performance that is qualified by high initiative and a strong drive to achieve and build in a concern for tomorrow in today's performance. A very dependable performer.

Average Performance

1. Objectives accomplished where objectives were relatively easy and exceptional facilitating factors were present.
2. Objectives not fully accomplished where exceptional inhibiting factors were present, but efforts were put into some extent to

overcome constraints in performance.

3. Performance which is qualified by very little initiative on the part of appraisee to seek out responsibility. High boss dependence, but a good follower.

Below Average Performance

1. A person who does not accomplish the objectives mutually set by him and his boss, with no inhibiting factors present.

2. Efforts to utilise facilitating factors to his/her advantage not seen.

CROMPTON GREAVES LIMITED
SENIOR MANAGEMENT PERSONNEL APPRAISAL

PERFORMANCE ASSESSMENT - I

TO BE FILLED BY THE APPRAISEE				Assessment of Immediate Superior
Key Performance Areas	Points	Results Achieved	Exceptional Factors Facilitating/Inhibiting Performance	

Signature of Appraisee : ____________

Date of Appraisal Interview ____________ Signature of Superior : ____________

Points

	GM	DH
Max.	70	80
Score		

LEADERSHIP & TEAM BUILDING - II

A. Leadership

1. Vision

- Vision to perceive mission of a unit, build, change and perpetuate.
- Sharing and developing this with team members.

2. Delegation

- Unit Responsibility/Accountability and its sharing with team members.
- Autonomy experienced by subordinates.

3. Empowering a subordinate

- Efforts put in by the boss towards developing his subordinates as better managers/performers and their confidence level.

	GM	DH
Max.	10	10
Score		

B. Contribution to Team Spirit & Unit Performance

Summary of Internal Customer assessment (Average score)

	GM	DH
Max.	10	5
Score		

OTHER BEHAVIOURS - III

1. **Idea Generation/Experimentation**
   – Capacity to generate new ideas (personally and through subordinates) and innovation efforts in unit.
2. **Risk Taking and Venturism**
   – Entrepreneurial flair and dynamism in building/changing.
3. **Unique Performance**
   – Performance that is not expected and does not fall in any of the categories above.

	GM	DH
Max.	10	5
Score		

CRITICAL ATTRIBUTES - IV

Critical attributes specific to each job (not exceeding five)
(Not included for purpose of rating)

1.
2.
3.
4.
5.

Good	Adequate	Inadequate

PEER ASSESSMENT FORM

CONTRIBUTION TO TEAM SPIRIT AND DIVISIONAL PERFORMANCE ASSESSMENT BY INTERNAL CUSTOMER

Name : ____________

Designation : ____________

	GM	DH
Max.	10	10
Score		

1.	Team objectives understood Puts Divisional performance/needs ahead of his department or personal concerns	______	Team objectives not understood Compartmentalised outlook. Insists on own dept/personal needs preceding overall organisational good.
2.	Open and direct communication	______	Closed/guarded in communication
3.	Trusting	______	Suspicious
4.	Plans ahead in anticipation & influences events. Peers are fully informed of what to expect.	______	Waits for crisis to happen and then takes decisions, thus disturbing linkages in the chain.
5.	Collaborative - 'We feeling' and high ownership of divisional objectives	______	Hostile - 'They feeling' and fault finding.

TRAINING & DEVELOPMENT NEEDS IDENTIFIED - V DURING APPRAISAL INTERVIEW

Training Needs	Comments of Corporate Personnel	Action Plan	
		Training	Development

Summary of Rating

Dimensions	SCORE
PERFORMANCE ASSESSMENT	
TEAM BUILDING	
INNOVATION & RISK TAKING	
TOTAL SCORE	

Reviewer's Comments :

Chapter 13

PERFORMANCE APPRAISAL IN STEEL AUTHORITY OF INDIA LIMITED (SAIL)*

About SAIL

SAIL produces about 9 million tonnes of crude steel every year, at 7 plants spread all over the country. It is, in fact, the largest manufacturing organisation in India. To give an example of its size - here is an interesting fact: the annual budget of SAIL is higher than that of any state barring U.P. and Maharashtra. The steel it produces goes into making an immense variety of products - from a teaspoon to a Vijayanta tank, from a sewing needle to an oil rig. SAIL utilises the skills of engineers of every discipline, plus professionals in marketing, R & D, finance, materials handling, personnel, medicine, education and more. It directly employs over 2,35,000 people, including 18,000 managers. And in recent years, it has pulled off, what can only be termed a financial miracle.

In the early eighties, SAIL was burdened with cumulative losses totalling Rs.276 crores. Over the next few years, the losses were progressively reduced. And in 1988-89, SAIL recorded a profit of Rs.358 crores. And wiped off all its cumulative losses. Fortune magazine of the USA termed it as one of the fastest turnarounds that year.

Objectives of Performance Appraisal

SAIL has changed its performance appraisal system in the year 1986. The new appraisal system was designed with the following objectives: .

- To integrate company and individual goals through a process of performance assessment linked to achievement of organisation objectives.

*The author thanks SAIL for their permission to include their appraisal system here.

- To increase awareness of targets/tasks and the responsibility of officers at all levels to ensure fulfilment of company objectives.
- To ensure a more objective assessment of performance and potential.
- To distinguish between differing levels of performance on relative basis and to identify officers with potential to grow in the organisation.
- To identify the developmental actions to be taken to enhance the performance of officers.
- To facilitate the process of Executive development through performance planning, self review, performance analysis and increased two way communication between appraisees and appraisers.

Components

Inorder to achieve these objectives the new appraisal system of executives in SAIL incorporated the following components:

1. **Tasks and Target Setting** : Each appraisee is expected to have a clear understanding of the tasks and targets assigned to him through a discussion with his appraiser in the beginning of every performance year. This exercise of tasks and target setting is to be done twice a year, first in the beginning of the performance year and second about six months after the performance year to make modifications in the tasks and targets set.

2. **Self-Appraisal** : The appraisee is expected to review his own performance every six months and identify their tasks and targets accomplished, constraints faced, suggestions for improvement and developmental needs. After such a self-appraisal, the appraisee is expected to pass this information on to his appraiser.

3. **Performance Review Discussion** : On the basis of this self-appraisal his reporting officer is expected to have a discussion with the appraisee to under stand the appraisee and his difficulties more, to prepare action plans for each of them to act and improve on the situation, to communicate expectations and to understand each other better. The performance review discussion is expected to increase the awareness about the tasks and responsibilities of officers as well as to identify the developmen-

tal needs and thereby to improve communication between the appraisees and appraisers.

4. **Performance Assessment** : After such a review discussion is over the reporting officer is expected to assess the performance of the officer concerned both in relation to job performance factors and in relation to managerial ability factors. The job performance factors consist of quantity of output, quality of output, job knowledge and cost/time control. The managerial ability factors included: planning and organising, initiative, commitment and sense of responsibility, communication, training and development of subordinates, team spirit, problem analysis and decision making, management of human resources, lateral coordination and discipline. The weight ages given to the managerial ability factors and performance factors varies between senior managers and middle/junior level managers. Performance factors were given higher weightage at junior levels. The appraisal rating are to be given on a 6-point scale, first by the reporting officer and then by the reviewing officer. The ratings may range from 30 to 180 as the total weightages equal to 30.

5. **Development Plan** : In addition to the assessment of the appraisee on Perform ance and Managerial Factors, the reporting and reviewing officers are required to prepare a development plan for the appraisee. The development plan may consist of development through training, job rotation, job enrichment, counselling/coaching. The developmental plan takes into account suggestions made by the appraisee in his appraisal during performance review discussion.

6. **Final Assessment** : The final assessment is to be done by the higher authority assisted by a performance review committee. In the final assessment the total scores (averaged between the reporting and reviewing officers) are to be combined along with a group of other appraisees working in the same or similar departments and to be arranged in discending order. On the basis of the relative standing of his scores the appraisee is classified into A category (top 25 per cent of performance in that group), B category (middle 50 per cent of performers in that group) and C category (bottom 25 per cent performers in that group, i.e., low performers). It is this categorisation of the appraisee into A, B and C categories that forms as an input into his promotions. The Performance Review Committee (PRC)

which consists of a group of senior managers also choose from among the top 25 per cent (i.e., from A category) a maximum of five per cent as star performers. Similarly the PRC may choose five per cent as bottom performers from among the C category of employees. Such bottom performers are to be counselled by the performance review committee. The top performers get high weightage promotions and stand the chance of fast promotions depending on their level and vacancies.

Such forced grouping of officers on the basis of their performance in the A, B and C categories was expected to facilitate distinction between differing levels of performance and to help identifying officers with high potential to grow in the organisation.

Context for Introducing the Appraisal System

The change in the performance appraisal system of SAIL took place at a time when the work culture at SAIL itself was undergoing a change. This change in work culture and turnaround was initiated during the year 1985-86 through a programme of action very well known in the country as "priorities for action project". Arising out of a feeling that SAIL has not measured upto the expectations of the country in terms of its performance as well as managerial contributions to its objectives, the top management initiated a series of meetings and discussions with unit management with a cross-section of middle management, frontline supervisors, work men on the shop floor and unions and associations. Based on the feedback and discussions a 'priorities for action programme' was initiated. This approach identified the following thrust areas for SAIL to devote itself, improve its operations and prepare itself for challenges in the future. These were:

1. Improving work culture
2. Optimal use of installed facilities
3. Increase in productivity
4. Generation of profits through cost controls and
5. Customer satisfaction.

As a part of this programme a number of changes were initiated in SAIL and there was concerted effort to create a new work culture. The changes in the appraisal system took place in this particular context.

Initially, the exercise began as a move to amend the promotion policy to make it totally performance oriented. Gradually, it was realised that the Promotion Policy would not be so changed without having an adequate/acceptable instrument for measurement of performance. This was an important step in the attempt to improve the work culture by convincing employees that their career growth was linked with the performance of the Company. Thus the Company reviewed its appraisal system and found that it needed drastic amendments.

The Old Appraisal System

Studies were conducted on the old appraisal system existing upto 1985. From the Management's points of view, it was found:

1. The appraisal system was not adequately distinguishing between different levels of performance. Analysis showed that ratings were skewed: 68% of the executives were being assessed in the top two ranks and no one in the bottom rank. With a large percentage of officers bunching at one level it became difficult to take administrative decisions on the basis of performance. It also raised doubts about the validity of a system which produces outstanding performers but not outstanding performance.

2. The system was not sufficiently grounded in the requirements of the Company. It did not reflect the Value System of the Organisation. It failed to communicate to the employee what set of activities or what qualities are considered desirable by the Organisation. The system of assessment also did not have a linkage to the job description and the requirement of the Industry.

3. Officers were not participating fully in the System. Basically officers did not see any value, because they did not see the output of the System being linked to any tangible decision making.

From the employees point of view the survey conducted on the appraisal system brought out the following major concerns.

1. Junior officers felt that there was no focus on what was expected from them. They did not know the areas in which they were expected to contribute so that their performance ratings could improve.

2. They felt that the system was not participative enough. They did not have a sufficient opportunity to be heard.

3. There were three assessment levels. Reporting Officer, Reviewing Officer and Higher Authority. Since each level could countermand the previous one, the Reporting Officer as the immediate supervisor felt that they had little role to play.

Process of Change

In response to these opinions, an exercise was initiated to revise the system. An initial draft was prepared and thrown open for discussions. Discussions were held at various levels with the Heads of Personnel, the Steel Executive Federation of India, the Chief Executives and in groups of executives. At each level there were suggestions and modifications made. They wanted very frequent performance review. In addition to the structured responses, indepth interviews were held with a cross section of officers.

On the basis of all their feedback and the discussions, a system was finally evolved during 1985-86 for implementation in the subsequent years.

As a first step, the new system was presented to groups of officers in each unit and the details explained. In the second step, 70 internal resource persons were identified. These internal resource persons were put through two "Training for Trainers' programmes conducted by IIM, Ahmedabad. Subsequently the resource persons trained 7000 officers in the essential aspects of the system. In each unit an Implementation Task Force was appointed to review the implementation of the system and provide guidance. At the Corporate level, an Inter-Plant Steering Committee was set up to oversee the process. The implementation strategy was designed keeping in view the following:

1. The large number of officers to be covered in various units. 2.The need to explain the various aspects of the system particularly target setting and performance review discussions, and convince officers of the need and rationale.

First Review of the System

After the new appraisal system was put into operation for two years, some minor modifications were made on the basis of the feedback received. The first two years of operation has thrown up a number of issues:

1. The system had been successful in correcting imbalances in the assessments which existed earlier.

2. Officers are actively participating in the system since they are now aware of its importance in the overall context.

3. Development aspects of the system such as performance planning and review discussion have not been fully implemented and needs much greater training effort.

4. The system throws up an immense amount of data about the problems faced by employees, their suggestions/views and their specific development needs. These can be utilised to design specific interventions.

Second Review of the System

SAIL has conducted a number of internal research studies every year to understand the extent to which the system is being implemented. In addition plant level groups were formed to monitor its implementation. A Central Task Force also was formed to monitor the implementation. After nearly four years of its implementation, SAIL started experiencing new problems in the performance appraisal system. While it was received enthusiastically and implemented well in the first two years the data generated through the appraisal system started throwing up some more anomalies in ratings arising out of inter-departmental groupings and comparisons. The internal resource persons and some members of the association were invited for a review workshop in early 1990 to take stock of the new problems being experienced by the review system. In this meeting the following problems were identified:

1. SAIL being a large organisation and the system covering about 18,000 officers it has become difficult to monitor effective implementation of the system with respect to each appraiser. While it has served a good purpose in the beginning the review discussion seem to become routine and executives were not giving sufficient time for the review discussions.

2. Some of the employees have not really understood the true spirit of the system and as a result have not internalised the advantages of the system.

3. There was a continuous need to educate and train the officers in

the system as the system is a developmental tool and aims at strengthening communication between officers.

4. Most of the executives were found to spend very little adequate time in performance review discussions as they have not seen the significance of the performance review discussion.

Recent Review

Arising out of these discussions the top management of SAIL has decided to re-educate the officers of SAIL on the appraisal system. In order to facilitate this process SAIL produced three films on Performance Appraisal and Performance Review Discussion which are being used in the Company.

SAIL also undertook another comprehensive review of its performance appraisal system. This review report is under discussion in the year 1991. The review recommends some minor changes in the appraisal system retaining largely the objectives, processes and format.

Chapter 14

THE STATE BANK OF INDIA EXPERIMENT*

The State Bank of India is a large organisation spread all over the country. It has about 6,200 branches grouped under 12 circles. Each circle (called "Local Head Office") is headed by a Chief General Manager who is assisted by a General Manager (Operations), a General Manager (Planning) and a number of other officers. The circle is further divided into modules for administrative purposes. Each module is headed by a Chief Regional Manager. Each module administers 3 to 4 regions each headed by a Regional Manager. Each region has about 50 branches and the Branch Managers report to the Regional Manager. In the country there are 23 modules and 123 regions. The total strength of the staff employed by the State Bank of India is about 1,70,000 including about 35,000 officers.

Performance Appraisal in SBI

The State Bank of India has been having a Confidential Reporting System of Appraisals. Under this system a confidential report on a prescribed format (known as C.O.S. 220) is submitted by every reporting officer on the officers reporting to him. This report is submitted in November every year and the reports are placed in a Service File which is maintained separately for each official of the bank. These reports are used for personnel decisions (salary administration, placement and promotions).

The forms for supervisors and middle level managers required assessment of the appraisee on dimensions like: general intelligence, job-knowledge, initiative and resourcefulness, supervision, business capacity, dependability, relationships with juniors and seniors,

---

* This chapter is based on a report of the experiment prepared by the HRD department of the State Bank of India, Ahmedabad, LHO. The author was associated with this experiment. Subsequent information provided by Mr R. Krishnan, HRD Manager and Mr. T.P. Raman, Chief Officer-HRD (Central Office) is gratefully acknowl edged.)

sociability, appearance, conduct, manners and health. In addition, the reporting authority is required to mention about any specially good work done during the year, any activity deserving warning or reprimand and special aptitudes. There were minor variations among the formats used for supervisors, middle managers and senior managers.

New Appraisal System

Recognising the need for paying increased attention to the development of its human resources, the SBI saw performance appraisal as a potential instrument for the development of its human re sources. In the year 1979 the Bank decided to adopt a new system of performance appraisal to meet this end. In a note circulated by the Central Office it was stated:

...HRD aims at optimisation of human resources. Optimisation depends upon the growth of the individuals in the organisation and the opportunities that the organisation provide for fuller expression and use of the potentials of the employees. Performance of employees can be improved through a process of helping them to identify their strengths and weaknesses and take steps to improve the strengths and eradicate the weaknesses. HRD also aims at the creation of an enabling organisation. The characteristics of an enabling organisation are organisation-wide openness, trust, mutuality and collaboration.

The proposed performance appraisal system will facilitate growth of an employee through performance improvement.

The objectives of the new appraisal system were formulated as follows:

i) Employee motivation development and growth - in terms of acquisition of new capabilities, knowledge, skills, experience, attitudes, etc., to perform his present job better and future jobs more effectively.
ii) To help the Bank to move towards a culture of mutuality and openness - with increasing mutual communication between the superior and the subordinate and development of helpful attitudes at all levels - leading to a climate of trust and collaboration.
iii) As a by-product, generate objective and accurate data about employees that could be used for personnel decisions like placement, promotions, transfers, training, etc.

In order to achieve the objectives the SBI evolved an appraisal format given in Appendix 14.1. The format consists of the following components:

1. Identification of Key Performance Areas.
2. Goal-setting through mutual discussions between the appraiser and the appraisee.
3. Common understanding on dimensions outside KPAs.
4. Self-appraisal
5. Performance analysis
6. Performance review and counselling
7. Identification of development needs

An important aspect of this format is the absence of any ratings. Performance is to be reviewed qualitatively stating the tasks accomplished, narrating incidents and making evaluative statements. This provision was made to facilitate review discussion and to avoid the distractions of the appraiser and the appraisee due to ratings during the discussion time. However, it was envisaged that subsequent to the discussion time. However, it was envisaged that subsequent to the discussion the appraising officer may send a confidential assessment of his subordinates' performance on a separate form having the same dimensions (KPAs and outside KPAs). He now uses a rating scale here and is free to show/not to show his ratings to his subordinate. However, the ratings he gives should be congruent with the comments he makes in the open form. His reviewing officer has the responsibility to help attain such congruence.

Objectives of the Experiment

Being a very large organisation the State Bank of India naturally wanted to be very careful in introducing large systemic changes like this. Here the Bank decided to experiment with this new system and understand it in depth. An experiment was undertaken in one of the regions with the following objectives:

a) to examine the feasibility and advantages of implementing such a system;
b) to assess the extent to which such a system can achieve the objectives it proposes to achieve;
c) to gain insights into the problems involved in implementing such a system so that the Bank can prepare itself better for a total implementation;

d) to determine the acceptance level of such a system by those who have to implement it; and
e) to gain insights into various other dynamics involved in using such a system.

The Experiment

Preparation

The Branch Managers of Region I of Ahmedabad Regional Office of the Ahmedabad Local Head Office were chosen for this experiment. The Region I chosen covers branches locally situated in the Ahmedabad City, with a good mix of branches (in terms of business mix) and varieties of Branch Managers (in terms of age, qualifications, experience, orientation, etc.). The original intention was to have the experiment conducted over a six-month period from January to June 1981 so that it could be reviewed by July-August 1981.

The first step of the experiment was an orientation workshop held in November 1980 for the experimental group of Branch Managers to explain the basic concepts and secure their involvement. Most of the Branch Managers were against the confidential system of appraisal existing at that time. The response from the Branch Managers was quite positive to the new system, though a few had reservations about the system's success in the context of the present culture in the Bank. Some die-hards felt this was one more gimmick Bank wanted to have to make them work harder. The idea, that the Bank is interested in their development as individuals and is prepared to create a machinery for the purpose, itself was so novel and unbelievable, that some of them took the exercise not seriously enough. The workshop was attended fully by the representatives of the Local Officers' Association who pledged their whole-hearted support for the new system and in fact indicated that they would have been happier if the Rating Scales had been built into the system so that this can replace entirely the present CR system. The workshop was also attended by CGM (HRD), and C.O. (HRD), Central Office, signifying the top management's concern and involvement in the experiment. During the month of January, a three-day programme on performance review and counselling was held to impart performance review and counselling skills to senior executives of the circle up to the level of Regional Managers.

After the orientation programme, the Branch Managers were required to identify their Key Performance Areas and settle objectives in consultation with their reporting officer (RM). Each Branch Manager was expected to have come prepared for the KPAs discussions having given thought to the KPAs and objectives relevant to his job and to himself (i.e., what direction he would like to develop himself). By the time they began this exercise two months had already elapsed since the orientation training due to civil disturbances in the city. Hence it was felt necessary once again to clarify the importance of KPAs and create a correct understanding of the objectives and role of KPAs in the new appraisal system. In order to provide this understanding a one- day orientation on KPAs and objectives was organised early in March 1981. As a part of this demonstration, discussions of KPA settlement were held between the MR and some BMs.

Settlement of KPAs

The seminar was followed by KPA identification and objectives settlement discussions. These were held in a guest room of one of the Branch premises - which is away from the Regional Office so that there was no disturbance to the Regional Manager as well as Branch Manager. The Regional Manager was assisted by one of the officials sitting outside the settlement room to assist the Branch Manager to complete the paper work of reducing his objec tives under each KPA into quantifiable, measurable terms, etc. HRD Manager was present during the discussions mainly as an observer and to clarify ideas and concepts, when it became necessary.

The following general pattern of discussions was observed during these exercises:

1. After the initial pleasantries, the RM encouraged the BM to talk about himself for about 10 to 15 minutes regarding his background, qualifications, achievements, his family, previous assignments held, his aspirations and interests, the circumstances under which he got posted to his present assignment, the condition of the branch when he took over, etc.

   This unfolding of the personality of the BM and his life in the Bank, with encouraging emotional responses for the RM, helped immediately to build a good rapport between the two and create a climate of trust and closeness conducive to further exploration and development planning. Besides this narration itself, often full of emotional release of re-living the past, brought out the inner strengths and weaknesses of the person, which many of them were not even aware of. In several cases this was the first and only time in the career that the Branch Manager had the opportunity of openly and frankly talking about themselves to their superiors and the very novelty of it had a therapeutic effect leading to a sense of euphoria in a few cases.

2. The second phase consisted of the Branch Manager identifying his KPAs and describing the objectives he proposes to set for himself under each KPA for the experimental period of three months and the time-bound action plan he has drawn for the purpose. Regional Manager's role here was to ensure, through convincing logic and friendly persuasion, that the objectives were challenging and realistic and relevant to the organisation as well as to the individual. In the atmosphere of rapport and closeness, Regional Manager helped the Branch Managers to explore the possibility of stretching themselves to the utmost within realistic limits. As the threat of punishment or censure for non-achievement or fail ure was not there (i.e., there is going to be only analysis of processes and not evaluation of results) many Branch Managers came out with new imaginative and so-far-untried strategies that they were prepared to experiment with. Regional Manager was also able to suggest several such innovative action points that were accepted readily by the Branch Managers.

   No doubt, there were a few Branch Managers who had deep-rooted cynicism and a sense of despair and helplessness, but even they were prepared to try out something new, though with considerable skepticism.

   There were several cases, where Branch Managers asked for specific support in terms of extra staff, expeditious decision-making at Regional Office level, more frequent visits by Regional Manager to Branch, etc., that would facilitate achievement of objectives. There were also cases, where this type of support was offered by Regional Manager voluntarily.

3. The third phase consisted of the Regional Manager and Branch Manager together summing up the objectives agreed upon and recording these along with the expected support from Regional Manager on the prescribed settlement form for purposes of review at the end of the experiment period.

One of the important features of these settlement sessions was the time that Regional Manager is required to invest thereon. Some of the discussions with the Branch Managers took as much as 2 1/2 hours while the minimum time taken was about half-an-hour, with an average of about 1 hour for each Branch Manager.

A new modular structure was introduced in the circle from May 1981. This resulted in 10 of the Branch Managers with whom KPAs were already settled moving into new positions and thus the number of 32 Branch Managers got reduced to 22.

Performance Counselling

In July, a one-day seminar of the Branch Managers involved in the experiment was held to make a quick assessment of the work done and to prepare the Branch Managers to "receive" counselling. The training included a Role Play of Review and Counselling session between the Regional Manager and one of the Branch Managers.

Actual Performance Review and Counselling of the Branch Managers took place in September. The time spent by Regional Manager for each Branch Manager varied from about 2 1/2 hours in certain cases to about 30 to 45 minutes in a few cases, with an average of about 1 hour per Branch Manager. In the normal course, this would have taken longer as the Review would have immediately been followed by settlement of KPAs for the ensuing period but, as this was only an experiment, the discussions stopped after Review and Counselling and a brief action plan for development in a few cases.

Most of these discussions were taped on cassettes and their transcripts have been made for future use. Some of the important features of the Review/Counselling discussions are as follows:

The discussions were held in a frank, free and friendly atmosphere and opportunity was given to the Branch Managers to analyse their performance in depth. The RM helped the BMs in their analysis through gentle probing. The recounting of the processes/strategies adopted by the Branch Managers, the narration of the difficulties faced and how they could overcome these or live with them, the sympathetic recognition and appreciation of the difficulties by the Regional Manager, the possible alternatives/solutions suggested by the Regional Manager for Branch Manager's consideration for the future, the positive strokes given by

Regional Manager in recognition of the good efforts made towards achievement, etc., are the highlights of these discussions. The Branch Managers seem to have appreciated these and felt more confident and close to the Regional Manager than ever before. There was, of course, evaluation of results, but non-achievement or partial achievement was not castigated or criticised. Instead, emphasis was on understanding the processes and difficulties in relation to the quantified and measurable action points/strategies earlier agreed upon and on assessing to what extent Branch Manager was able to adhere to and put into practice the action plan and with what success. Such an analysis is also aimed at helping the BMs examine their goal-setting and work behaviours.

Daily 3 to 4 Branch Managers' reviews were handled by the Region al Manager and these were also held in the Guest Room of branch premises so as to avoid disturbances.

One of the research scholars of the Indian Institute of Management, Ahmedabad, interviewed the Branch Managers before going in for counselling and after completing counselling to assess their reactions and the benefits that Branch Managers have gained in the process.

Results

Two studies were conducted as a part of the review of the experiment of the new system - one by a doctoral student of the Indian Institute of Management, Ahmedabad, using "interview" method, and one by the HRD department of the LHO using "structured questionnaire" method.

The focus of the first study was to capture the "general experiences and reactions" of the BMs in relation to the new system being experimented; while the questionnaire survey aimed at studying the BM's reactions to each component of the system and have their assessment as to what extent these components have fulfilled their intended objectives. A brief summary of the findings that emerged during the studies and the related observations are furnished below:

Interview Study

Since this study was mainly aimed at identifying the various experiences and reactions of Branch Managers to the new appraisal system, it was felt that an informal but somewhat loosely structured interview would help to probe and elicit dominant reactions of the participants.

A total of 19 BMs were interviewed. Of these 12 were interviewed before review and counselling discussions and 7 were interviewed after the discussions.

As everyone did not answer exactly the same number of questions for each item mentioned above, there would be less than 19 responses, as at least some of them have repeated the same idea. Each response represents the focal point made by one BM. The following excerpts are only distinctive responses to the queries and they give a flavour to what the BMs felt about these aspects of the performance appraisal experiment.

Overall Impressions

The overall total impression was positive towards the concept of having a system wherein the BMs can participate and share their views and opinions and also seek help without the fear that their weaknesses might be exposed or looked down upon.

Key Performance Areas and Their Settlement

The responses were as follows:

a) There must be commonality in KPAs for all BMs.
b) Some BMs are setting superficial or easily achievable objectives.
c) KPAs help in obtaining some results.
d) The KPAs selected cover all the areas which a BM must look into.
e) KPAs have helped me in focussing on specific areas of action.
f) As a result of this exercise we come to know what we have to do and what's wrong with our administration.
g) There can only be 3 KPAs: develop business, house-keeping and team spirit.
h) The RM said, "You should do some advance" and so this was included as a KPA.
i) KPA must be a challenging task and not related to budget.
j) KPAs have helped me to involve my staff in deposit mobilisation.
k) Too many person present during KPA settlement inhibited by speaking out.
l) KPAs were accepted without any argument, as my colleagues had told me not to ask any questions.
m) KPAs are helpful to those who are career-oriented.
n) Many KPAs were formed, for the performance of which the BM had to depend on his subordinates. This puts the BM in a disadvantageous position.

These reactions indicate that there are some definite advantages in identifying KPAs like focussing attention on important areas of performance, clarifying "what we have to do" etc. However, there appears to be scope for improvement in relation to the nature of KPAs and targets set as well as the process of settling them.

Review and Counselling Sessions

The following responses were given:

a) Counselling sessions are useful particularly for those who are not so vociferous but are mild.
b) I was thrilled to hear someone representing the bank ask me, "What are your training needs?"
c) I was glad to see on record that RM was full of praise for my achievements.
d) Quick feedback helps and creates greater awareness of job requirements.
e) Two of the branch managers suggested that the review sessions should be held fortnightly, one suggested that it should be quarterly and another suggested that it should be six-monthly.

Overall Positive Impressions (Encouraging Factors)

a) Yes, the system should be continued, as it brings the RM and BM close together.
b) In the normal course, no one volunteers to come (to meet the RM) but if called they would come.
c) As I have no speaking practice, in a meeting or seminar I would not be heard, but during a counselling session I could be more vocal and express my difficulties.
d) KPAs have made us more duty bound and conscious.
e) Organisational memory-concept can be implemented.
f) Earlier, people have been bluffing about their performance, but now they are not hiding their faults.
g) I appreciate the KPA idea as it gives some guidelines to us.
h) The system should be given a fair trial.
i) HRDs help in planning and can be used as a checklist.
j) In the present system (CR) I do not know why the RM is not impressed with my performance; in the new one I can know about it.
k) Performance improved in areas which were earlier ignored.

Overall Suggestions, Problems and Negative Impressions

a) The forms must be simplified. What is meant by decision-making, conflict resolution or innovation? They need to be explained.
b) Whatever is being done is not because of the KPAs, but how it is being systematised.
c) In spite of the help given by the RM there is nothing that can be done (helplessness).
d) Bad points are not being written by BMs in their self-appraisal.
e) Anyway it is going to be introduced and so why resist (apathy).
f) Do the head office people really think that such gimmicks would work?
g) I had to take guidance from another BM is filling up the forms.
h) Knowledge of KPAs has not altered my routine work in any way.
i) There must be some muscle built into the system. The BMs must be told, "You do this or else..."

Except two or three BMs who seem to have some resentment and negative attitudes to the system, others are only making suggestions and pointing out problems/limitations. There appears to be a need to clarify the various dimensions (non-KPA areas) used in the new forms.

Other Comments

a) Linking KPAs to personnel policies is very essential.
b) This system should be implemented for clerical staff also.
c) Sundays must be avoided for any such meeting, seminar, etc.
d) Award staff should also be involved and given more responsibility.

Questionnaire Survey Conducted by HRD Department

The HRD department of the Ahmedabad circle conducted a question naire survey to assess the experiences of the Branch Managers with the experimented system of appraisal. A questionnaire was sent to the 22 Branch Managers who participated in the KPA settlement and review exercise and the replies given by them were analysed. A summary analysis of the responses given by the managers is presented below.

New Systems vs. CR System

Nineteen of the 22 Branch Managers were of the opinion that the proposed appraisal system is certainly better than the existing confidential report system. None of the Branch Managers felt that the present CR system is better than the proposed one. Nine of the Branch Managers suggested strongly that the proposed system should be implemented immediately after experimentation, while a similar number felt that the Bank should implement the new system with rating scales. This leads us to conclude that the majority of the Branch Managers are actually aware of the shortcomings in the existing system and are looking forward to the introduction of a review/appraisal system which would be free of these shortcomings.

Advantages of the Proposed System

In response to an open-ended question requiring them to mention the various positive points and advantages in the experimented system, they mentioned the following:

a) Creates more openness between Branch Manager and Regional Manager (more than 10).*
b) Provides lot of scope for self-development, as the Branch Manager gets constructive feedback (10).
c) It serves as a means of identification of the strengths and weaknesses of the Branch Manager (7).
d) Provides a means of communicating the difficulties of the Branch Managers (internal and external) to the Regional Manager so that the latter is able to assess the performance in a more objective fashion (7).
e) Increases self-confidence of the Branch Manager (6).
f) Make the Branch Manager closer to the Regional Manager (5).
g) Helps improving staff relations at the Branch by making the Branch Manager aware of the constant need for interaction with the staff (1).
h) Has less subjectivity than the CR system (1).
i) It is an effort-oriented and not a result-oriented system of assessment (1).
j) Helps in identifying the right man for each post (1).
k) Incorporates an organisational memory and record system (1).

* The number in the parentheses indicate the number of Branch Managers mentioning the strengths.

Weaknesses/Limitations of the Proposed System

In response to a question on what weaknesses or disadvantages they saw in the proposed system the Branch Managers have given the following responses:

a) Only the Branch Manager is included, at present but the exercise should be made applicable to all officers in the Branch (7).
b) The Branch Manager may set objectives that are easy to achieve (4).
c) The Branch Managers' personality traits such as dress, manners, relationship with colleagues, general intelligence, etc., are not covered under the new system (1).
d) Interim transfer of Branch Managers or the regional Manager may hamper assessment of performance (1).
e) The exercise of KPA settlement and review is too time consuming (1).
f) The regional Manager should be honest and fair in his as sessment (2).
g) The system is too superficial and does not make an in-depth assessment of the Branch Manager. It needs more "muscle" (1).
h) No method of periodically cross-checking to see if the Branch Manager is achieving the KPA objectives (1).

General Conclusions

Studying the responses presented above, it is evident that the Branch Managers experienced more positive things in the new system. In spite of certain misgivings, 16 Branch Managers (70 per cent) felt that the proposed system will have less subjectivity than the existing system; while an equal number felt that the system would definitely lead to their self-development. However, 4 Branch Managers (17 per cent) felt that it would only partially lead to self-development. Seven Branch Managers (30 per cent) felt that the system would work equally well if rating system is introduced, while 4 Branch Managers (17 per cent) were categorically against this view. However, 11 Branch Managers (48 per cent) felt that introduction of a rating system would create conflicts between the Regional Managers' ratings and the Branch Managers' "self-ratings" but these could be resolved satisfactorily once the Regional Managers' concern for the development of the Branch Managers was established.

Process of Setting KPAs and Objectives

According to the questionnaire responses given by the Branch Managers, the average time taken for the KPA settlement discussions between the Regional Manager and Branch Manager was 55 minutes. The highest was 135 minutes and the lowest was 15 minutes. The frequency distribution of the time taken for the discussions is given below:

Time taken in minutes	No. of Branch Managers
30	8
45	8
60	3
90	1
120 and above	2

It will be observed that the majority of the Branch Managers settled their KPAs between 30 and 45 minutes. Fifteen Branch Managers (65 per cent) stated that they identified and settled their KPAs jointly with the Regional Manager after discussions, while the remaining 7 Branch Managers stated that they decided their own KPAs and objectives and the RM had merely approved them.

All the Branch Managers felt the objectives agreed upon were challenging and realistic. Of these, 18 (78 per cent) of the Branch Managers felt that they had a better understanding of their role and the areas they need to focus their efforts on, as a result of their discussions with the Regional Manager. Some of the Branch Managers also felt that the discussion helped them in other ways as stated below:

a) Helped them to identify priority areas (2).
b) Boosted their enthusiasm and commitment (3).
c) Helped in explaining achievements to Regional Manager (3)
d) Helped in giving direction and in quantifying the efforts required to achieve agreed objectives (2).
e) Improved staff relations at the Branch (1).

Significantly, none of the Branch Managers felt that time was wasted on discussions or that the KPAs and objectives did not add anything new. After setting the KPAs and objectives with the Regional Manager, 15 Branch Managers (65 per cent) felt a new sense of direction while 12 Branch Managers (52 per cent) felt a sense of confidence. Only 3 Branch Managers (13 per cent) felt apprehensive about not being able to achieve the objectives set by them, since they involved a high degree of challenge. Two Branch Managers (9 per cent) felt a sense of commitment while another 2 felt a sense of challenge.

Communication Between Branch Manager and Regional Manager

As a result of the KPA discussions 14 Branch Managers (61 per cent) felt that they had an understanding of the Regional Manager's expectations. Seventeen (74 per cent) Branch Managers could communicate their difficulties to the Regional Manager. A large majority of the Branch Managers (83 per cent) felt that there was better communication between them and the Regional Manager after the KPA discussions. Significantly, none of the Branch Managers, not even those who were always close to the Regional Manager, felt that their understanding with the Regional Manager had remained unchanged or has not improved as a result of the discussions.

Working on KPA Objectives

Fourteen Branch Managers (61 per cent) felt that setting up of quantifiable time-bound action plans gave them a direction towards which they could work and thereby made achievement of the objectives easier. More than 50 per cent (13 of the Branch Managers) stated that they got the necessary support from the Regional Manager for achieving their KPA objectives (this does not mean that the remainder did not get support but that the support may not have been required. A good number (65 per cent) were able to share the objectives with the staff members and 48 per cent of the Branch Managers were able to secure the active cooperation of the branch staff in achievement of the objectives. Three Branch Managers were partially successful in this regard. Another three Branch Managers had fortnightly review meeting with the Regional Manager while four Branch Managers had no review sessions at all, except for the final review and counselling sessions, because they felt it was not called for or there was no occasion for such meetings.

Performance Review and Counselling Discussions

As stated by the Branch Managers, the average time taken for these discussions was 70 minutes, the maximum being 3 hours and the minimum being 30 minutes. The frequency distribution is given as follows:

Time taken in minutes	No. of Branch Managers
30	4
45	6
60	6
90	3
120	1
150 and above	2

Fourteen Branch Managers (65 per cent) were able to come to the discussions fully prepared with their self-appraisal of performance and performance analysis while the remaining 8 (35 per cent) could not do so, as they found the forms and the terminology employed too complicated. Perhaps there is a case for simplification of the forms or for building up the necessary understanding and expertise in the Branch Managers.

The Branch Manager's responses to the various questions based on the review and counselling discussions are as follows:

a) I benefited a great deal from the performance counselling discussions I had with my Regional Manager (10)*.
b) The counselling helped me to communicate my difficulties to the Regional Manager (16).
c) The performance appraisal discussion helped me to discover areas of my strengths (11).
d) The discussion helped me to understand areas that need my attention for improvement (10).
e) The discussions helped me to come closer to the Regional Manager (15).
f) I felt happy that the Regional Manager appreciated my good performance in certain areas (18).
g) I felt that the Regional Manager appreciated my problems and difficulties (19).
h) The discussions were completely frank and open (19).
i) I was feeling uncomfortable with the probing done by the Regional Manager (none).
j) I felt that the probing by the Regional Manager helped me to analyse my performance in depth and understand the real issues (5).

*The figures in parentheses indicate the number of responses.

Regarding self-appraisal (through Performance Review forms) and Performance Analysis, Branch Manager's responses were as under:

a) It helped me to present my performance in proper perspective to the Regional Manager (14).
b) It helped me to identify where I was right and where I had gone wrong (11).
c) I could understand my strengths and limitations and plan for my development (15).
d) It helped me to overcome my anxieties and apprehensions about shortfalls in performance, if any, as I could provide convincing explanations/reasons therefore (6).
e) It helped me to learn from the analysis of my performance so that I can avoid earlier mistakes and develop my strong points further (11).

Analysis of Facilitating and Hindering Factors

A number of facilitating and hindering factors emerged during the performance anlaysis. They were tabulated for use by the Regional Manager.

Analysis of Results Achieved under Various KPAs

Another interesting study made was in regard to the extent to which the objectives the Branch Managers had set for themselves were achieved. No doubt, the focus of the system is on process and not on results, but it is encouraging to note that in quite a good percentage of cases the objectives were achieved, proving thereby that the objectives were in fact challenging as well as realistic. The results are summarised below:

S.No.	Objective under KPA	No. of Branch Managers who have achieved	No. not achieved	Total
1.	Business development	14	8	22
2.	House-keeping	9	3	12
3.	Customer service	13	3	16
4.	Quality of advances	6	8	14

Note: 1. Not all Branch Managers had objectives under each KPA and hence the total does not come to 22.

2. "Not achieved" implies only that the process of performance is not completed within the 3 months' period of the experiment; the process initiated was already on and continuing and would get completed later; this is particularly true of the objective of improving the quality of advances, which does take him.

Conclusions and Implications

On the basis of these studies and their own observations the HRD department summarised the impact of this experiment as follows:

1. The lengthy KPA discussions and the counselling sessions let to the strengthening of a close dyadic relationship between the Regional Managers and Branch Managers based on openness, mutuality, trust, collaboration, etc. Branch Managers felt free to communicate the problems and difficulties to the Regional Managers and were able to understand better the expectations of the Regional Managers from them and also appreciate his difficulties/limitations. In the process, better role clarity and understanding also emerged.

2. Regional Manager was able to get a much clearer picture of the Branch Manager's personality, his strengths and weak nesses, his problems and difficulties, his motivating factors, etc., than ever before. He was able to secure their involvement in the fulfilment of his own goals as "partners" and not as "assistants". This contributed to the development of the Regional Manager himself and his own inter-personal and leadership skills.

3. The identification of the strengths of the Branch Managers helped the Regional Manager to make more effective postings and placements where their strengths could be effectively utilised by the Bank. The identification of the weaknesses helped the Regional Manager to attempt to eradicate them, again through proper placement, training, etc.

4. The Branch Managers felt an increasing sense of involvement and participation in "management". They could feel their share in the "goal" of the Regional Manager and become "partners" in his performance.

5. The Branch Manager felt an increasing ability to take on challenges without fear of failure or admonishment and to work

through them with a sense of purpose. In the process they were able to feel the support the Regional Manager was giving them.

6. The Branch Manager felt an increasing ability to analyse the process (of their performance) and to have an objective look at their own performance and learn lessons therefrom.
7. The Branch Managers felt an increasing ability to introspect and reflect on themselves and their work behaviours and to identify their own strengths and weaknesses through an analysis of the processes leading to their successes and failures.
8. The Branch Managers felt that the system led to their own growth and development through experimentation with new processes which they have never attempted before. They were also able to explode some of the old myths (like "certain things cannot be done in the Bank"; "only Branch Manager is responsible for everything"; "award staff are irresponsible"; "award staff cannot be involved in business development", etc. they have been living with all along and that usually arises out of - as well as leads to - a sense of helplessness and despair. For example, one Branch Manager by himself, conducted a "market survey" of his area of operation for the types of services required by the customers; he was also able to secure the involvement of his staff (including clerical and subordinate staff) in business development by apportioning his total business commitment to the various members of the staff and made them achieve it. Many Branch Managers attempted similar staff involvement in business development for the first time with surprisingly encouraging responses, particularly from the award staff. Some Branch Managers tried for the first time to approach the customers of other Banks with encouraging results. These are some of the areas where Branch Managers have been spurred on to gain new experiences and learn from them and develop themselves.
9. Clear developmental and training needs emerged in a few cases. Some Branch Managers expressed their inadequacy of job knowledge in areas of advances, foreign exchange etc., which would be necessary for their effective functioning. Some of them would need to go through behavioural science/TA programmes to develop leadership, motivational and team- building skills.

Post-Experiment Work

The Deputy Managing Director (Personnel and OD) of the SBI met the Regional Manager and the Branch Managers involved in this experiment and reviewed its impact. Seeing the utility of this it was decided to introduce this system in stages. In the year 1982 it was extended as an experiment to 9 modules covering about 27 regions. In Ahmedabad itself it was extended to 4 regions. In 1983 it was further extended to 19 modules and by 1984 the SBI plans to cover the entire country. The feedback received from the subsequent coverage is very similar to the feedback received from the first experimental group. however, in 1983, the Bank started experiencing some variations in the experiences of different circles with this system.

APPENDIX 14.1

A Manual on Performance Appraisal and Review (SBI)

1. Performance Appraisal

1.1 Performance appraisal is a critical and effective tool in the development and optimisation of human resources in an organisation. It helps people in the organisation to consciously aim at and improve upon individual performance and thus organisational effectiveness. It also facilitates developing an organisational culture of mutuality, openness and collaboration towards realisation of individual as well as organisational goals.

2. Objectives of Performance Appraisal

2.1 The primary objective of performance appraisal is optimisation of human resources through development of individual employees. It should help the employees to identify and eradicate their weaknesses and improve upon their strengths in the performance of their current and future jobs.

2.2 The next important objective is generation of valid data to help decision-making authorities for taking personal decisions like placement, promotion, transfer, training, etc.

2.3 Another objective is to develop an organisational culture of mutuality, openness, trust and collaboration in the achievement of individual and the organisational goals.

3. Requisites of a Performance Appraisal System

3.1 The organisation believes in the development and optimisation of its human resources. It also believes that such a development is in its own interests of improving productivity and effectiveness and that all employees have the potential for development.

3.2 The organisation will create and provide reasonable opportunities to every one of its employees for improving his performance and development.

3.3 The organisation believes in developing a climate of openness, trust, mutuality and collaboration through appropriate training and other strategies.

3.4 Performance appraisal system needs to have the active support and involvement of the corporate management. They should, besides articulating the organisational goals and values, demonstrate their belief in and efforts for management development, as managerial example influences behaviour down the line in the organisation.

3.5 At managerial levels, there should be willingness to understand human behaviour and get along with people. Genuine concern for and efforts towards development of subordinates, ability and willingness to communicate clear-eyed, honest observations and judgements about individual competence and performance, a spirit of dynamism, and sense of personal involvement in the affairs of the organisation and an effective leadership are the other managerial inputs in a performance appraisal system.

3.6 There must be employee willingness to develop and continually improve performance through realistic and challenging goal setting. They should commit themselves to the furtherance and achievement of his objectives of the organisation. Organisational goals are to be perceived as personally relevant. He should perceive and accept the superior as one genuinely interested in his development and not as one "playing God".

3.7 A performance appraisal system presupposes role clarity and responsibilities.

4. Definitions

4.1 Key Performance Areas are critical functions distinctly characteristic of a job or role.

4.2 Objectives are specific quantifiable/observable tasks/ targets to be completed/achieved by an employee during a year, under each of the mutually identified Key Performance Areas.

4.3 Appraisee. An employee/officer whose performance during the given period is appraised.

4.4 Reporting Officer or Appraiser is the immediate boss of the appraisee.

4.5 Reviewing Officer is the boss of the reporting officer.

4.6 Appraisal is a critical evaluation both by the appraisee and the appraiser of the extent and the process of performance of the appraisee under each of the agreed objectives.

4.7 Year is usually January to December.

5. Process

5.1 Before the beginning of each year, preferably along with the budget settlement discussion, the appraisee and the appraiser will identify the Key Performance Areas (KPAs) for year as also specific, quantified/observable objectives under each of the identified KPAs. As an example, some of the possible KPAs and objectives thereunder for positions like Branch Manager, Regional Manager and Development Manager are given in the annexure. The identified and agreed KPAs and objectives will be recorded in a settlement form, in duplicate, and signed by both the appraisee and the appraiser. A copy of this form will be retained by the appraiser, the original being given to the appraisee.

5.2 During the year, as and when the appraisee and the appraiser meet in the course of discharge of their functions, the extent and the process of performance of the appraisee under each of the settled objectives will be informally discussed.

5.3 Immediately after the completion of the year or latest by the end of the succeeding January, every appraisee will appraise his performance in the formats enclosed and also analyse the how of his performance.

5.4 The KPAs and the objectives, as per settlement form, will be carried out to the appropriate columns of the appraisal form (Part I-A; p. 199). The appraisee will indicate the actual performance against each of the objectives and furnish brief comments also. Simultaneously, will also appraise his performance outside KPAs under each of the dimensions indicated in the format (Part I-B; p.200). He will indicate the performance through a brief description of a task achieved/incident. In Part-C (p.201) of the format, he will analyse his how of the performance, briefly mentioning those factors that facilitated and those that hindered performance. Factors from within (personal) as well as outside (others) will also be analysed and recorded briefly. He will then indicate therein his ideas/suggestions (i.e. steps to be taken by himself as well as the organisation) for improving his identified strengths and eradicating the observed weaknesses.

5.5 After completing his (self) appraisal as above, the appraisee will forward them to the appraiser, preferably before the end of January of the following year.

5.6 After this, the reporting officer will arrange for an Appraisal Review discussion with the appraisee. At this meeting, the appraisee and the appraiser will discuss the what and the how of the performance of the appraisee. The reporting officer will also give feedback to the appraisee and suggest ways and means of improving his performance. Development and training needs will be discussed. These will be recorded. At the end of the discussion, the reporting officer will, in the presence of the appraisee, furnish his brief comments on the performance of the appraisee under each of the objectives and the other specified dimensions in the formats (Part I-A and Part I-B; pp/199-200). In Part I-C (p.201), the appraiser will briefly comment upon the appraisee's analysis of his performance and actions suggested. He will add, if necessary, his suggestions/views also.

5.7 A brief summary of the performance review and feedback will be recorded in the format Part I-D (p.202) which will thereafter be signed by both the appraisee and appraiser.

5.8 The review will be done in Part I.E.- (p.203) by a reviewing officer - one above the appraising officer. The reviewing officer will, as far as possible, have a brief discussion with the reporting officer before completing his review. Thereafter, he will record his review in the format and sign it.

5.9 After review, the reporting officer will pass on his recommendations to the appropriate authorities for necessary action.

5.10 The Part I (A to E) will be returned to the appraisee who keep it at least for a period of three years and produce it for perusal as and when required by the controlling authorities/reporting officer.

Objectives

6.1 KPAs and objectives thereunder are to be identified by the appraisee and the appraiser.

6.2 KPAs, which are to be largely in conformity with the organisational objectives, can vary from time to time and from one appraisee to another.

6.3 KPAs and objectives once identified should not normally be changed during the year.

6.4 KPAs should not normally be more than 4/5 and should distinctly characterise the appraisee's job. Stated otherwise, they should be those tasks for which the appraisee can normally be held responsible.

6.5 The objectives should correspond to the responsibility areas identified. Specific targets/observable activities will have to be decided and indicated for each objective. It is preferable that before settlement discussion, every appraisee prepares a list of objectives so that all critical areas of performance are covered.

6.6 The objectives should be realistic and achievable. An element of challenge has to be willingly built into them so that the appraisee stretches for his own good and the organisational excellence.

7. Feedback and Performance Review

7.1 The appraiser should, based on the performance data provided, extend a helpful and positive feedback. A constructive and honest appreciation of the performance and a free and frank expression of the observations are essential components of a feedback.

7.2 Counselling helps an appraisee to be more aware of his own strengths and weaknesses. In the process of counselling, an appraisee identifies ways to improve upon his strengths and eradicate the weaknesses. A climate of mutuality, openness and trust should prevail in the process of counselling. Counselling rendered with genuine interest and accepted with trust contributes substantially to the growth of an appraisee.

7.3 Counselling is a continuous process. While it is normally extended at the time of performance appraisal, the reporting officer should endeavour to counsel the appraisee as and when occasion arises.

7.4 Counselling requires appropriate skills and attitudes in the appraiser. The appraisee should perceive it as a genuine help and accept it with trust.

CONTENTS

(in duplicate)

PERFORMANCE APPRAISAL

Settlement of KPAs and Objectives for 19

Name of the official : ______________________________

Name of the reporting official : ______________________

KPAs		Objectives (under each KPA)	
S.No.	Description	S. No.	Description

Supports, if any, required

	Official :
Signature of the	Reporting :
	Official :

Date :

Part I - A

APPRAISAL OF PERFORMANCE

Performance Under KPAs

KPAs		Objectives (under each KPA)		Actual performance & comments by the appraisee	Comments by the appraiser on the performance
S.No.	Description	S.No.	Description		
	Each of the mutually settled KPAs to be stated		(To be stated under each of the KPAs)	Against each of the objectives	Against each of the objectives

Part I - B

PERFORMANCE OUTSIDE KPAs

S.No.	Areas of performance	Brief description by the appraisee of the performance (through a task achieved/incidend)	Comments by the appraiser
1.	Innovation		
2.	Team building		
3.	Public relations		
4.	Delegation		
5.	Conflict resolution		
6.	Staff management		
7.	Decision-making		
8.	Any other significant area of performance		

Part I - C

PERFORMANCE ANALYSIS

	Personal	*Others*
Factors facilitating	*1.* *2.* *3.* *4.*	*1.* *2.* *3.* *4.*
Factors hindering	*1.* *2.* *3.* *4.*	*1.* *2.* *3.* *4.*

Action suggested by the appraisee :

Brief comments by the appraiser :

Part I - D

PERFORMANCE REVIEW & FEEDBACK

A brief summary of the perfomance review discussion and feedback will be recorded here.

Name of the appraisee official : *Signature :*

Name of the appraiser official : *Signature :*

Part I - E

REVIEW OF APPRAISAL

Remarks of the Reviewing Authority

Name of the reviewing authority : ____________________

Signature of the reviewing authority : ____________________

Date :

Chapter 15

INTRODUCING PERFORMANCE APPRAISAL SYSTEMS : THE CASE OF A LARGE ENGINEERING COMPANY

NEW Performance Appraisal Systems cannot be established in short periods of time as appraisal practices cannot be changed over night. Performance appraisal is a matter of importance and concern to every employee. This is mainly because most of personnel decisions that are of tremendous significance to the personal and professional life of employees are made on the basis of appraisal reports. At least these are perceived to be so. Even when employees make verbal statements indicating that their appraisal systems are highly routinised, every one gets high ratings, there are too many biases etc., when it comes to actual appraisal of their own performance employees tend to take it very seriously. Ironically, employees may not tend to take the appraisal of their subordinates as seriously as they take their own appraisals. On the other hand they expect their bosses to take much more interest in them. Because every one treats his own appraisal with importance, changing appraisal systems would require preparing the employees not only intellectually but also emotionally to new appraisal systems. As the kind of appraisal discussed in this book requires high levels of emotional investment in appraisals by the employees, motivational and emotional readiness needs to be established for introducing new appraisal systems. This requires the organisation to pay enough attention to the process of introducing or changing the appraisal systems. It is not uncommon to find organisations changing their appraisal systems without paying enough attention to the process of changing and landing themselves in trouble and quickly reverting to their old systems of appraisal.

---

*This case is presented in detail in Udai Pareek and T.V. Rao, Designing and Managing Human Resource Systems, New Delhi, Oxford & IBH, 1981, Chapter 12.

Some Mechanisms of Introducing new Appraisal Systems

The processes to be adopted in changing the systems of performance appraisal depend upon the extent to which the new intended system is close to the already existing system. If the new system is far away from the existing system in terms of objectives, components, complexity, time investment, preparation, emotional investment required etc., the process of introducing it should be slow, step by step and carefully monitored. Training of a few change agents within the organisation becomes very crucial for its introduction. These change agents should have high credibility within the organisation and should be drawn mostly from line jobs. They should be helped to thoroughly understand the system and their commitment to it should be gained. Then all those who are going to use the new system should be oriented to it through training workshops and seminars. In these seminars as well as in subsequent implementation the change agents play an important role by acting as facilitators, resource persons, trend setters, etc. If system being introduced is far away from the existing system, there is no substitute to such preparation.

Another strategy that is useful in introducing such systems is the strategy of experimentation. In this strategy the new system may be experimentally tried out in some parts of the organisation. Alternately the new system could be introduced in the organisation on an experimental basis for some period (during which period the old system continues) and after the organisation is satisfied that its employees have reached the level of readiness to implement it, it may decide to formalise the new system.

Another strategy is to evolve the system through a process of discussions in the entire organisation. Every one may be involved in this process of evolution. Discussions may be organised department or unit-wise, and suggestions may be gathered. Representatives of these units gather together for a workshop to evolve the new system synthesising all the suggestions. Subsequently people could be trained to acquire the skills needed to effectively participate in the new system.

In organisations that have already well developed systems only minor changes are required. For such organisations the process may be simple and may involve merely organising a series of orientation workshops or short sessions. If only minor changes are involved, of course, even a circular letter may serve the purpose.

The following case of a large engineering company illustrates some of the processes that could be followed in changing from confidential report form to open systems.

The Organisation

The organisation manufactured heavy engineering equipment. At the time of introducing the new system of performance appraisal it had an annual turnover of about Rs.100 crores. It had about 14,000 employees including about 1,500 managerial staff. The organisation had five divisions including two manufacturing units. For personnel and financial matters these were grouped into three divisions and had three separate departments of Personnel and Human Resources Development (HRD). Some attempts were made to review the performance appraisal in early years. Some new dimensions were added to the confidential report form. The confidential report had dimensions like: knowledge of work, punctuality, leadership, dependability, etc. These qualities were being assessed on a 10 point scale for a total of 100 points. Every officer was being assessed by two of his superiors (one and two levels above him) in a confidential form. Employees scoring below 33 per cent on any dimension or on their overall score were being given a feedback by the personnel department. The appraisal ratings formed one of the important inputs for promotions.

The culture of the organisation differed slightly among various divisions. Particularly, one of the two manufacturing units had little more conservative and conformistic orientations than the other divisions. The top management, however, continuously kept on stressing the importance of developing human resources. The full-time directors and chief executive of the company used to spend considerable time with their senior executives in planning and guiding their activities. A somewhat informal climate existed in the organisation. Seniority-cum-merit was followed in promotions. Meritorious employees got ahead in the organisation in several departments.

Decision to Adopt the System

The first step taken by the company was to decide firmly and clearly that they needed a system of the kind described in this book. This decision was taken by the top management on the basis of a report submitted to them by a group of external consultants and an associated internal task force. The external consultants were called into look into the organisational structure, control systems and personal function in the context of the fast growth of the company. The consultants along with their suggestions on corporate plans and organisational structure for growth also suggested the establishment of a HRD department and change of appraisal systems to focus on the development of people.

The corporate management of the company had always emphasised the philosophy that development of human resources was one of its important responsibilities. The corporate management had been making efforts in the past to communicate to managers their strong points and their weak points and helping them prepare for handling higher level responsibilities. However, the corporate management was apprehensive that these concerns remained only with it and did not percolate down the line. They wanted that every manager in the organisation should consider it as a part of his responsibility to develop his subordinates. HRDs and the new appraisal system were perceived as a means of providing a set of formalised mechanisms to ensure this.

Performance Appraisal as Entry Points for HRDs

Performance appraisal was identified as a critical component that could be revised and used to introduce HRDs. This was done for the following reasons:

1. There was already a system of performance appraisal existing in the company and employees were very dissatisfied with it. It was felt easier to start with a system already existing and change it rather than to start by introducing altogether new systems like potential appraisal.
2. Of all the sub-systems of HRD, performance appraisal was considered as an important tool for developing human resources. This system offers a unique opportunity to people to know their strengths and weaknesses.
3. Performance appraisal also brings out the need for other sub-systems like training (for developing those whose performance is poor on some dimensions), potential appraisal (for transfers, placement and promotions for which performance appraisal data are not sufficient), organisation development activities, data storage, etc.
4. It offers a unique opportunity to introduce the spirit of HRDs to all employees in the organisation.

Besides starting with performance appraisal it was decided also to streamline the training function and slowly start working on the potential appraisal and OD sub-systems.

Experimental Trial of new Forms

After it was decided to start with performance appraisal, a format incorporating all the components of the open appraisal system (outlined in this book) was developed. This format consisted of three forms. The first form was to be used for recording KPAs, objectives, self-assessment on KPAs objectives and behavioural dimensions, performance analysis assessment by the reporting officer, training needs and action plans. The second form was to be filled by the reporting officer identifying training needs. The third was a summary from where ratings given by a reporting officer for all his employees were summarised.

Four departments were selected two each from two of the manufacturing units for experimentation. The experiment aimed at the following:

1. To test out the preparedness of the employees for an open system of appraisal.
2. To test out the appropriateness of the forms and to evolve a final format of appraisal that should be used by the company.
3. To anticipate and experience the problems involved in introducing the new system and develop strategies of dealing with these problems.
4. To develop internal resources to introduce the system later in the company.

A two-day orientation programme was conducted to orient the employees in the four departments to the new appraisal system. The programme included inputs to develop skills for identifying KPAs, target setting, assessment on behavioural dimensions, performance analysis and counselling, performance counselling role plays and case discussions.

The experimental period for these four departments was about six months. During the orientation programme the employees sat with their reporting officers and identified their KPAs and set targets for the next six-month period.

Doubts were expressed by a few employees about introducing such an open appraisal system. Generally these comments came from two to three individuals in each group of about 20 to 25 officers. A most frequently raised doubt was expressed as follows: "Can this system do anything if people are stagnating in the same job without promotion for a long period?" Pessimism and doubts were expressed particularly by people, who were either not promoted or were suspended. Generally however the response in the training programme was curiosity or neutrality in attitudes. Adequate care was taken to see that the officers did not treat this as a special job given to them. This was necessary to avoid any experimental effects. Looking back, we feel that the experimental effects were more in the negative direction in these groups, i.e., the experimental groups expressed more negative attitudes and raised more doubts about this system than the subsequent groups.

The post-orientation programme of exercises was monitored by the newly joined DGM (HRD). He also participated in the training programmes. Besides, he individually met all the participants after the programme to check whether they had correctly identified the KPAs.

When the time period was over he also monitored the performance appraisal discussions and counselling sessions.

In the overall analysis, the experience indicated that there were not any major problems associated with the introduction of a system of this kind. A few of them responded very well. Some had problems of review discussions particularly with one or two troublesome employees. In one case conflict between the reporting officer and the appraisee came out into the open. This did create some problems but due to the positiveness expressed in most of the cases, confidence was gained by the HRD department in introducing the system.

After this experiment one of the consultants associated with this experiment was appointed on a full-time basis as Advisor in General Manager's capacity to introduce the system.

Orientation Programmes in the Company - Identification of Trainers

After the experience of the experimental try-out, the final format of appraisal was evolved. The format was shown to the corporate management. After its approval it was decided to conduct orientation programmes throughout the company.

Since about 1,500 managers were to be oriented, and not more than

30 could be taken in each batch, about 50 programmes would have to be conducted. Conducting these with the help of only two trainers who were equipped with the skills would take about 100 working days. Thus, practically 6 months would be required only for this purpose. Therefore, it was decided to train a group from different divisions of this organisation who would in turn become "trainers" for other groups.

These trainers could also act as internal change agents later and help in monitoring the system. As trainers they would be equipped with more information and more skills than what every employee would be equipped with. However, training requires certain basic skills and orientations. Some faith in a system of this kind, ability to communicate, some ability to conceptualise, etc., are needed to become trainers. A list of these qualities and purposes of the exercise were given to the divisional heads. The divisional heads identified a group of officers from their respective divisions for this purpose. Most of these potential trainers were drawn from higher levels, i.e., a level above or below that of the heads of departments.

These officers were put through a four-day training programme. Two days were devoted to train them exactly the way they would be required to train others and two days were spent on helping them develop trainer skills. Two member-teams were formed to conduct orientation training. Their job was simplified by evolving self-instructional material for use during the training programme.

The objectives of these two-day orientation programmes were:

1. To orient the employees to the new HRDs the company has decided to introduce with all its components (performance appraisal, potential appraisal, training, research and organisational development of data storage systems).
2. To introduce in detail the new performance appraisal system and its components.
3. To develop skills in identifying KPAs and setting targets, assessment on behavioural dimensions, performance analysis and performance counselling.

In all 34 "trainers" were trained. The training of the rest of the employees was done by these trainers. Those in higher levels (i.e., level 14 and above) were trained by the Advisor and the DGM (HRD).

The Trainer Reactions

In the initial stages after their selection and the first day of orientation some of the potential trainers were not sure of their own capabilities as trainers. They felt that training was a specialised job and that they may not be able to do as good a job as a specialist would do. However, by the time they were through the fourth day of training most of them felt confident. Each of them was supplied with a detailed trainer's manual. Besides, they had some practice sessions where they were training employees generally junior to them in hierarchy. They were also paired up to support each other during this training. All these factors helped them in gaining confidence as well as doing a good job as trainers.

During their own training they asked a number of questions. This helped them to be clear about various issues. Some of them who still did not have confidence sat through the practical training given by their colleagues of the first few batches.

On an average each trainer participated in training two to three batches. Thus a maximum of 10 days was spent by each trainer in introducing the system.

Later discussions with these managers indicated the following:

1. As a result of working together as trainers a feeling of togetherness and a new identity as change agents in introducing this system had developed among these 34 managers.
2. As they had to continuously clarify and defend the system they themselves had become clearer about the system and had started appreciating the system better.
3. They took the various tasks associated with the new appraisal system more seriously than others. As most of them were senior managers this greatly facilitated in developing seriousness in their departments.
4. The role of clarifying doubts had been distributed all over the organisation among senior managers.
5. Some of them liked and enjoyed the diversion in their work for this short period of time, very much. They developed self-confidence as trainers and some of them enjoyed this role very much.

Almost everyone in the organisation was trained in a period of about two months. At the end of the programme a questionnaire was sent to a randomly selected group of employees to study the extent to which they were clear about the various components and procedures involved in the new appraisal system and also to get a feedback on the effectiveness of the trainers. The feedback thus obtained was sent back to each individual trainer. This feedback contained, on the one hand, an assessment of the particular trainer's training abilities assessed by those who attended his programme and on the other hand, average ratings scored by other trainers (without giving the identity of these trainers). This feedback was another significant step because symbolically it is what has been talked about in performance appraisal. (Every individual should understand his own strengths and weaknesses and feedback is one good mechanism to help people understand their capabilities so that they can continuously make efforts to do better.) The trainers enjoyed such a feedback and found it useful. Most of the feedback was positive and it contributed further to their level of confidence.

Survey of Attitudes to Performance Appraisal

During the initial experiment as well as the first few orientation programmes a few officers vehemently opposed the new open system of appraisal. Although it was only a few officers who had been raising objections and pointing out problems it became difficult to sense whether they were reflecting general attitudes or their own problems and frustrations. Therefore in order to find out the general trend of attitudes to performance appraisal, and to examine if some of the basic attitudes required for open performance appraisal were present or not, a survey was conducted. This survey was conducted before the orientation training programmes were organised. The survey established beyond doubt that most employees in the organisation did have the required basic orientations for such a system. The results of the survey are presented in Exhibit 13.1.

The results indicate that some basic facilitating orientations were present in the employees of the company for introducing a new open appraisal system (high percentage on items 2, 4, 6, 10, 11, 12, 13, 14, 15 and 17). The survey also indicates the need to clarify the limitations of performance appraisal (e.g. responses on items 1 and 5 indicate the tendency to directly link performance appraisal with promotions in a sizeable percentage).

Exhibit 15.1

Managers' Attitudes to Performance Appraisal (N = 163 officers in unit 1 and 425 in unit 2)

S.No.	Statement	Percentage of officers agreeing with this statement			
		Levels I & II officers Units 1 and 2		Levels of III & above Units 1 and 2	
1	2	3	4	5	6
1.	A good performance appraisal system is sufficient to decide whether an employee deserves to be promoted.	71	58	43	51
2.	One of the objectives of performance appraisal should be to help the employee understand his strengths and weaknesses relating to his performance so that he can make efforts to improve and grow.	95	99	100	100
3.	It is very difficult to have objective ratings by any officer (for himself or for others) as human nature is such	60	43	68	67
4.	A good appraisal system should help the company to identify and provide opportunities for development	98	97	97	95
5.	Promotions should not be based on performance appraisal ratings as the main input.	61	65	70	57
6.	Appraisal ratings should be made known to the employee.	79	94	84	90

1	2	3	4	5	6
7.	My reporting officer generally communicate his perception of my strengths and weaknesses to me.	55	52	60	48
8.	I feel that my company at present is taking care of developmental needs of employees through training, etc.	49	60	38	56
9.	The present system of appraisal through confidential reports serves no useful purpose.	68	80	46	77
10.	In a good appraisal every employee should be given an opportunity to rate his own performance	84	93	86	90
11.	If an employee's performance is appraised by his boss, the employee should know his boss's thinking and get an opportunity to have a dialogue with him.	84	94	92	98
12.	I would like to know from my boss more about his appraisal of my performance, my strengths, weaknesses, etc.	87	96	92	100
13.	Unless employees plan periodically the kind of work they are going to undertake in a year, appraising performance becomes impressionistic.	85	87	84	95
14.	Any good appraisal system should take into consideration the problems the employee faces in performing his job.	95	96	97	68
15.	Appraisal of performance should use clearly defined quantitative ratings.	88	82	84	79

1	2	3	4	5	6
16.	I am very dissatisfied with the existing system of appraisal	71	73	46	75
17.	There is scope for providing enough opportunities in this organisation for a junior officer to grow and develop as an effective manager.	58	73	84	89

The Training Programme

As mentioned earlier the orientation programmes were conducted throughout the company. The programmes were conducted over a two-month period. The officers chosen from the organisation and trained as trainers themselves, in turn, trained most of the officers. The senior officers were trained by the Advisor and the DGM (HRD). Each training programme lasted for two days. Before the training began the candidates were supplied with a brief write-up on the HRDs and the new appraisal system. They were given this material a day or two in advance and were requested to go through it and note their doubts, comments, questions and suggestions for discussion during the programme. A brief outline of the programme design appears in Exhibit 13.2. There were some variations in this design from group to group.

As indicated by the programme design, case-discussions, skill practice exercises, role plays, feedback on psychological tests and films were used in the training programme. Performance appraisal and counselling manuals developed by the authors were used, during these programmes. As these manuals provided step-by-step guidelines for trainers, the trainers were able to organise and manage these programmes without much difficulty. Most of the inputs suggested in the above design including cases, self-tests, role-play briefs and concept explanations are presented in these manuals.

Each programme was conducted jointly by two trainers. Each pair of trainers may have conducted about three to four programmes. For each trainer the programmes meant an absence of about six to eight days from the work place. As all of them were in the managerial cadre (the nature of work being mostly administrative and supervisory), and as the training rooms were close to the work place and as the training programme was being handled by two persons, some of them did have the opportunity to attend to any urgent work for about an hour in a day. So it did not create any major disturbances in the work.

During the training programme the trainees were encouraged to raise questions. All the questions raised in various programmes were noted and later a manual was prepared clarifying them.

Exhibit 15.2

Outline of the Orientation Programme

Day 1

Session 1	Introducing the System: HRDs - need for the system, its objectives, operational details and clarification of doubts.
Session 2	Identification of Key Performance Areas: practice exercises.
Session 3	Basic attitudes required for an appraisal system that would contribute to development: openness, spontaneity, giving and receiving feedback, etc. - exercises.
Session 4	Effective counsellor attitudes - test and feedback on test.
Session 5	Developing managers as managers - film; manager wanted.

Day 2

Session 1	Experiencing feedback - feedback on tests relating to managerial effectiveness.
Session 2	Effective performance counselling process: three cases in performance counselling.
Session 3	Communication in performance counselling: film - person-to-person communication.
Session 4	Skill practice in performance counselling: role plays.
Session 5	Concluding session: clarification of doubts and explanation of steps involved in introducing the system and the roles to be played by managers.

Note : A minimum of eight hours a day was required for this programme

Training of the Top Management

Introducing a new performance appraisal system would be incomplete without the active involvement of the top management. The seriousness attached to the system depends on how the employees perceive the top management's commitment. The top management should not merely be committed but must also make efforts to communicate its commitment. In order to be committed and to communicate this commitment to others, the people at the top themselves need to be trained thoroughly in the system. Since it was difficult for them to make themselves free during working hours a series of evening sessions were arranged for the executives comprising top management. The design was slightly altered for this group. Instead of focussing too much on skill training, the focus was shifted to policy issues and operational issues. These sessions were conducted more in a workshop form. However, this group also had exercises like each one identifying his own KPAs, getting feedback on psychological tests, case discussions on performance counselling, discussion of films on communication and developing managers as managers, etc. The discussions in these sessions were of a much longer duration than those in the regular training sessions. Thus, short of having role plays the top management group had all the inputs that are described in the schedule presented earlier.

All the officers at the level of DGM and above including the directors were present in these discussions. It is in these discussions that apprehensions were expressed by two of the GMs that to switch over to a completely open appraisal system may be too premature for managers who have been accustomed to confidential reporting over a long period of time. It was argued that due to past conditioning most managers may start with apprehensions and this apprehensiveness may influence their counselling skills. It was also argued that in the minds of employees, performance appraisal will continue to be associated with promotions and thereby it may interfere with appraisal discussions. It was felt that employees should have enough practice in counselling and in operating before it is formally introduced.

In order to give enough practice and a full experience of the system it was decided to introduce trial runs all through the company. In order to give practice it was decided to have three-monthly appraisals for one year before the new appraisal system is actually introduced. In order to remove any inhibitions and fear associated with appraisal and to facilitate review discussions it was also decided not to send any of the completed forms of ratings to the personnel departments nor to maintain any record of the discussions.

Appointment of Task Forces

In the initial stages a good deal of attention needs to be paid to the implementation of the system. While training and orientation programmes introduce the system and provide some skills necessary for participation in appraisal, etc., when the actual implementation occurs employees are likely to seek clarifications on a number of doubts and various issues. While the HRD department may play an active role it may no be able to cope with the demands. Moreover, everyone may not like to go to the HRD department. Some employees may not even take the initiative of expressing their doubts unless some formal opportunities are provided. Thus there is need to closely monitor implementation of the system.

Internal task forces are very helpful to ensure effective implementation of the new systems. Such task forces should be drawn from different levels (hierarchy levels) and from different departments. Since it is better to have a small size task force of only five to seven officers, only critical departments (large size ones) may be represented. It is advisable to include technical people, those who command respect and have accessibility to the top management. The chairman of the task force should be from among the top management levels of the division. Inclusion of the top managerial levels in the implementation task force creates an image of seriousness and time pressures for the members. The HRD department should provide all the help to the task force. The role of the HRD department may include: drawing up the agenda for task force meetings; developing questionnaires to assess periodically progress of implementation; tabulation of data; preparing circulars; developing manuals; etc.

In this company, HRD implementation task forces were appointed separately in each division. In each of the divisions the task force was headed by a senior officer of the level of the DGM. The officer from the personnel and HRD department of that division was appointed as secretary of the task force. The task force had other three to four members thus making a total of five to seven members. The briefing given to the task force appears in Exhibit 13.3.

Exhibit 15.3

Briefing for the Task Force

The main objective of the task force is to facilitate more and ensure the speedy and effective implementation of the system.

While the execution of the processes and details lies with the personnel department, the task force is a thinking, advising, monitoring and policy-formulating body in relation to major issues involved in HRDs. The members of the task force should be fully aware of the various systems, sub-systems and procedures that are being introduced, should be able to clarify to other officers in the company and questions and doubts raised, receive feedback about how the various systems are working and suggest corrective action strategies to be implemented by the personnel department. The task force would be dealing with only establish ment of systems and procedures and not with minor details and individual cases.

The following are some of the tasks on which the task force may need to give immediate thinking:

1. *Monitor the progress of the implementation f the new appraisal system. This includes designing mechanisms to get reactions to training, reactions to the new system, review ing the data collected on attitudes to performance appraisal, reviewing the effectiveness of the training programmes, devising mechanisms to monitor identification of KPAs, devising mechanisms for guiding employees in identification of KPAs, reviewing the effectiveness of actual counselling sessions and planning corrective action in each of the above.*

2. *Monitor the identification of training needs and deciding priorities of roles and areas needing attention. This includes devising mechanisms for the identification of training needs, reviewing the data compiled by the training department, indicating priorities and providing a focus to the training strategies.*

3. *Finalising the interim system of potential appraisal and monitoring the same. This would involve finalising the potential appraisal forms, finalising the processes of potential appraisal, ensuring that the data are made available, monitoring the process of potential appraisal, reviewing and moderating the systems.*

4. *Facilitating the long-term potential appraisal system. Appointing role set groups, arranging demonstration sessions for potential appraisal, reviewing the system, clarifying doubts and planning systematisation of the long-term appraisal.*

5. *Monitoring the use of data feedback and other systems of organisation development.*

6. *Suggesting topics and areas of concern for research by the personnel department (Research and Organisation Development Cell).*

7. *Feedback to the personnel department about the problems in the new systems and planning corrective action.*

8. *Planning self-renewal for various systems.*

9. *Other issues that may come up from time to time (e.g., assessment of subordinates, training in motivation, creativity, etc.).*

Feedback on Performance Appraisal and Training

By the time the task forces came into operation training of all the officers was completed. The task force, therefore, decided as a first step in monitoring to assess the extent to which those who attended the various training programmes had understood the HRD and the new appraisal system. The task force members designed a short questionnaire and sent it to all officers for their responses. The questionnaire elicited information on the following components:

1. clarity of procedure involved in the new appraisal system;
2. issues or questions on which more information is required;
3. reactions to the new appraisal system;
4. extent of confidence in handling the new system;
5. usefulness of the orientation training in gaining insights into the new systems; and
6. assistance required to implement the system.

The results of one such survey are presented in Exhibit 13.4.

The task force discussed the results of this survey. Reactions to the new system appeared positive. The training programmes also seemed to have served the purpose they intended to serve. However, since a sizeable portion of the officers stated that they were not absolutely clear in their minds about the procedures, KPAs, objective setting, etc., components, it was decided to pay some attention to each of these components as and when a particular component came into operation. For example, for the first trial run, the immediate step involved was identifying KPAs and objectives. Therefore the task force decided to go round from department to department clarifying the mechanisms and helping them identify the KPAs and set targets.

Exhibit 15.4

Effectiveness of Orientation Training for Performance Appraisal (Number of questionnaires sent = 473; number responding = 397)

Questions asked	Percentage of respondents answering		
	Yes	No	Can't say or not sure
1. Are you clear about the procedures involved in the new appraisal system?	95	5	0
2. Do you think that the new appraisal system offers an opportunity for officers in this company to discover more of their strengths and weaknesses?	74	2	24
3. Do you feel confident that you will be able to benefit as an appraisee from the performance review and counselling sessions you will have with your reporting officers?	25	44	32
4. Do you feel confident that your subordinate officers will benefit from the review and counselling sessions you are going to give them?	67	2	32
5. To what extent do you think that you have benefited from the training programme in relation to the following?	To a extent	Some great	Not at whatall
(a) Clarity of procedures		44	55 1
(b) Identifying Key Performance Areas	42	55	4
(c) Setting objectives		37	58 5

		To a great extent	Some what	Not at all
(d)	Understanding the concepts of creativity, initiative, team spirit and developing subordinates	51	47	3
(e)	Performance Analysis	38	58	3
(f)	Criteria for self-rating	44	51	4
(g)	Developmental needs	40	55	5
(h)	Role of forum III	31	65	5
(i)	Role of Reviewing Officer	42	55	4
(j)	Use of data by personnel department	26	64	10

6. Given the existing situation in the company what do you think is the probability of success (measured in terms of development and increased understanding) of the system?

	Percentage of officers giving this response
a) Self	
i) I am very confident that this will succeed	31
ii) I am somewhat confident that this will succeed	65
iii) I do not think this will succeed	5
b) Others	
i) This may succeed with a few officers but not with most	22
ii) This may succeed with some officers	56
iii) This may succeed with most officers	25

	Percentage of officers giving this response
7. All in all what do you think of this system?	
a) Comparison with the earlier system	
i) The previous system is better than this	5
ii) This is definitely an improvement over the previous system	95
b) New system	
i) This is an excellent system	5
ii) This is good but depends on how it is implemented	86
iii) There are a few merits but there are more problems	9
iv) There are no merits in this system and there will be problems	0
v) This system is not desirable for the company	0

In order to give feedback to the trainers it was decided to tabulate the data trainer-wise (grouping all the respondents trained by each batch of trainers together), and pass it on to them. While giving the feedback data to help each trainer to see himself in relation to others, the data of other trainers were given trainer-wise but keeping the names anonymous. Since the feedback was uniformly positive it should have boosted the morale of the executives as trainers.

Other Monitoring Efforts by the Task Forces

The HRD-implementation task force served as the main vehicle of implementation of the system. Wherever the chief executive of the division took more interest, that task force worked very well in spite of the time pressures on the members and the chairman. All the task force chairmen were busy people holding charge of some crucial departments. Their time was very valuable to the organisation. In spite of the work pressure, however, they took interest. On a few occasions when their bosses asked them to attend to other important issues rather than the HRD they would become a little apprehensive and express doubts as to whether the organisation was serious enough about the system. When such doubts came up it was necessary for somebody from the top levels of the HRD department to spend time with task force chairmen and members and have long discussions. Such discussions helped in reassuring them and are provided by someone at the top level who is in charge of HRD. The position of this person becomes important as unless such assurance comes from the top, task forces may get demoralised and may take the task easy.

The following are some of the other significant monitoring tasks undertaken by the task forces:

1 Clarification of KPAs and Target-setting Procedures

For initiating the first trial run, officers had to identify KPAs and set targets for the first three-month period. The task force members requested different departments to do the exercise and send one copy of the KPAs and targets to the task force chairman. These were reviewed by the task force. In cases where some departments had problems the task force members went to these departments and helped them in finalising their KPAs. Those departments that did not do a good job of identifying KPAs also were helped through discussions. Wherever needed, one or two members of the task force would go and provide the help. This reduced the demands on the time of all task force members. The task force thus ensured that there is a maximum understanding about KPAs. The KPAs collected during this period were edited and a compendium was prepared by the HRD department.

2.Pre-review Preparation

After the first three-month period the task force members went round the departments holding brief sessions and explaining about appraisal discussions. This task included clarifying the rating scale for self-assessment, behavioural dimensions, performance analysis, identifying training needs, comments to be made by the reporting and reviewing officers, etc. The HRD department played an active role in assisting the task force members in these tasks.

3.Assessment of Training Needs

The task force also helped the HRD department in identifying areas for in-company training and outside training after collecting training-needs data from employees.

In addition the members played an active role in some of the tasks described as follows.

Feedback on the First Trial Run

In the early stages of introducing systems like this, continuous monitoring is necessary. Such monitoring helps in designing corrective action. As soon as the first appraisal reviews were over the managers from the HRD department as well as a few task force members met the other managers to interview and find out their experiences. Besides getting such feedback on a select basis through interviews, structured questionnaire was sent to all officers requesting an assessment of their experiences. An analysis of the responses from one of the divisions is presented in Exhibit 13.5.

Exhibit 15.5

Survey of First Experience of New Performance Appraisal System

1. The consensus

Do you think we should continue with this system?

31% I think this system is useful and we should definitely continue it.

55% I think we should give it a try and review it after wards.

10% I think we should continue it with some modifications.

4% I prefer the old system of Confidential Reports (ESRs) over this system.

2. The preparation

(a) Have you prepared yourself well for the interview?

30% Yes, very well

50% Yes, somewhat

9% Yes, a little

2% No, it was a ritual

(b) What problems did you experience during self-appraisal?

79% found self-appraisal easy or had no problems.

21% stated having problems. The problems frequently mentioned include:

i) Rating on the behavioural dimensions, initiative, creativity, etc.

ii) Self-appraisal needs thinking and analysis and is time-consuming.

iii) KPAs had changed, new work came up or work got postponed.

iv) Did not keep detailed records, so could not convince reporting officer about performance.

3. The interview

(a) How much time did you both spend for the discussion?

27 minutes = Average time (actual varies from 2 hours to 1 minute)

(b) How do you rate psychological climate of the performance review discussions you had with your reporting officer?

	To a great degree	To some degree	To a little degree	Not at all
	(Percentage of responses)			
There was mutuality and respect between the two	73	25	2	0
The climate was open and free	76	18	6	1
There was good rapport between the two of us	69	20	9	1
The climate was cordial	69	25	5	1
The climate was emotionally charged	2	6	21	71
The climate was inhibitive and I could not express all feelings	3	8	11	78

(c) Who do you think talked more during the interview?

85% Both equally

8% Reporting Officer

6% Myself

(d) Have you been able to express all the difficulties and problems you had been facing regarding your job and achievement of KPAs?

35% Yes, all difficulties without any problems

31% Most of them

9% Some of them

2% Only a few of them

0% Not at all

23% Not needed during the interview, as we keep talking of them every day.

(e) As a Reporting Officer when you had discussions with your subordinates.

% ticking the statement	Statement
82%	I found my subordinates to be receptive to feedback
79%	I am satisfied with the appraisal discussions I had with my subordinates.
63%	I could communicate my disappointment or happiness with their work.
16%	There was a great difference between my assessment and the appraisee's statement.
13%	Intended to over-rate him to maintain good relations.
5%	I had difficulty in giving negative feedback.

4. As an appraisee, do you feel the discussion has helped you in any way? Tick the statements that are true with you.

% ticking the statement	Statement
75%	Our understanding of each other has increased in a positive direction.
75%	I could express my difficulties to my Reporting officer.
64%	I came to know about some of the areas where I should do better.
56%	I understood more about the expectation of my Reporting Officer from me.
54%	I understood some more strengths that I have
44%	I have got to know of areas of improvement for my own development.
31%	The discussions were more a ritual and nothing new
25%	For the first time, I have had an opportunity to sit and talk to my Reporting Officer about the job, difficulties, etc.
15%	I started thinking over biases of my Reporting Officer.
10%	These discussions have not helped me at all.
4%	Our relationship is strained now.

5. As a Reporting Officer if you had performance review discussion with your subordinates, tick the statements true with you.

% ticking the statement	Statement
66%	I came to know more about the difficulties and problems experienced by my subordinates
66%	Some of my appraisees have understood themselves
42%	The interviews have improved our relationship
8%	The interviews have affected slightly our relationship.

6. Suggestions
Please give your suggestions for improving this system; your answer will help us in reviewing the system (a sample of suggestions are presented below).

Exhibit 15.6

Hindering Factors in performance
(From Analysis of Appraisal Forms)

Category of hindering factors	No. of officers mentioning this (percentage in brackets)	
Environmental		
1. Waiting for inputs (delay in material or job cards or data from other departments, non-availability of materials or tools)	50	(27)
2. Shortage of staff	45	(25)
3. Subordinates (go-slow or incompetent)	16	(9)
4. Shortage of material-handling equipment	10	(5)
5. Shortage of transport	8	(4)
6. New to job	8	(4)
7. Non-cooperation of other departments	6	(3)
8. Procedures or material flow bog down	6	(3)
9. Others	14	(8)
Total :	163	(90)
Personal		
1. Ill-health	8	(4)
2. Lack of experience, practical knowledge, etc.	7	(4)
3. Others	4	(2)
Total :	19	(10)

Use of Data from Appraisal Forms

Completed performance appraisal forms can throw up a lot of significant data that could be used by the organisation for its effectiveness. The HRD department can play a significant role in ensuring that these data are analysed and used. After the first appraisal discussion the HRD department collected the forms for monitoring. They compile the data on training needs to check with previous assessments and to identify in-company programmes needed as well as the areas where outside training may be required. Besides this the performance analysis parts of forms were analysed and tabulated. Such an analysis provided insights into areas that needed improvement. Exhibit 13.6 provides an example of an analysis of hindering factors found in one of the divisions. After such analyses are done it may be feedback to the divisional head for initiating improvements.

As a step in this direction, data were collected on the following:

a) The training needs of each employee in relation to the existing jobs they were performing; and

b) the training programmes attended by each employee.

An analysis of the performance appraisal data of four years prior to the introduction of this system: this was done in order to identify reporting officers who had tendencies to rate their subordinates either too liberally or very conservatively. The analysis assessed the extent to which "halo effect" has been working in the past. The study also isolated the candidate who got consistently high ratings over the four year period and communicated the same to the top management.

Joint Task Force Meeting

Since the implementation task forces were working in different divisions there was no communication between them except through the central office, HRD managers or the GM, conveying to each other the developments and experiences. After a couple of months some of the members felt that they must learn from each other's experiences and must know what is being done by other task groups. As a result they decided to exchange copies of minutes of their meetings and reports with other groups. Besides, they decided to have periodic joint meetings. The first meeting was held after the first trial run to discuss issues and work out future strategies. This meeting proved very helpful in sorting out issues. The chief of HRD took active role in helping the task groups get clarity on the problems raised after the first trial run. Such meetings are likely to be very useful. For example, it was decided in the first meeting that as the quality of KPAs is still not up to mark the HRD officers should meet all executives individually and help them improve the quality. This task was later undertaken by the HRD department and they even brought out a compendium of KPAs.

Top Level Involvement

There is generally some resistance shown by employees for introducing any system that would require change of habits and change of culture irrespective of the benefits. In introducing a system of this kind a most often asked question is, "how much is the top management committed?" In a system like this the human resource department sometimes has to undertake the task of taking not only the employees along but also the top management. It has to play a change agents' role. This becomes particularly critical if the top management is changing or is likely to change (which is so in most public sector undertakings). Therefore, there is a need to stabilise the system by involving as many members of the top management as possible. If the top management has faith in the new HRD department and is left on its own, then the department should make efforts to keep the top management informed of all developments. As the company attached quite some importance to this system, it was decided to keep the top management posted with progress. As there was an institution of a weekly get together of GMs and Directors (called GM's meeting) it was decided to have review of progress of HRD implementation as a permanent topic in GM's meetings. For certain reasons when there were no GM's meetings a special meeting was called after the first trial run to review the progress. This was attended by the Chairmen of the task forces with the Chairman and MD in the chair. It was in this meeting after reviewing the progress the following decisions were taken:

1. To expand the rating system from 5 points to 9 points in view of liberal self-assessment and narrow range observed.
2. Finalising the training policy.
3. Action to be taken on those not completing appraisal discussions.
4. Finalising potential appraisal forms, etc.

Besides such meetings the HRD department used to issue a periodic progress report on the implementation of HRD to all the top management and senior managers (DGMs, GMs and Directors).

Thus the system was fully introduced in this organisation in a period of two years. The experiences of this organisation indicate that public sector undertakings are not closed to innovations as many people think and that some of them can take an active lead and produce wonderful results. It takes time for systems to be stabilised. In the opinion of authors public sector undertakings have strengths which can be used for innovative work.

Transition Management and Stabilisation

This case describes so far the process involved in introducing an open system of performance appraisal for managerial staff. Subsequent experiences of this organisation as well as a few other organisations indicate that equally intensive efforts are required to monitor the implementation and stabilisation of the new system. In this organisation, for example, immediately after the introduction of the system the adviser left. In that very year there were a series of changes that took place in the top management and the composition of the top management changed substantially. The HRD department could not monitor the subsequent implementation as rigorously as it did during the process of introducing. As a result the rate of return of completed forms to personnel department came down. This transition period created a vacuum in personal data systems creating difficulties for the top management to take personnel decisions. About two years subsequent to the introduction of the new system disappointed with the gaps created in the personnel data systems, the top management had to decide to further modify the system and reintroduce confidential form of ratings although counselling was retained. They assumed that forms were not being completed because of difficulties in the openness involved. In another organisation, however, when similar difficulties were experienced the HRD department and the top management took active interest in contacting the managerial staff and filling the data gaps without changing the system. Periodic reviews and minor modifications from time to time to suit other organisational needs is a part of any system and this was followed in this organisation also. It is important to note from these experiences the need for continued rigorous efforts to stabilise systems after introducing them.

Chapter 16

APPRAISAL PRACTICES IN INDIA

PERFORMANCE appraisal practices in Indian organisations are quite varied. They vary from almost "no appraisal" to a "sophisticated multipurpose, multi-component based appraisal systems". In some of the small and medium sized organisations it is not uncommon to find that there are no formal mechanisms of appraising performance. Informally appraisal reports are given by senior officers to the top management. At the time of promotion decisions the top management takes the views of appraisers into consideration. At the other extreme there are organisations that have performance appraisals that aim simultaneously at different objectives, like data generation for personnel decisions like rewards, promotions, job-rotation, transfers, etc., and creation of a new organisational culture of openness, trust, mutuality, etc., and generation of enabling capabilities and employee development on the job, etc., and that use different components (KPAs, objective setting, managerial and behavioural dimensions, self-assessment, performance analysis, counselling, identification of training needs, etc.). A good example of such a system is the one followed by Larsen & Toubro Limited and the one being experimented by the State Bank of India and its associate banks. Between these two extremes, on one side are organisations having annual confidential reports which take into consideration only certain traits to be shown by the employee (e.g., sincerity, punctuality, hard work, appearance, leadership, drive, loyalty, etc.) and ignore fully the job-related accomplishments of the employee. On the other side of the continuum are organisations that have semi-confidential formats and that require the appraisee to state his accomplishments, and that take into account such statements of the appraisee for final assessment by the boss which is on work-related dimensions as well as behaviours of the employee and that require the appraiser to discuss with the appraisee before his final assessment. Most of the government departments fall into the earlier category whereas forward looking private and public sector industries tend to fall in the latter category. (Here the government departments like the department of health and family welfare, education, energy, etc., are to be differentiated from public sector industries like BHEL, HMT, BEML, IOC, SAIL, etc.). In between these two sets there are again organisations having appraisals with various degrees of sophistication. Some have a performance-cum-trait based confidential report formats whereas some others have performance-cum-trait based appraisals open to the appraisee for discussion and requiring him to make his comments before they are sent to the reviewing authority and then to personnel department.

Appraisal Practices

Recently the author (Rao, 1982) conducted a survey of appraisal practices in 45 different organisations (34 private sector and 11 public sector). The following observations could be made from the results of this survey:

1. About 50 per cent of the organisations seem to profess the purpose of their appraisal as regulating employee behaviour as well as developing employee capabilities. About 30 per cent of them still use appraisals only for controlling and regulating employee behaviour whereas only about 10 per cent seem to use appraisals mainly for development purposes.
2. A fairly high percentage of the organisations seem to use one or more components of appraisal discussed in this book. Table 14.1 presents the percentage of organisations using different components as a part of the appraisal system they have.

Table 16.1

Components of Performance Appraisal used by Different Organisations (n = 45)

Sr. No.	Components	Percentage reporting the use of this component
1.	Some form of agreement between a boss and his subordinate on tasks or targets or functions forming a basis of appraisal	62
2.	Appraisal discussions aiming at helping the appraisee to recognise his strengths	49
3.	Appraisal discussions aiming at helping the appraisee to recognise his weaknesses	53

Sr. No.	Components	Percentage reporting the use of this component
4.	Appraisal feedback (written or verbal) to tell the employee the areas he needs to improve	69
5.	Self-appraisal to communicate to the boss the accomplishments of an employee	44
6.	Appraisal on managerial qualities required to perform any managerial job (e.g., leadership, coordination, etc.)	73
7.	Identification of training and developmental needs	87
8.	Appraising potential for promotions	78
9.	Identification of factors affecting performance and communicating them to the boss for his assistance and future action	44
10.	Signature by subordinates on the form after assessment by the boss	33
11.	Confidential ratings by an officer one level above or reporting officer	71
12.	Confidential ratings by an officer at least two levels above the appraisee	40

This table indicates a very encouraging trend in the performance appraisal systems being used by different organisations. Particularly, performance review feedback to help the employee recognise his strengths and weaknesses, use of appraisal for identification of training needs, basing the appraisal on mutually agreed tasks, targets or functions and self-appraisal seem to characterise about half of the organisations. All these components, if monitored well, are likely to facilitate employee development. In spite of this trend it appears, that in a large number of organisations (71%) the final assessment appears to be that of confidential nature.

3. The survey also revealed some interesting practices being fol-

lowed in different organisations. These practices are different from the usual ones. In 11 of the companies surveyed the executives mentioned these as unique components of their appraisal systems. Each item below relates to a different organisation. .ls1

(a) Appraisal of a person falling under the category "outstanding" should be accompanied by a brief citation of the individual's performance with specific details which earned him the grade.

(b) The final ratings are given by an officer three levels above the appraisee. He gives his confidential ratings on the basis of the independent ratings by the reporting and reviewing officers of the employee.

(c) To avoid biased assessment by the immediate supervisor, the appraisal form is sent to employees from other department one level above the appraisee and with whom the appraisee is interacting.

(d) Appraisal forms are simple (one page) for workers and staff. For officers and managers they are lengthy and go into depth.

(e) The appraisal reports by reporting officer are shown to the appraisee and his comments are obtained. The reviewing officer gives his final ratings confidentially. From this year onwards even these are going to be shown to the appraisee.

(f) A "merit award" system is operating for those whose performance is praiseworthy.

(g) The ratings are given for various qualities in a printed form. There is a co-efficient factor for each of the ratings. The ratings are multiplied by this co-efficient factor and final number is arrived at the personnel department.

(h) First assessment is finalised by the reporting officer after discussions with the appraisee. These are then sent to the head of the division who may make changes based on his knowledge about the performance of this employee and others of his level in the division working at other locations. These are then sent to the divisional director for his own analysis and transmission to personnel department.

(i) The reporting officer of the appraisee and the reviewing officer discuss the performance of the appraisee before the reporting officer discusses with the appraisee. Then the assessment is sent to the head of the department who sends them to the manpower planning and development managers for review.

(j) Appraisee is assessed by two officers two levels above the appraisee. The appraisee is informed of his strengths and weaknesses and is allowed to defend himself. His comments and suggestions are recorded.

(k) The senior managers of the company are expected to give a minimum of four objectives per year and plans as to how they will be achieved. The MD along with the divisional head will review at the end of six months and at the end of the year the progress achieved. Improvements needed are verbally communicated to the employee.

Appraisal Systems in Banks

Banking services is one sector where a great degree of attention is being paid to performance appraisal systems. Several of the nationalised banks have changed their performance appraisal systems or are in the process of changing them. The State Bank of India is in the process of adopting an open system of appraisal like the one described in this book. Its associate banks like the State Bank of Bikaner and Jaipur, State Bank of Mysore, State Bank of Hyderabad, State Bank of Indore, State Bank of Patiala, State Bank of Saurashtra, State Bank of Travancore, etc., are likely to follow the same after detailed experience of the SBI are available. In fact, about five years ago a common task force of HRD managers of these associate banks was appointed to evolve a common system of appraisal for the associate banks. The task force evolved a system similar to that being experimented by the State Bank of India at present. Once the SBI experiences are available it might become easier for the various associate banks to revise and adopt the new system. Till that time these and a few others may continue to follow traditional annual confidential report form of appraisals. In most of the Banks that follow the traditional system, their officers are being assessed on the following characteristics: (i) general intelligence; (ii) job knowledge; (ii) initiative and resourcefulness; (iv) supervision; (v) business capacity; (vi) ability to assess sound business propositions; (vii) dependability; (viii) relationship with junior and senior colleagues; (ix) relationships with public; (x) sociability; (xi) appearance and dress; (xii) conduct; (xiii) manners; (xiv) managerial ability; (xv) health; (xvi) special aptitudes; (xvii) any significant achievements; and (xviii) failures that attracted issue of warning by superiors.

Those of the banks that have already changed their appraisal systems have normally performance-related as well as trait-based appraisals. Several of the banks also have self-appraisal as a part of performance appraisal, although mostly such self- appraisal is more of a communication of achievements.

For example, Allahabad Bank has introduced a system that aims at helping officers to identify their strengths and weaknesses and encourage improvement of performance on the job. In this system officers are assessed in three specific areas: (i) job performance; (ii) job knowledge/skills and personal characteristics; and (iii) potential ability and development. The appraisal is to be initiated by the appraisee with a self- appraisal. In the self-appraisal, the appraisee gives details like the training courses attended, job performance (deposits, advances, profit/loss, etc., for Branch Managers, Chief Managers and Regional Managers), contributions made in the job during the year, achievements, deficiencies pointed out, training needs, areas of aptitude and interest for future work, efforts made for self-development and efforts proposed to be made, etc. Ratings are then given by the reporting officer of the appraisee on factors relating to job performance, job knowledge/skills and personal characteristics and potential ability and development. For example, under job performance each Branch Manager has to be assessed on 15 different factors (deposits, advances, advances to priority sectors, profit/loss, quality of deposits, quality of advances, position regarding sticky advances, balancing of books, submission of important returns, reconciliation of accounts with RBI/SBI, etc., rectification of irregularities, cash management, staff management, general administration and customer service) and an overall rating given on that basis. In relation to job knowledge/skills and personal qualities each BM has to be as sessed on 8 dimensions (knowledge of banking law and practice, knowledge of bank's procedures and instructions, general knowledge and intelligence, accuracy and dependability, timeliness, power of expression, personality and behaviour, and discipline and punctuality) and an overall rating is to be awarded. Under potential ability and development each BM is to be assessed under 12 factors (initiative and resourcefulness, planning and organising ability, decision-making ability, leadership, loyalty and devotion to duty, integrity and honesty, health, ability to work under adverse circumstances, special work done, irregularities observed, etc.) and an overall rating is to be assigned. The reviewing authority can moderate the assessment made by the reporting officer.

The Indian Overseas Bank has a system in which Branch Manager gives a self-appraisal on Business Growth (deposits, advances, profit/loss, etc.), Customer Service, Internal Administration and Training Requirements in great detail. The reporting officer makes comments on each of these areas and gives his final assessment using a 5-point scale on seven factors (general intelligence, job knowledge, managerial ability, business development, public relations/customer service, expenditure control and dependability). Along with his assessment for Branch Managers, the Regional Manager is also expected to send branch inspection report.

The Union Bank of India has an appraisal system in which the reporting officer is required to assess each of his appraisee officers on technical skills (consisting of job knowledge, job performance, and dependability), human skills (consisting of emotional stability, power of expression, inter-personal relations and leadership), and conceptual skills (consisting of mental alertness and grasping power, job relation, judgement/decision-making, and initiative). All these are defined for different categories of roles and the assessment has to be made on a 5-point scale.

The Punjab National Bank (PNB) has a primarily development-oriented appraisal form. There are ten different formats available for ten different categories of employees. The system PNB has started with a self-appraisal by the appraisee. For example, in the self-appraisal to be made by Regional Managers/AGMS/DGMS working in zones they are required to comment on the following:

1. Job satisfaction in discharging duties during the review period.
2. Suitability of duties to skill, talent and capacity.
3. Important achievements.
4. Compliments received or deficiencies pointed out by superiors.
5. Willingness to move out of the station of posting.
6. Training attended.
7. Growth needs and plans for improving capabilities.

In addition actual achievement figures are to be given on business indicators like deposits, advances, priority sector advances, sectoral distribution of priority sector credit, advances under DRIS, etc. In addition break-up of loosing officers for the past 2 years and details of various activities (like CRs overdue, sanctions overdue for renewal, number of complaints outstanding, number of offices visited, number of villages adopted, etc.) are to be given. Lastly, the self-appraisal also includes a statement of efforts put in by the appraisee for business development, control measures and staff matters. On the basis of this self-appraisal and his own assess ment his reporting officer is expected to rate the appraisee on growth of business, quality of advances, demonstrated managerial abilities (separately on realistic budget formulation and submission, staff control through delegation and development, developing mutual understanding and team spirit among staff, clarity in instructions, upward communication and others), and ten different qualities dealing with potential and growth (job knowledge, dependability, cooperativeness, emotional stability, decision- making, initiative and resourcefulness, flexibility, communication and creative abilities).

Similar self-appraisal formats have been introduced by Corporation Bank, United Commercial Bank, Central Bank of India, Bank of India, Dena Bank, and the Bank of Baroda. Self- appraisals introduced by these organisations vary from a brief statement of achievements during the year to be made by the appraisee to a somewhat detailed description of achievements on various business and other parameters. Of these banks, the Bank of Baroda has recently introduced an elaborate development- oriented appraisal system. Every appraisee (officer/executive) is expected to initiate the appraisal process through filling a self-performance recording form. In the self-appraisal the appraisee is expected to indicate: (i) his job responsibilities; (ii) his satisfaction with the way he has been able to carry them out; (iii) his major achievements; (iv) an analysis of factors preventing better performance; and (v) factors that may help him to be a better performer (job rotation, training, etc.). The reporting officer is expected to rate his work performance factors (for example, under advances seven different factors are spelt out in the form and for house-keeping eight different factors are spelt out in the form for Accountants/Branch Manag ers). Demonstrated Managerial Approach (for example, 20 different factors are spelt out under the headings - planning, organising, staffing, directing and controlling) and Development Aspects (for example, ten different dimensions like readiness to learn, knowledge, conceptual skills, decision-making, stress tolerance, creativity, initiative, etc., were spelt out for Branch Managers). In addition to these, recommendations are to be made for training, etc. A special feature of the Appraisal System in BOB is the requirements for performance review discussions to be conducted by the reporting officer after his appraisal. Apart from the State Bank of India where counselling is being experimented, the Bank of Baroda probably is the only bank having a requirement of performance review discussion as a part of the appraisal system.

As the discussion so far indicates, the Banking Sector is making serious efforts to have systems of appraisal that improve their efficiency, effectiveness and image through development of their employees. In the coming few years they are likely to progress further in the direction of multi-objective and multi-component- based open systems of appraisal.

Managerial Preferences and Attitudes to Appraisals

Given the above trends of appraisals in Indian organisations let us now examine the managerial reactions and preferences; for appraisal system depends upon how well the users of the system understand the purposes, accept these and strive for achieving these purposes. Also in designing any system managerial preferences should be taken into consideration. Some evidence is available from unpublished surveys conducted in the last few years on the reactions of managers to the existing systems of appraisal and their preferences. Mostly such studies are conducted for internal consumption by industry and therefore these are not widely publicised. Some of the observations from these surveys and experiences of the author from various appraisal workshops and training programmes are presented below.

Surveys conducted seeking the opinions and preferences of managers indicate that managers themselves are interested in open appraisal systems. As far back as in 1974 when the author was involved in designing a new performance appraisal system for managers of a large private sector company, a number of managers (about 50) were interviewed. There was dissatisfaction expressed uniformly by all of them to the closed system of appraisal exist ing at that time in that company. Each of the managers wanted to know what their boss thought of them and their strengths and weaknesses in performing various tasks. They wanted more communication from their reporting officers to help them improve their performance.

In another survey conducted by the author in 1978 in a large public sector company having a confidential report form of performance appraisal, of the 588 officers surveyed about 98 per cent of them felt that the appraisal system should help them to recognise their strengths and weaknesses. A fairly high percent age of them (over 60 per cent) recognised that it is very difficult to have objective assessment in any form of appraisal because human factors is always involved. Interestingly about 50 per cent to 60 per cent of them from different levels indicated that even in the confidential form of appraisal their reporting officers communicate their perceptions of the strengths and weaknesses of the appraisee to him. However, about 88 per cent of them wanted to know more from their boss.

In this organisation an open appraisal system of the kind discussed in this book was introduced subsequently on an experimental basis. A year after introducing the new system a second survey was conducted to assess the opinions of officers. The survey indicated the following:

1. About 63 per cent of the officers stated that they were willing to show the full report to their appraisees while the remaining preferred not to show full support.
2. However, 84 per cent of them preferred to have performance review discussions and the remaining were against such discussions.
3. About 53 per cent of them preferred trait-based assessment of their subordinates to performance-based assessment. (It was probably easier to assess them on traits where there could be less arguments. Performance or task-based assessment also holds the reporting officer responsible by supplying the infrastructural assistance.).
4. The average time the officers felt that they could spend on each appraisal was about 30 to 40 minutes.

In a recent survey conducted in Jyoti Limited, Baroda, 70 managers responded to a questionnaire on performance appraisal system (Gangotra, 1983). Of these, 37 responded as appraisers and 33 responded as appraisees. Jyoti's have an evaluation system requiring each appraiser to assess his subordinates on performance-related qualities (e.g., planning, speed and accuracy, prompt decision-making, contribution of new ideas, job knowledge, etc.). After completing his assessment, each appraiser is ex pected to discuss with his appraisee before the form is sent to the reviewing officer and then the personnel department. The survey revealed the following:

1. About 94 per cent of the appraisers stated that they always give a formal feedback whereas only 36 per cent of the appraisees said that they are being given feedback.
2. Only 10 per cent of the respondents stated that the assessment should be kept confidential from the employee.
3. About 84 per cent of the respondents felt that the opinion of the appraisee also should be recorded on the appraisal form after completing appraisal.
4. About 73 per cent respondents preferred to have self-appraisal as a part of the system.

5. About 86 per cent of the respondents did not think that giving positive and/or negative feedback would reduce motivaiton. However, 92 per cent felt that their subordinates do react to negative feedback. At the same time 84 per cent felt that such feedback should be given.
6. About 32 per cent respondents spent less than 15 minutes on each appraisal. In all about 70 per cent took less than an hour for each appraisal including discussions.
7. About 73 per cent of the respondents preferred to rate their appraisee on the main areas of work assigned to him rather than on general qualities.
8. All the respondents (100 per cent) wanted to know their areas of weakness requiring improvement.

Kulkarni, Nangia and Prakasam (1980-81) of the National Institute of Bank Management conducted nation-wide opinion survey of the bank employees of various personnel issues. Their survey of 6,800 bank employees drawn from various nationalised banks re vealed the following perceptions and preferences with respect to performance appraisal practices:

1. Only about 14 per cent of the employees stated that they were aware of the basis on which their supervisor evaluated their work in the Annual Confidential Reports. Of the remaining, 55 per cent had no idea at all of the criteria used and another 31 per cent had some general idea but not aware of any special criteria.
2. About 68 per cent of the employees felt that the data filled in the Annual Confidential Reports do not focus on the job performance.
3. About 73 per cent of the employees felt that the appraisee should be interviewed about his performance and given an opportunity to provide inputs for his performance assessment.

General Trends

A series of workshops and training programmes were organised by the author at the Indian Institute of Management, Ahmedabad. Starting from the year 1979 three workshops and training programmes were arranged. More than 100 executives from private and public sector industries, service institutions and banks participated in these programmes. The participants were from personnel and training departments as well as line functions. In each of these programmes the participants had lengthy discussions sharing their experiences about the appraisal system followed in their respective organisations, presenting their perceptions of the merits and demerits of these systems and sharing the thinking of their organisations relating to the future of performance appraisal in their organisations. From the deliberations and experiences shared in these programmes the following conclusions could be drawn about the present situation of Performance Appraisal Systems in India:

1. A sizeable number of organisations both in the private and the public sector continue to follow trait-based, confidential formats of performance appraisal.
2. Almost all of them however are dissatisfied with such forms of performance appraisal, particularly for assessing managers.
3. Their dissatisfaction arises mainly from the following factors: high subjectivity in appraisals, lack of correlation with job-related factors, the appraisee not having an opportunity to project his performance, the appraisee some how getting to know about his ratings and diminishing value of appraisal as an instrument of controlling or monitoring employee behaviour.
4. With increased recognition being given to the personnel function a few organisations have already begun to experiment with new systems of appraisal. Such experiments are taking place both in the private and the public sector and these experiments are focussing on the role of appraisals as instruments for developing human resources.
5. A few organisations that have merely changed the format of appraisals from closed to open ones, and introduced them without reorienting the managers to the new systems have run into serious difficulties. For example, introducing counselling as a part of appraisal without training the managers in counselling skills, introducing open assessment without having a committed HRD philosophy, etc., have resulted in problems leading to rethinking on the part of the organisations about the new appraisal systems.
6. Managers are increasingly wanting open systems of appraisals and personnel departments are still struggling to find appraisal models suitable for their organisations.
7. While employees are wanting open appraisal systems, at present, their objective of asking this seems to be limited to having a knowledge of the assessment given by the boss and to argue about it if it is not to one's disadvantage. Most of them still do not recognise the full potential of good appraisal systems. Even those who recognise the potential of appraisal systems, accept

the development objective intellectually but find it difficult to practise it skillfully due to motivational and emotional blocks.

8. A large number of manager still seem to be excessively oriented to ask the question "what am I going to get from the new appraisal system?" rather than asking the question "how do I use this system to develop my subordinates and to increase my own managerial effectiveness?".
9. A large number of executives including those at senior levels see the role of developing human resources as mainly that of the personnel or the HRD departments. This lack of recognition of their HRD role prevents most executives from effective use of development-oriented appraisal systems whenever they are being introduced. This managerial culture should change for the new systems to become more useful. Such change is only beginning now and may take time.
10. In some of the organisations the symbols are taken more seriously than the purpose or the spirit behind these. For example, if the appraisee is required to sign on the form as an indicator that he had discussion with his appraiser, the signature becomes more important than the discussion. Similarly form filling becomes more important than the process of filling it. Personnel departments are still struggling to overcome such problems.

Future of Performance Appraisals

There is a great degree of awakening taking place in the managerial world about the potential uses of performance appraisals. The role they can play in developing employee capabilities, creating an open culture, strengthening superior-subordinate relationship, developing process skills and paving way for increased managerial and organisational effectiveness is being slowly recognised. Unlike in the West where training is perceived as the most important mechanism of developing employees, in India appraisal systems are being recognised as an equally (and sometimes a much more) potential tool for development. In the coming decade there is likely to be more and more experimentation with new appraisal systems that contribute to improvements in the quality of work life as well as to the development of human resources. The seeds have already been sown at several places.

Chapter 17

APPRAISAL PRACTICES IN SOME ASIAN COUNTRIES

SOME of the Asian countries have similar state of affairs like India in relation to performance appraisal systems and practices. On the one hand there are unique systems like those in Japan that have evolved over the last several years as integral parts of the Japanese Management Philosophy and Styles; on the other side there are countries that have a mixed bag of performance appraisal systems like those in India. Countries like Singapore, Malay sia, Philippines, Pakistan, Indonesia and Sri Lanka could be categorised under the latter. In this chapter an attempt is made to present some of the major trends that could be observed in some of these countries. The purpose of this chapter is mainly to point out that Indian organisations are probably somewhat better off in terms of the appraisal systems they have or those they are experimenting with as compared to other Asian countries (if we do not consider the multinationals present in these countries whose appraisal systems are decided largely by their western counterparts). No exhaustive survey could be conducted for this purpose. As most of these countries still do not have well established institutions to conduct management research, published literature is rather limited. For example, from the various journals published from Singapore (by the Singapore Institute of Management etc.) in the last few years, one finds hardly one or two articles on this topic. However, due to the great public interest that was aroused in the last two years in Singapore on appraisals, there are quite a few reports, articles and workshop summaries that appeared in local newspapers. The observations made in this chapter were drawn from such sources. In addition the author's visits to some of the institutions in Philippines, Malaysia and Singapore, and discussions with professional colleagues from these and other countries provided more information. Even in a country like Philippines where there is the Asian Institute of Management it was difficult to find literature and case studies on performance appraisal practices in Asian countries. This itself is an indicator of state of the existing appraisals and the neglect of this area by managers and the management profession in the past. In contrast, management literature from the West has been giving some attention to this area. For example, the Journal of Applied Psychology hardly has a number in the last three years that does not have atleast one article dealing appraisal related topics.

Singapore

Until recently, performance appraisal in most Singapore companies involved merely the filling out of confidential forms by supervisors. Appraisees (particularly busy managers) dreaded the year- end to fill several confidential report forms of assessment. Recognising the potential of open appraisal systems, the National Productivity Board of Singapore started promoting open appraisal systems through a series of seminars. The open appraisal systems that they have been promoting require a half-yearly or quarterly discussion of the employee's performance with the appraisee with a final end-of-year assessment. During the discussion the appraisee is told what is written about him and is given a chance to have his say on his supervisor's reports. Strengths and weaknesses are communicated. Both sides agree on the final assessment and joint action plans are drawn up to improve work effectiveness.[1]

The National Productivity Board of Singapore has been pursuing the use of open appraisal systems in the last 2-3 years by being in close touch with companies. In spite of this it appears that several organisations continue to have a closed system of appraisal. Some companies that have adopted open-appraisal to promote people-centred management are still struggling to over come the problems associated with such systems. In fact quite a few companies in Singapore did not have appraisal systems before 1980, until the National Wage Council recommended appraisals to be used by companies. Some of these companies hastily put to gether some appraisal forms and started using them.

From a study of performance appraisal methods in 120 organisations in Singapore, Joseph Putti of the National University of Singapore made the following observations:[2]

1. There is a lack of support from senior management for the design and implementation of appraisal systems. Managers still consider it as an unimportant aspect of their work.

---

1. "Job appraisal comes out into the open", The Strait Times, Singapore, February 23, 1983, p. 13.

2. Work appraisal through professorial eyes, Business Times, May 24, 1982.

2. There is a lack of coordination between personnel and other departments on appraisals.
3. Managers lack the training to participate in and use appraisals effectively.
4. Companies take a "copy cat" approach gathering several rating forms from other companies and try to combine them.
5. A good number of organisations were using some form of graphic rating method.

During early 1982 the Government of Singapore constituted a high powered steering committee for bringing about reforms in the personnel management philosophy and practices in the civil services. The government accepted the importance of employee centred philosophy with focus on long term career plans t bring the best out of civil services people and ensure a good man-to-job match.[3] A team visited London to study the personnel management practices of 'SHELL'. Subsequent to the report submitted by the team on SHELL's practices and their implications for personnel management in Singapore, many organisations are showing interest in using open systems of appraisal like the one used by SHELL, oriented to HRD philosophy.

SHELL people at all levels believe in a consultative and participative approach to management. This open easy management style encourages frank discussion between superior and subordinate in all matters, especially the performance and development potential of the supervisee.[4] SHELL has two annual staff reports - one on performance and another on development. The performance report is openly discussed with the subordinate who can record his comments and objections. The report on development is not generally shown. SHELL does not use assess ment by points or performance categorisation into "good", "excellent" etc. This is because they observed the ratings to be most often on the higher side. In the development report appraisal ranking of CEP (Currently Estimated Potential) is done by a team of those who have knowledge of the employee. This is facilitated by the SHELL's organisational culture of openness and consultation and heavy uses of matrix structures, task forces, study groups and presentations.

3.Civil Services with Human Face, The Straits Times, April 19, 1982.

4. It is the man that matters, The Straits Times, April 19, 1982.

Singapore Tobacco is one example of the changes being brought about in the appraisal systems followed by Singapore organisations.[5] For about 10 years they have been using two appraisal systems - one for management and another for the non-executive and non-bargainable staff. The managers were being. assessed on 17 factors (like job knowledge, organisation and planning skills, initiative, verbal expression, ability to motivate and train subordinates, etc.) on a 5-point scale (outstanding to poor). This system was replaced by descriptive reports with emphasis on joint work planning by managers and subordinates. In the old systems the second group were being assessed on seven traits (mental capacity, sense of responsibility, temperament, etc.). In the revised system work-related factors have been included replacing the traits. Employees are being trained to use the new system. The new systems also provide for a performance discussion between the appraiser and the appraisee. The Singapore Tobacco Company evolved the new system with the help of an external consultant who conducted a series of surveys and workshops before finally designing and adopting the new system.

ESSO (Singapore) is another organisation that has interesting personnel management practices. In their performance appraisal they give high importance to the time the appraisee spends on developing their subordinates in terms of giving directions, counselling and training.[6] The supervisor discusses with each subordinate his goals, reviews past work, decides whether targets have been met and whether the job could have been done better in other ways. These interviews are seen as good opportunities for feedback between supervisor and subordinate. The subordinate may suggest a transfer to another division or make other suggestions from the personnel growth stand point of view. Training needs are determined on the basis of appraisals. ESSO appraises potential of their employees separately.

The Singapore Automotive Engineering introduced an open system of appraisal recently.[7] It took for them a year of hard work to change over from confidential report form to an open system. In this system the employee is given two weeks' notice to psychologically and emotionally prepare himself for the appraisal interview. Every appraisee (even workers) is allowed to see how he has been rated and is given a chance

5. Work appraisal through professorial eyes, Business Times, (Singapore), May 24, 1982

6. ESSO takes a long-term view, Business Times, Singapore, February 28, 1983, p.3.

7.Away with form-filling ritual within a year, The Strait Times, Singapore, February 23, 1983, p.13.

to explain why he is not doing well or what he would like to do to improve his work. "This form of stock taking is done three times a year." In the beginning many appraisers tried to play the "good guy". Many workers were praised but seldom criticised. That was put right through constant reminders to appraisers that they would do more harm than good to their workers if their weaknesses were not highlighted and solved. The appraisal form is designed in such a way that the final evaluation is not done by the appraiser. The appraiser merely gives marks for certain factors considered important for doing a job well. The final scores are assigned on the basis of weightages of these factors. The workers were nervous and felt a little threatened about the open appraisal, but a trial run corrected that. Some supervisors complain that the appraisal interviews take too much of their time as such session lasted one to three hours. In the appraisal forms scope is provided for the appraisee to say about their jobs and the company's welfare officer follows-up with them subsequently.

Malaysia

The Malaysian situation is somewhat similar to that of the situation in India. The performance appraisal practices vary from annual confidential form of appraisal to fairly open systems being practised, by some companies (particularly multinationals). A great deal of debate and thinking has been in process on "what should constitute a good performance appraisal system". A number of seminars and workshops have been conducted in the last few years on this topic. Several private consulting organisations like CREDO, Malaysia, and professional training institutions like the Malaysian Institute of Management as well as government bodies like the Institute of Public Administration, Institute Bank, Bank Malaysia and the National Productivity Centre. The Malaysian government is already in the process of changing its appraisal systems from traditional trait based reports to more participative responsibility oriented and somewhat open systems of appraisal. However, it may take some time to fully implement and stabilise such systems.

Rao and Iqbal (1982) surveyed the appraisal practices of over 25 banks and financial institutions. From the results of this survey the following observations were made:

1. All the banks have some form or other of performance appraisal. However, almost all of them use appraisal for salary and reward administration. Its potential as a development mechanism is not being used by most of them.

2. In one of the banks, the appraiser is expected to counsel the appraisee at the end of the year in the presence of another senior officer. The purpose of this counselling is to ensure uniformity of standards. The appraisal ratings and comments are shown to the employee and he has to sign it. This appraisal is different from the appraisal form used for deciding increments. The appraisal form used for increment purposes is kept confidential. The main problem this organisation has been experiencing in its open appraisal system is the "defensiveness" of employees. During counselling, instead of trying to learn from their supervising officers, the employees tend to become defensive.
3. In another bank, the supervising officer and his boss sit together and rate their subordinates. The ratings are used mainly to decide increments and rewards, and the employees are informed of their weaknesses in the increment letters. This is a very impersonal way and this may be quite demotivating to an employee to get his weaknesses in writing at the end of the year. The possibility of human development taking place when such impersonal mechanisms are used is very much diminished.
4. In another bank, there are separate forms used for executives and clerks. The appraisal data are shared with the employee and his strengths and weaknesses are highlighted. He is also given an opportunity to make comments on the assessment.
5. One bank uses key job areas as a base on which performance is assessed. In this bank also, the appraisee is shown the assessment on him made by his manager and is encouraged to comment on it.
6. Another institution is using self-appraisal as a component of the performance appraisal. The form is initiated by the appraisee through a self-appraisal on the various aspects of his job, his training needs and an indication o the jobs he is interested in. His supervising officer comments on this and also grades the appraisee on several personality traits and attitudes. Then, there is a performance review discussion in the presence of another officer of a higher rank than the appraisee. However, employees from this bank feel that performance discussion is generally a one-way communication and it does not create a completely open climate.
7. Another organisation has started an open system of appraisal including counselling. However, it has not worked as well as they anticipated because the line managers were not trained in the new system, particularly in counselling skills.
8. The survey reveals that about 50 per cent of the banks are

continuing with the traditional confidential assessment system, and are not happy with this. There is a desire to change. The remaining 50 per cent are at different stages of having open systems of appraisal that may eventually contribute to staff development. The main indicator of this openness is showing the appraisal ratings to the appraisee and getting his comment.

9. Almost all banks use appraisal for reward administration. But very few use it for identification of training needs. In fact, in some organisations, the appraisal forms are not accessible to the training department. As a result, the training department does not get the opportunity to plan training programmes that might help improve performance in areas of weakness indicated by the appraisals.
10. A few organisations have performance feedback and very few have counselling. Those that have these systems may need to periodically reorient their line managers to understand the purposes and dynamics of counselling and make counselling an effective instrument.
11. A good practice that is prevailing in almost all the banks is performance rewarding through salary increments. Besides giving increases in salary, annual cash awards, promotions, sponsorship for overseas, field visits and conferences and giving higher responsibilities are rewards commonly used by the banks.
12. The Survey indicated that while rewards are given, there is very little attention paid to the way in which these are administered. Intimating to an employee of his salary increase for effective performance through a circular letter may not have the same impact as and when a senior executive calls him, points out the areas of his contributions, compliments him and then informs him, of the management decision to reward him. It appears that very few banks are practising this kind of a personalised reward system. As a result, much of the impact of reward is lost. If reward has to serve development goals, the person receiving the reward should know which of his behaviours or accomplishments are being complimented.

These trends are probably quite reflective of the appraisal situation in Malaysian industry also.

Other Countries

Philippine. is in the process of introducing several management systems and practices like the Management by Objectives, Management

Information Systems, Budgeting Financial Controls, etc. There is a high degree of awareness of the need to introduce professional management in government systems. Even in the government separate functionaries are being appointed to handle the personnel management development functions. For example, the Ministry of Education, Culture and Sports has a separate office to look after the Personnel Management and Development function headed by an Assistant Secretary. Innovative schemes are being adopted to promote competence and high performance among employees. For example the Ministry of Education has a scheme for promoting competent and innovative teachers who desire to remain as teachers because they are not interested in handling supervisory and administrative functions. The scheme designed is such that the teachers can equal the salary of senior level schools administrators without being appointed as Principal I, II, III, etc. They are called "Master-Teachers" and the "Master-Teacher" concept is being adopted to give recognition to teachers who excel in performance. There are two appraisal systems in use by the Education Ministry keeping in line with the guidelines issued by the Civil Services Commission. The Performance Appraisal System for Teachers (PAST) attempts to assess each teacher in relation to four areas; (i) learners' achievement, (ii) teachers' competence, (iii) teachers' personality and human relations; and (iv) additional factors. In relation to student achievement the specific functions of the teachers are defined and planned targets are set jointly by the supervisor and the teacher in the beginning of the year itself. The teacher is assessed in relation to these. Teacher competence is measured on a number of variables including the efforts he made to create national consciousness among students, to develop himself professionally, to do community services, to manage records etc. His personality and human relations are assessed on personal qualities like morality, integrity etc. Specific indicators are prepared for these. The assessment has to be reviewed and signed by both the rater and the ratee. The ratee can express his disagreement. Different factors (like planning, organising, promptness in submitting reports, decision-making, leadership, etc. are as sessed for the administrator groups although other components of the system are same as PAST.

In Philippines outstanding performers in civil services are rewarded with promotions and salary increases. Because of this personnel strive hard to give best of themselves and achieve goals of their unit or organisation.

Performance appraisal practices in Pakistan appear to be still traditional using confidential report formats. However, innovations and changes can be found here and there even in public institutions and government organisations. An example is the appraisal system used to appraise faculty members of the Institute of Education and Research, Allama Iqbal Open University, Islamabad. Tasks are assigned to faculty members at the beginning of the year. Faculty and the Director of the Institute meet to decide the targets to be achieved. A self-assessment proforma is given to each faculty member, who at the end of the year are expected to complete it and present it in a faculty meeting indicating his tasks, achievements, failures, causes and ratings he would give himself. The exercise continues over a few weekly meetings. The Director gives his own self-assessment at the last meeting and also gives his impressions about the overall performance of the faculty. He goes on to give a general description of the faculty in such a way that each faculty member can make out as to how he is being rated. Faculty have been found to work hard to achieve good ratings. Those getting poor ratings can meet the Director separately and ask for assignments where they are likely to do better. The faculty of this centre feel that this process helps them tremendously to develop themselves.

Although not an Asian country it might be appropriate to mention here an appraisal system being followed in the Soviet Union by one of the companies. Elektrosila, a heavy electrical works at Leningrad has an interesting system of managerial appraisal by their subordinates.[8] The company has some 20,000 employees. A few years ago the top management decided that the subordinates should be involved in assessing their boss's managerial ability because the company recognised that the opinion of the superiors alone was frequently inadequate. For example one workshop chief of considerable ability was consistently rated badly by his boss with whom he did not get on well. After his peers and subordinates rated him his potential was seen more clearly and subsequently he got promoted. Elektrosila used a 30-item appraisal questionnaire to assess the manager's political consciousness, self-discipline and attitude to work, his level of technical and financial knowledge organisational ability, moral qualities, communication ability, general style of management, authority etc. Questionnaires on each of the firm's 500 managers are completed by 20 people, including his superiors, several colleagues at the same level who know his work, and a number of his subordinates. The identities of all taking part are kept secret to prevent them from feeling inhibited. Each question's score from all 20 questionnaires is added together with the aid of a computer to create a "socio-gram" of the manager that indicates his strengths and weaknesses.

8.Soviet Workers appraise their managers, International Management, December 1977, pp.51-52.

The appraisal committee uses the socio-gram to determine the areas where he needs to improve. Training needs are thus, identified from this. This technique has been found to aid development of the employee as well as help the organisation in making various personnel decisions. The system has worked so well at Elektrosila that a number of other enterprises in the Soviet Union are following it subsequently.

Performance appraisal in Japanese organisations need to be understood in the context of Zen Philosophy and the Japanese Management Styles. Performance appraisals are so integrated into organisational life that it is difficult to isolate and talk about appraisal systems appraisal mechanisms. Appraisal of individual performance is underplayed in Japanese organisations and group work and organisational identity are promoted. At the same time human needs are so well attended to through a variety of practices like life-long employment etc., that individual employees need not bother much about the psychological, social and economic needs and focus their attention on performance. Describing Zen Philosophy Pascale and Athos (1982) remark - "the Japanese see each individual as having economic, social, psychological and spiritual needs, much as we do when we step back and think about it. But Japanese executives assume that it is their task to attend to much more of the whole of the person, and not leave so much to other institutions (such as government, family, or religious ones). And they believe it is only when the individuals' needs are well met within the subculture of a corporation that they can largely be freed for productive work that is in larger part outstanding."[9]

The Japanese accept ambiguity, uncertainty, and imperfection as much more of a given in organisational life and this results in dealing with each other in an entirely different ways than that of others. As a result of this, egoism and defensiveness are likely to be much less. Performance feedback is smooth and indirect.... "the Japanese see themselves as far more interde pendent. They are prepared to make far greater investments in people and in the skills necessary to be effective with others.[10]

The following personnel principles outlined in a manual of Matsushita Electric illustrates the importance given to people and their development in Japanese organisations.[11]

9.Pascale, R.T. and Athos, A.G., The Art of Japanese Manage ment, London, Penguin Books, 1982.

10.Ibid, p. 89.

11.Personnel Principles, Matsushita Electric, 1957.

1. It must be realised and accepted that the source of all good management rests in the personnel ... our people are our most important asset.
2. Managers must be sincere and show a warm concern for their personnel. Falsity and pretense can only buy mistrust and lay the foundation for a future loss of confidence.

No matter how difficult the encounter, is sincerity must be maintained and, if it is, the other person can certainly not help but definitely influenced by it. This will be the source from which a strong bond of trust will emerge.

In addition to sincerity it is important to have a genuine concern for your subordinate.... If you are really thinking about the other person's future progress, improvement and stability, you must treat severely all that should be so treated, but all the while demonstrating your concern by explaining patiently and completely why whatever is being done is being done, until the matter is satisfactorily understood. In this way a mutual warmth will grow up between you.

3. Without using our power of authority, we must work to gain cooperation by trust and understanding.... Realising that we have common goals, it is important that we influence people by standing on understanding and trust. To gain this position it is necessary to say all that should be said and listen attentively to what your subordinates have to say, so that by discussion and deepening understanding, everyone can be satisfied.
4. In order for the individual to develop, we must supply appropriate demands.

.... The managers must not forget to provide appropriate demands to each of his subordinates within the limits of their abilities, so that each is encouraged and stimulated to actively participate in the creative process.

5. Each person must be given some responsibility and authority.

..... Mistakes should be looked upon as a kind of tuition fee. We must see that the person realise the cause for the error so that it can be turned into a learning experience.

6. Harmonious cooperation is essential for good management..... To encourage this, small gatherings will be held atleast once a month at which each person may air his complaints, ideas and demands and submit them for thorough discussion.

..... The purpose of these meetings will be to deal with all proposals which arise thoroughly, respectfully and satisfactorily. It is important, therefore, without regard to rank or position, to be very honest and frank in our discussions, always showing respect for the other persons' opinions, always aiming towards the furtherance of good understanding among all employees.

"Part of the complex of intertwined features of the Japanese organisation are approaches to evaluation and promotion. (Ouchi, 1982, p.22)." Formal evaluation and promotion is a very slow process in Japanese companies. "The Japanese organisation takes in only young people who are still in formative stages of life, subjects them to multiple group memberships, and inculcates in them the kind of devotion to co-workers that one sees in the United States Marines. It is not external evaluations or rewards that matter in such a setting, it is the intimate, subtle, and complex evaluation by one's peers - people who cannot be fooled - which is paramount" (Ibid., p.25).

Using Ouchi's theory Z based on Japanese Style of Management, Starling (1982) suggests the following five features that might provide insights into how performance appraisal systems can be designed to fit into a smoothly running organisation.

1. Acceptance of the subjective-individuals want to identify with the organisation, but identification can occur only if the purpose of the organisation is linked to spiritual values like service, fairness, harmony, betterment, courtesy, humility and gratitude. "Shared values" is a great facilitator for getting things done.
2. Recognising the importance of interdependence - i.e. of relying on others for team work. Independence in Japanese organisations means selfishness. Japanese organisation charts show collective units and not individual positions. As a result managers who rise to the top also treat individual employees with respect and trust and possess skills for committee work and consensus building.
3. Employees should be willing to go long periods without a major promotion or formal evaluation.
4. Performance feedback should be smooth and continuous. Mentor-protege relationship should be encouraged. Mentors should teach their protege how to be effective in the organisation.
5. Delink the performance appraisal from compensation.

In sum, this brief survey of appraisal systems in different countries indicates that there is a good deal of awakening in different countries on the need for paying attention to people and their performance. It looks as though organisations want to move in the direction of Z organisations. In order to move in that direction a new culture needs to be created - a culture that encourages openness, trust, mutuality, collaboration and team work. Appraisal systems are still not being seen as potential mechanisms for promoting such a cultural change. In countries like Japan where there is already such a culture existing appraisal becomes a part of the process and one does not need to talk of "appraisal systems" but talk more in terms of "organisational culture", "values", "personnel philosophy" etc. The success of open appraisal systems therefore seems to be when they cease to exit as formats and systems but quite alive as norms, culture values and processes. Organisations have to go a long way to reach this goal. The movement has begun now only in some of the Asian countries and a few are yet to begin.

Chapter 18

MAKING PERFORMANCE APPRAISALS WORK

PERFORMANCE APPRAISAL systems are not going to be successful in our country for some more time to come. For that matter performance appraisals have not succeeded anywhere in the world if the indicators of success are 100 per cent timely returns of forms and 100 per cent satisfaction on the part of employees with their appraisals. As long as human beings are going to be assessed by human beings certain amount of subjectivity can never be eliminated. Appraisers would continue to assess their appraisees in the light of their own experiences, perceptions, understanding, insights values, and attitudes. As no two persons' perspectives would be the same, there are always likely to be differences in assessment even when they assign the same rating (number) to the appraisee. So long as such differences exist appraisees would continue to be dissatisfied with their appraisers although they may be highly satisfied and defend themselves as appraisers. Hence there can never be a 100 per cent satisfaction with appraisals. Such dissatisfaction with performance appraisals is likely to be high in organisations that link appraisals with salary and other forms of rewards. This dissatisfaction is likely to be even higher when sophisticated and open systems of appraisals are used. This is because sophisticated systems raise managerial expectations in unnoticeable ways. Most employees would not like to admit to themselves or to others that their performance has not been reward-worthy. So everyone expects some form of recognition. Those who have been ignored for some reason or the other also start expecting some form of recognition when new appraisal systems are introduced. Their yardstick for measuring the goodness of the new appraisal system is the extent to which their personal expectations are met. In those cases where such expectations are not met there may be more dissatisfaction. In cases where their expectations are met, managers rarely speak loudly. But in cases where there is dissatisfaction employees may express loudly, clearly, and openly partly because the new appraisal system also claims to promote openness. So what gets talked about in the organisational grapevine is the disappointment with the new system much more than the good things it has done. At intellectual level and in discussions among themselves and with consultants while managers agree that the new systems have brought in a lot of role clarity, more interpersonal as well as organisational communication that aids their efficiency and effectiveness, more understanding between them and their bosses as well as subordinates, more of problem-solving, more understanding of their own strengths and weaknesses etc., at emotional level several of them may continue to feel ambivalent or negative. This is because emotionally rewards and recognition of their work are more important and the new appraisal system by itself may not be able to fulfil this need. In order to counter this problem if an organisation decides to delink appraisal from rewards and decides to use it only for development purposes, managers take it very easy and do not participate actively in appraisal process resulting in poor return of forms to HRD department. It appears that for Indian Managers even at top levels growth needs appear to be of much less important and emotionally less meaningful that recognition. Somewhere in our organisational life the development needs have been starved and killed and recognition needs have been overplayed with. Given this situation it is safer to conclude that performance appraisal systems are not likely to succeed in our country for some more time to come if satisfaction and return of forms are taken as indicators. Managerial maturity has to come to the level where managers start feeling the need for developing their capability as managers much more intensely than their need for "recognition" and "status".

How do we reach that stage? The process has already begun. A decade ago we rarely talked of performance appraisal as a means for employee development. Today most organisations are restating their objectives of performance appraisals to include development. New appraisal systems like the one described in this book are being experimented and have even taken roots in some organisations. The next decade is going to be a decade of transition. More and more organisations are likely to be experimenting with new appraisal systems. It is important to manage this transition. In order to manage this transition we should recognise the problems that are likely to arise during this period. In this chapter an attempt is made to highlight some of these problems of transition that are likely to be faced by organisations changing from closed and control-oriented to open and development-oriented appraisals. These problems if not recognised and talked well may prevent organisations from effective use of such a potential instrument like performance appraisal.

These problems can be conceived in terms of top management's response to the new appraisal systems, managerial responses to the new appraisal systems, role of personnel and HRD departments in relation to appraisal systems, union reactions to appraisal systems, and organisational responses to the appraisal systems.

Top Management Response to New Appraisal Systems

For the new appraisal systems to be successful a high degree of commitment is required from the top. The following should be recognised by the top management:

1. First of all the corporate managers and top level decision-makers should recognise the link between development of the capabilities of their employees and organisational growth and dynamism.
2. They should recognise the need for paying special attention to and making investment of developing their human resources in directions that facilitate the achievement of organisational objectives and growth plans.
3. They should recognise the extent to which human capabilities can be developed and multiplied and the condition required to be created in the organisaiton for nurturing the development and utilisation of human capabilities.
4. They should recognise their responsibility in humanisation of organisational environment to make the employees feel that the organisation where they work and spend a large part of their working life is theirs that it is their second family, and that they are taken note of, valued and cared for.
5. They should encourage their managers at all levels and particularly those at senior levels to recognise their hitherto neglected role of development of their subordinates and should release a part of their time for investment on human resources development. Particularly during the transition period they should be able to contain a substantial investment of managerial time for this purpose.
6. They should be willing to encourage upward communication in the organisation, willing to receive negative feedback, view such feedback with understanding and use it for corrective action.
7. They should be willing to examine their personnel policies and streamline them, if necessary, to be in consonance with their human resources development philosophy and policies.
8. They should have the capability to recognise and appreciate the not easily noticeable change. This is because the positive consequences of adopting a HRD philosophy and introducing new

appraisal systems may not be noticeable in terms of visible symptoms like improved productivity, profits, cost-reduction etc., in short periods. There may be less visible changes like more problem-solving at different levels, more healthy interpersonal relationships; increased managerial confidence, more initiative, better managerial action, strong superior subordinate relationships, less tension, more role clarity etc. Such changes may not occur in short periods of time and may not also be noticeable unless proved.

9. They should be willing to state openly and clearly the culture they want to establish in the organisation, the values they want to promote and the processes they would like to encourage. They should then promote this by setting personal examples for others to follow.

Managerial Response to New Appraisal Systems

If the new appraisal systems do not work, it is most likely to be attributable to the managers. The same managers who do not like confidential report form of appraisals, who express their preference for open systems that give them a feedback about their strengths and weaknesses, as seen by their reporting officers, fail to use them properly to their advantage when they actually come. Managers tend to sabotage their own development when opportunities actually come. If new appraisal systems have to succeed, the managers at every level should recognise their own role in making them successful. Managers have been found to take the following instances in organisations that change their appraisal systems. While expressing views and apprehensions are understandable, taking negative stances prevent the managers from experiencing the full advantages of the system and benefiting themselves.

Stance 1: "Our organisational culture should change before we introduce such systems. We are not yet ready for an open system."

Managers who take such a stance perceive that there is not enough of openness and trust in the organisation to be able to discuss performance openly with the appraisee. Partly it is a reflection of their own insecurity in discussing the performance of their subordinates with them or a lack of faith in their seniors to give performance feedback without hurting the feelings. This is a very understandable situation. Managers should recognise how their own insecurity or lack of trust is leading them to view the implementation of the system suspiciously or with pessimism.

It is true that certain minimum level of openness and trust is required to use development-oriented open systems. He does one build trust and openness? If one has to wait for the day when such a climate exists, the day may never come. The best way to create a climate of openness and trust is by being open and trusting. The new system should be taken as an opportunity to initiate a new culture in the organisation or to strengthen the already existing culture rather than to wait for a day of change which may never come if the managers do not work for it.

A related issue in this context is "whether to introduce systems first to initiate certain new processes or to initiate the processes themselves first and introduce systems later." Some argue that before new appraisal formats are introduced the managers should be helped to initiate counselling, interpersonal feedback and communication etc., processes. Only after such processes are established should the new systems be introduced. While there is some merit in this argument, the counselling, interpersonal feedback and communication processes do not stand by themselves. They have to take place in a context and such a context has to be provided by the development-oriented appraisal system itself with all its components. If counselling and communication processes are introduced independently, then also managers are likely to ask the same question - "Why this now?" Even for introducing these some formalisation has to be done. So why not introduce the entire system in its perspective rather than bit by bit? No doubt there are problems and difficulties associated with initiating new processes through systems but the alternatives are time-consuming and are not encouraging. However the possibilities are not ruled out completely. Particularly in highly traditional organisation some processes may be introduced first before systems involving process change are introduced.

Stance 2 : "Top management is not committed" or "There should be more commitment from the top"

Managers who take this stand generalise either out of their limited observations or speak out of their past frustrations and disappointment with top management. If occasionally someone at the top is unhappy that things are not moving and too much attention is being paid to performance appraisals, immediately the executives use this as an excuse for not spending enough time on appraisals. Managers should recognise what could be expected from the top management in realistic terms for systems like this. The corporate management is not in the business of making appraisals successful. They would have a number of other things to attend to in order to make the organisation moving. If managers expect them to take a high degree of interest in appraisals, their expectations are unrealistic. Top management need not (and in fact should not) go on issuing circulars asking executives to complete their appraisals on time. Nor would they be spending their time properly if they start telephoning those who have not completed appraisals. It is the job of the personnel department.

In one organisation when the new system was introduced several executives were doubting the seriousness of the top management. In that organisation the chairman himself was the first to use the new appraisal system and complete his appraisals and counselling discussions. Not knowing it they continued to delay their appraisals looking for instructions from him. The Chairman himself was upset and started wondering whether the system should be continued given the poor response of managers.

This illustrates clearly how managers can kill innovations that are likely to benefit them by looking more for the commitment of others rather than showing their non-commitment. If the top management shows a high level of commitment then managers may say - "It is the top management's system. They are interested in it, but why should I be interested?" Thus, whatever the top management does can be held against the system. Unless executives realise what they are doing to themselves in this process the systems are not likely to succeed.

A related concern is when managers say that "such systems should start from the top". No doubt that the senior and top level managers should start using the system. However, it should not come in the way of others starting it. Unless efforts are made simultaneously at all levels it may be difficult to stabilise the system. Managers should learn to ask the question "how can I use this system for my own learning and growth?" rather than asking "how others are reacting to this system?"

Stance 3 : "Promotion policies, reward policies, transfer policies and support mechanisms should be streamlined before introducing this system."

When new performance appraisal systems are introduced, they are introduced with certain purposes. These purposes may or may not have nay relationship with other personnel policies. Normally they do have a relationship but not necessarily always. For example where new PA systems are introduced as a part of an integrated HRD plan. potential appraisals are separated and rewards are delinked. Promotion decisions are to be made mainly on the basis of potential appraisal taking into consideration performance appraisal reports also. A development oriented performance appraisal is very much linked with training, job-rotation, placement, promotion, transfer and such other decisions. The appraisal data provide inputs to these. Unless the inputs are generated other systems may be difficult to be streamlined. While top management and personnel departments should take note of this and act on this, managers should be patient. They should not put the cart before the horse and make streamlining other things as a pre-condition for introducing new PA systems.

Stance 4 : "Top management's style should change."

In some organisations where some of the top level managers have authoritarian or coercive styles, managers start arguing that these styles should change for making the new system successful. Any manager's styles cannot change overnight. Styles are consistent patterns of behaviour acquired over time. Awareness of such consistencies and an examination of their impact on the organisational health and morale is the first step in change. Receiving feedback from those affected by the styles helps in creating such awareness. Defensiveness is likely to be higher at the top levels than below. So change may take a longer time. In fact, change may be required at every level and instead of waiting for others to change, managers should start the process themselves at their own levels.

Stance 5 : "Boss subordinate distance may decrease resulting in loss of control over subordinates."

Quite often open systems of appraisal are interpreted as promoting "softer" approaches to deal with employees. It is not really so. This feeling arises because of the softness and understanding (empathy, acceptance, listening to feelings and concerns, etc.) required to be shown by managers in counselling. Counselling is a part of the appraisal process and appraisal itself is a mechanism of achieving some of the process objectives. Either counselling or performance appraisal are not substitutes for "executive action" or "administrative action". If erring employees have to be dealt with administratively or through executive actions like warning the employees, pointing out their defects, transferring them etc., they should continue to do so. Just because there is a new system of appraisal, all other forms of human resources management should not be suspended. In fact the new appraisal system should facilitate the effective use of "executive" and "administrative" actions. Managers should be clear about this and should continue to exercise their executive powers whenever needed. Task- orientation combined with human touch is likely to strengthen the respect and commitment of subordinates to their bosses rather than weaken it.

Stance 6 : "KPAs is another form of achieving business goals of the organisation and the new appraisal system is another way of making us work hard."

Employees who ask such questions seem to be shying away from hard work or are suspicious of the intentions behind the introduction of the system. The purpose of KPAs is to bring about more role clarity and have a common understanding between the appraiser and the appraisee from the beginning. The purpose of identifying objectives is to establish mutually acceptable work standards that may reduce subjectivity in final assessment. This forms the basic framework (task framework) in relation to which development efforts (identifying capability gaps, training need etc.) are to be directed. Without these a sharper focus on the capability requirements to perform various tasks cannot be achieved. The process certainly may result in better performance over time but performance improvements come only after the individual acquires more capabilities. So individual gains first and organisational later!

KPAs are also often confused as business goals themselves. It is necessary to recognise that KPAs are "individualised role related task priorities" and not the business goals themselves. They focus on individual efforts and challenges. They are individualised "means goals" or "task related process goals" that may lead to achievement of business goals but not business goals themselves.

Stance 7 : "KPAs are not easily understood. They may become too much binding and kill the creativity and flexibility. There may also be problems in the event of the appraisee or the appraiser getting transferred."

Sometimes there may be confusion in relation to Key Performance Areas Managers may not be able to distinguish in some cases performance areas from result areas. In Key Performance Areas the stress is more on the effort and the nature of effort to be put in by the appraisee in relation to the various critical or important tasks he is to perform. The performance areas should provide clarity to the appraisee and the appraiser about the various tasks to be accomplished by the appraisee and establish standards against which the performance of the appraisee may be assessed more-objectively. It must be remembered that KPAs are means, means for gaining increased understanding about one's role and about the areas where one should put more efforts. Any time a boss observes his subordinate during the performance period, he should be able to relate the activities of his subordinate to one of the KPAs or objectives. KPAs are flexible. If, during the period of performance, some urgent and unplanned tasks come up, both the appraiser and the appraisee can change the Key Performance Areas and identify new areas on which both of them may agree. Once identified, KPAs are not likely to change unless such emergencies take place. However, what is more important is a joint understanding between the boss and the subordinate. As long as they have this understanding, they can keep on changing the priorities according to the task requirements. If the appraisee changes, the appraiser has to work out new KPAs with the new appraisee. If the appraisee has worked with the appraiser before he changes for a substantial period in a performance year (about 4, 5 or 6 months) then the appraiser can complete his assessment of the appraisee before the appraisee changes. If the appraiser changes, the appraisee will continue to have the same KPAs. However, as soon as a new appraiser comes, the new appraiser and the appraisee should get together and the appraisee should brief the new appraiser in relation to the KPAs identified with the previous appraiser. Promotions and transfers are normal phenomena in large organisations. Organisation cannot stop taking transfer and other kinds of personnel decisions to suit the requirements of the appraisal system. The normal organisational life will go on and the appraisal system should be able to respond to these changes. That is why enough of flexibility should be built into the system. The important thing is joint understanding - understanding of the performance areas - and the appraiser and the appraisee should not become slaves in the hands of what they themselves have identified for clarity purposes, KPAs are instruments, but not ends in themselves. Managers should recognise this.

Stance 8 : "Objectives are not always quantifiable and behaviour dimensions are not easily understood"

Some of the objectives may not be quantifiable. Particularly in service areas, it may be difficult to set quantitative targets. However, it is useful to have some common understanding about the standards of performance between the appraiser and the appraisee. Quantification per se is not important. Quantification is done mainly to have the same kind of understanding between the appraiser and the appraisee so that the objectivity in the final assessment increases. Studies have shown that wherever quantification of objectives is possible, the agreement between the appraiser and the appraisee in the final assessment was high. In relation to the question on behaviour dimensions, it is important that both the appraisee and the appraiser have a common understanding of what is expected from the appraisee in relation to each of the behaviour dimensions. The appraiser should point out to the appraisee at the time of identifying KPAs itself the kind of expectations he has from the appraisee on each of the behaviour dimension listed in the form. He should also point out the opportunities the organisation offers to the appraisee to show these behaviours. The focus should be on helping the employee develop behaviours that contribute to the employee as well as organisational growth.

Stance 9 : "Nobody admits his weaknesses. So open systems of appraisal fail to develop people."

This is very understandable concern of managers. This concern comes from the fact that the appraisal system has performance analysis as an important component. Under performance analysis, the appraisee is expected to identify personal as well as environmental facilitating and inhibiting factors. In the process of identifying the personal inhibiting factors (i.e., weaknesses of the appraisee), some managers feel that their subordinates do not admit their weaknesses. If the subordinate does not admit his weakness, it either means that he does not see what the appraiser sees as a weakness or that the subordinate is being defensive. Identifying personal inhibiting factors does not mean that every appraisee should keep on exhibiting and stating all his weaknesses. It is quite human to hide one's weakness. However, if the performance appraisal can stimulate thinking on the part of the appraisee about his weaknesses, it has done its job as the individual would then look for more data and subsequently he is likely to try and improve himself. Managers should not be overconcerned that their subordinates do not admit their weaknesses. They should encourage their subordinates to speak of their strengths and slowly once a climate of trust and emotional acceptance is built up, the appraisees are likely to come to the point of talking of their weaknesses. If the subordinate does not admit his weaknesses, it may also partly be a failure on the part of the manager to build a climate. Managers who insist that their subordinates should admit their weaknesses run the risk of damaging their relationships which are important for productivity and healthy climate. Managers as appraisers can give feedback to stimulate self-reflection on the part of the appraisee and leave it for the appraisee to use it.

Stance 10 : "Self-appraisal is Self-glorification"

Studies have shown in the past that in open systems of appraisal, there is quite a bit of leniency in appraisal rating. When a person is asked to appraise himself, it is quite likely that depending upon his own personality and his own emotional security, he may over or under project himself. Let us imagine that an employee over-projects himself. It is an employee over-projects himself, the appraiser always has an opportunity to point this out to the appraisee. Even if he does not point this out to the appraisee, once an employee over-projects himself, soon he may realise that he has raised the expectation of his appraiser and that he has to meet these expectations subsequently. This is something useful both for the appraiser as well as the appraisee. The purpose of self-appraisal is to ensure that the appraiser records a number of things which he has done or accomplished and about which the appraiser may not be aware of. If that is so, then the appraisee has every right to bring to the notice of the appraiser a number of things which may look as self- glorification. A healthy way of looking at this is to say that "there is more communication and more understanding" rather than to say that "there is self-glorification" taking place. Who does not want his strengths to be recognised by taking place. Who does not want his strengths to be recognised by his seniors? If a manager wants his strengths to be recognised by his seniors, he should be willing to recognise the strengths of his subordinates.

Stance 11 : "People tend to rate leniently in open appraisals. So appraisal ratings tend to get inflated."

This is true. Several research studies conducted in other countries have shown this. One may not be very much worried about such leniency in ratings. In a development-oriented appraisal system, ratings are means but not ends in themselves. Ratings are means to exchange expectations, to exchange evaluations and judgements. Ratings form a basis on which more and more communication may take place between an appraiser and the appraisee. Ratings stimulate discussions. Quite often managers get worried when there is a difference between the ratings of an appraiser and the appraisee, that there is something wrong going on with them or with the system. This worry is unnecessary. In fact when there is a difference between self-appraisal ratings and the ratings assigned by the boss, it may be indicator of a healthy climate existing between the appraiser and the appraisee. This shows that they can have differences and sort these differences out themselves. When people rate themselves or each other leniently, and that helps in establishing a cordial atmosphere between them, we can tolerate the leniency in the ratings. However, problems may arise if these ratings have to be used for personnel decisions. That is why it is necessary to examine and see if a different form of appraisal is required for making personnel decisions.

Stance 12 : "Training needs are not met by the organisation in spite of doing serious exercise and identifying them, taking pains"

Some managers complain that in spite of their mentioning the training needs in the new appraisal system, the organisation has not done anything to take care of them. They quote this as an example of lack of seriousness on the part of the top management. It is important to recognise that no organisation can meet completely the training needs expressed by all its employees. Training budgets are somewhat limited. Only certain kinds of training programmes that fit into organisational priorities are possible in some organisations. Of course, some organisations have so huge training budgets that they can afford to organise more training programmes for their employees than what their employees ask. Expression of training needs should not be taken automatically as a right on the part of the employee for training. If training needs are not identified and expressed, the organisation would not have an opportunity to meet these. But if the training needs are identified, it does not mean the organisation should meet each of these, nor does it mean that the organisation will be able to meet all of these. Managers should recognise the limitation their organisations may have in meeting the training needs. In addition our understanding of the technology of identifying training needs has not come to such an extent that we are able to say definitely what is required and what is important, when and to what degree.

Stance 13 : "I take trouble to complete my appraisal follow meticulously whatever the appraisal guidelines say. Once I complete and send my forms up, I do not hear anything from anybody. I do not even know if any one looks at my forms. This discourages me from investing more time in the next appraisal."

Some managers, when they do not hear anything from their reviewing officer or from the personnel HRD department, start getting disappointed. Such managers seem to have high expectations from their reviewing officers or from personnel departments. A few of them probably are merely seeking reassurance from someone that everything is all right. Reporting officers should be sensitive to such expectations and should communicate any remarks or suggestions made by reviewing officers. At the same time managers should realise that performance appraisal is essentially a process between them and their appraisers or appraisees. All that happens should happen between them and should be happening between them. The reviewing officers or the personnel/HRD departments come into picture only in problem cases, for training needs and for other development decisions about which the appraisee may hear once in a while. Reviewing officers may not review each individual case. So managers should not be concerned about what is happening to their forms. If they have some expectations in this regard they should voice these to their appraisers and take initiative in getting to know more about what is happening to their forms. It is possible that the appraisal forms are not collected by the personnel or HRD departments in some organisations where the appraisal is left entirely between the appraiser and the appraisee.

Stance 14 : "Other systems have not worked in this organisation. They become rituals over time. How can this work?"

Any dynamic organisation is constantly alive to new developments and technology and may be involved in trying out new technology, structure, systems, work methods and so on. Generally when changes are introduced people talk about it a lot - particularly if the changes affect them directly. In the event of uncertainty of outcomes, they are even likely to resist the change. The success or failure of a system like the one described here may vary from dyad (appraiser-appraisee) study conducted at the Indian Institute of Management, Ahmedabad indicated that when systems like these are implemented, the extent to which they were utilised and the benefits derived varied from department to department depending on the leadership styles of the heads of these departments, the organisational climate existing in these departments etc. (Nagabrahmam, 1980). In another internal study conducted in a large private sector company a large percentage of managers opined that the system is not working well in the company. However, when asked to indicate whether they themselves are using the system well, almost all of them stated that they have benefited a great deal from it personally. This experience indicates that perceptions of managers about organisational experiences are likely to be highly biased and mostly based on rumours. Those having negative experiences may be few but they spread the wrong message fast. In one company that introduced a new open system of performance appraisal, when a survey was conducted after a few years of its introduction, about 50 per cent rated that they benefited from it, for another 45 per cent it did not make any difference but about 5 per cent of them said that their relationships with their boss or subordinate were strained. However, most of the employees in the organisation perceived that the system created more problems than solved. This was because the 5 per cent that had experiences went round talking about it and spreading the negative side whereas each of the 5 per cent that had useful experience thought that the experience is only limited to them individually and kept quiet. Managers should learn to measure the success or failure of systems of this kind at their own levels rather than looking for generalities in the organisation. When this happens, the question of the systems not working may not arise, because similar systems have not worked in the past. Those in the top management or in the personnel and HRD departments are there to take care of these issues.

Personnel/HRD Department's Response to New Appraisal Systems

Successful implementation of new appraisal systems also depends to a great degree on the personnel and HRD departments. Most often the responsibility for initiating and monitoring the implementation of new appraisal systems is given to these departments. The following responses on the part of these departments are likely to facilitate effective implementation of these systems:

1. The managers of these departments should have a thorough understanding of the new systems and should have a high degree of commitment to it. They should have much more conceptual clarity than what the line managers have and should attempt to practise the new systems even before they are used by the line managers.
2. They should anticipate employee resistance and be prepared to break this resistance through persistent efforts.
3. While the effectiveness with which ultimately these systems are implemented depends on the line managers, and may vary from manager to manager, personnel and HRD departments can be instrumental in helping the managers in effective implementa-

tion. For this purpose the Personnel and HRD staff may do the following :

a) Initiate a process of education for managers about the new appraisal systems, its objectives etc., and help them develop skills required for effective implementation through orientation programmes etc.
b) Be available to assist the line managers in implementation.
c) Take initiative and keep contacting line managers during KPA identification and counselling times.
d) Monitor the system by maintaining information about the progress of implementation and taking corrective action.
e) Keep counselling to line managers about how their appraisal ratings have been used for various personnel decisions.
f) Compile and use performance analysis for organisation development purposes by communicating to the top management organisational constraints identified by employees in their appraisal.
g) Preparing supportive personnel policies, getting them approved by the top management and implementing them.
h) Acting on the training needs identified and developmental suggestions made in the appraisal forms and communicating back to reporting officers wherever the personnel department cannot comply with the suggestions and recommendations made by the line managers.

4. The personnel and HRD departments are likely to be the targets of criticism during transition time. The managers of these departments should recognise this and should be able to contain this. A great degree of patience is required on their part. They should not get easily discouraged when line managers as well as the top management criticise them. At the same time they should be open to suggestions and should be willing to make changes when needed.

Union Responses to Performance Appraisals

Officers' unions exist only in a few organisations. Whenever they exist, they have an important role to play in making appraisal systems successful. In fact in organisations that still have traditional confidential forms of appraisals, officers' unions can play an important role in pressurising the top management to have a HRD outlook and change the appraisal systems to encourage employee development. There are instances where the officers' associations have raised such demands. Since the new appraisal systems are good for the employees and aim at promoting their development, the unions and associations should be happy to have such systems and even demand them from top management.

Strategic Considerations in Introducing New Appraisal Systems

Change of appraisal systems should be carefully planned. Organisations having traditional trait based confidential report systems should prepare themselves a great deal before they go in for open systems of appraisal. The employees may not be able to respond well for sudden changes. Several strategic options are available for introducing change. Some of these are outlined below:

1. Introducing Change in the Systems Step-by-Step all Through the Organisation

In this strategy, the organisation may make modifications in the appraisal system step by step over a period of time. For example, in the initial years trait based assessment may be supplemented with performance based assessment (using PAs or KPAs). After some period of time self-appraisal could also be introduced. Subsequently performance analysis could be introduced. A few years later counselling could be introduced. Finally the system could be made partly open or semi-confidential. This kind of change may take a few years. However the dimensions on which performance assessment would be available for personnel decisions will remain the same from the time the first change has been made (i.e. KPAs, managerial qualities, behaviour dimensions etc.).

2. Introducing Change Level-by-Level in the Managerial Hierarchy

In this strategy the new system could be introduced for a particular level of managers in the initial stages and slowly it could be extended upwards and downwards to all officers. In such a case it is useful to start at higher levels of the hierarchy because at higher levels the number of managers to be oriented to the system is generally small and more attention could be paid in the initial stages to help the managers gain a thorough understanding of the system.

This strategy of introduction is recommended if the organisation is adopting a system which is totally different from the existing system.

3. Introducing Change Department-by-Department or Area-by-Area

In this strategy the entire organisation is divided under different departments, or geographic units on the basis of the nature of work they do, on the basis of departmental levels they have or on the basis of geographical proximities. The appraisal system in its totality could be introduced in one entire unit or department over a short period of time (1-2 years). The experiences of this may be used to make modifications in the system and it could then be extended to other departments or regions.

Where the manpower in the personnel department is limited and their monitoring capabilities are limited this strategy may be used to facilitate effective monitoring. Line managers from those departments where the system has already been experimented could serve as resources for the new departments where it is being introduced.

4. Combinations of the Above

The above three strategies could be combined and used. A variety of combinations are possible. It is possible to go very slowly using a step-by-step, level-by-level and region-by-region (or unit-by-unit) strategy. In this strategy only a few managers at a particular level of hierarchy in one of the organisational units may be involved in the initial stages and subsequently it could be extended vertically and horizontally simultaneously increasing sophistication.

Whatever is the strategy to be used, the organisation should plan it rather than making systematic change in total at a time and not being able to cope up with the pressures and demands created by such a change.

Chapter 19

FROM APPRAISALS TO PLANNING, ANALYSIS AND DEVELOPMENT : RECENT DEVELOPMENTS IN EXECUTIVE APPRAISALS

In this chapter an attempt will be made to update the reader with some of the recent developments in performance appraisals. In the last 10 years a large number of organisations have started reviewing and revising their appraisal systems. In almost all these cases there is a welcome change and movement towards development-oriented and open systems of performance appraisal. This is reflected in the public sector organisations like the Steel Authority of India Limited (SAIL), National Dairy Development Board (NDDB), Life Insurance Corporation of India (LIC) and private sector organisations like the Sundram Fasteners Limited (SFL), Crompton Greaves Limited (CGL), Tata Iron and Steel Company (TISCO) and the Construction Group of Larsen & Toubro (L&T, EEC). In this chapter an attempt has been made to describe the trends and innovations. Specially the unique issues addressed by each of these organisations through their performance appraisal systems are highlighted.

From Appraisal to Planning, Analysis and Development

A significant shift in emphasis can be noticed from the titles given by organisations to the appraisal systems. Organisations are slowly avoiding the use of the term "appraisal" and increasingly emphasising Planning, Analysis, Review and Development. For example L&T (ECC) calls their system as "Performance Analysis and Development System (PADS)", NDDB titled its revised system as Performance Planning and Review (PPR), LIC calls it as Work Planning and Review System (WPRS) and CMC call their system as Performance and Development Review (PDR). In all these the emphasis is on Planning of Performance, Analysis of Performance, Review and Development. This change is definitely symbolic of the shift in focus and is undoubtedly the first step in re-orienting appraisals to development.

Emphasis on Planning

The emphasis on Planning by most of these organisations stem from the following needs and assumptions:

1. In the absence of a work or performance plan, managers tend to lose direction over a period of time and increase the chances of their getting sucked into routines. Performance planning through key performance areas, tasks, targets, objectives, key result areas and the like gives a sense of direction to every manager by helping him focus his atten tion on important aspects of his work. The performance plan helps him to remind himself periodically of the key activities or important tasks that should engage his attention.

2. Over a period of time in most organisations employees develop a tendency to keep doing things they are familiar rather than doing things they are not familiar. As a result higher level executives tend to underutilise their potential. Partly this happens because employees have a tendency to carry with them habits, work patterns and tasks they have performed well as they go up the managerial hierarchy. Thus when a person gets promoted to next higher level he may have a tendency to continue to do things that he has done in his previous role due to familiarity and past success. This continues down the line and thus over a period of time higher level executives may be doing things which their juniors far lower in the hierarchy should be doing. To avoid this, performance planning provides an opportunity to examine periodically whether the tasks executives perform are appropriate to their role and for their level. Performance planning helps an executive to examine the nature of activities he is involved in and the extent to which he is able to utilise his capabilities in the job.

3. Performance is more easily measurable at the departmental or unit levels rather than at individual levels. Most organisations have a variety of mechanisms for measuring such departmental performances rather than individual performances. One of the problems of measuring collective performance is that the individual identity may get lost. Hence performance planning and

analysis system is being used as an instrument to focus attention on individual output and thus give significance to the individual.

4. Performance planning helps in identifying the "distinctive" contributions of every employee to the organisation and gives the employee a sense of accomplishment. This also enhances his accountability. It is due to the fear of accountability some employees avoid performance planning. The distinctive contributions are identified by expecting every employee to distinguish his performance and contributions from those of his boss, subordinates and colleagues.

From Performance Counselling to Performance Review Discussion

The term "Performance Counselling" seems to create some unintended negative images. Some line managers find it difficult to get accustomed to the idea that counselling is not meant for only troubled employees or difficult cases. As a result organisations are preferring to use the term Performance Review Discussion or PRD. The SAIL system is an example of this.

A few organisations are even going to the extent of suggesting quarterly or half-yearly PDRs for senior executives.

From Performance Assessment to Performance Development

There is also an increasing trend to emphasise performance development much more than performance assessment. It is increasingly being recognised that assessment and ratings are instruments for development rather than ends in themselves. A result of this realisation is delinking appraisals from rewards and promotions. There is a continuous debate going on about the merits and demerits of linking appraisals to rewards. Organisations are realising that both ways there are problems. While good performance should be recognised and reinforced in many ways, mechanical linking of rewards and promotions leads to serious problems. Some organisations have delinked appraisals from rewards temporally and through forms. Rewards are being given on the basis of simple confidential form of recommendations. These forms are filled a few months after the development-oriented review discussions are conducted. Such temporal separation of open developmental appraisals from confidential reward appraisals is being used reasonably well.

As a result of this, emphasis on performance development is increasing. Organisations are emphasising that PRDs should themselves have an educative value. A variety of development decisions could be taken during PRD time. PRD itself is being considered as a developmental tool.

This is reflected in Sundram Fasteners where annual PRDs take place between the appraisee, his reporting officer, reviewing officer and the HRD Manager. In L&T Construction Group, internally trained facilitators are used while PRDs go on between an appraisee and the appraiser. The development plan outlined in the performance appraisal system of L&T is illustrative of the increased development-orientation in performance appraisals. Development plans are becoming integral and important parts of appraisals as reflected in the systems of most organisations.

Peer and Subordinate Appraisals

There is a growing trend to use appraisal by peers and internal customers. For example in the appraisal system used by Crompton Greaves every senior manager is appraised also by his colleagues who are his internal customers on certain dimensions.

A few organisations like TISCO have started experimenting with upward appraisals or appraisal by subordinates. In this system every senior executive is anonymously appraised by a group of his juniors or subordinates. The data are compiled and fed to the appraisee officer. This method has been found to be a very useful tool for development.

Role of Committees

Another significant development in the last few years is the use of committee system in reviewing performance. Those organisations that still emphasise objectivity have been using teams of senior executives to review the performance appraisals, decide rewards and significant development activities.

Acceptance of Subjectivity

A significant change that seems to be coming in performance appraisals is realisation of the fact that appraisals are bound to be subjective and subjectivity is a part of life. Such a realisation seems to reduce emotions and tensions associated with appraisals and increase the potential for development.

Some caselets described here highlight the appraisal systems in some of the organisations.

Work Planning and Review System· L.I.C.

The WPR in LIC is designed to achieve the following objectives: (i) to provide clarity of role to the manager, (ii) to enable the manager to think about his work in all aspects including his own strengths and weaknesses, (iii) to enable the manager to identify his achievable results, (iv) to enable him in systematic planning and execution, (v) promoting healthy superior-subordinate relationships and (vi) helping the manager identify his development needs.

WPR consists of the following steps:

Step 1 Surveying the Job in which each manager is required to carefully survey the environment for an operating unit like a branch in terms of the socio-economic and customer profiles. For managerial jobs such a survey may involve an examination of the state of affairs in his department as they evolved historically. Some form of SWOT analysis is done.

Step 2 Planning Results and Activities in which the manager lists the activities he needs to undertake and achieve results relating to his role. A role analysis is done for this purpose, range of activities listed result areas identified, and a time- bound plan prepared for achieving results.

Step 3 Assessing Effectiveness in which each manager is expected to indicate how he will assess the results in each area. This is done at the time of planning itself.

Step 4 Identifying Areas of Self-Development in which step each manager reviews his strengths and weaknesses and identify the areas in which he needs additional knowledge, skills and other competencies.

Step 5 Planning Interview in which step he is required to discuss the result areas, activities, measurements and work plan with his superior and record the same.

Step 6 Reviewing the Plan in which each manager is required to review his work plan with his superior. It is assumed that the Reporting Officer with his greater experience and more holistic perspective would be in a position to help by raising the right questions which might have the effect of improving the work plan.

The following is a summary of how the WPR System works:*

I. Understanding Role*Awareness of role boundaries

* Understanding purpose of position
* Understanding prescribed elements
* Understanding discretionary elements

II. Survey of Job-Scanning environment, e.g., socio-economic profile, customer profile etc.

* Looking at past performance of office/department.
* Taking a look at people, practices, conventions, inter-relationships, systems, attitudes, morale, problems, etc.
* Analysing strengths and weaknesses in department/office.

III. Prioritise for the Year-Listing weaknesses and strengths in office/department

* Assessing importance of competing needs based on overall needs of office
* Deciding on areas to be taken up based on assessment of priority

IV. Identify Result Areas-Seeing clearly what you want to achieve i.e., sharp focus on end result

* Narrow down on the problem-zone through segmentation
* Arrive at quantitative indicators for measuring achievement

V. Plan Activities-For each result area chosen, trace all aspects of problem based on data

*(Courtesy: HRD Department, Life Insurance Corporation of India, Central Office, Bombay).

- * For each result area arrive at sequence of actions proposed
- * For each result area, arrive at time frame for activities
- * For each result area, check whether the activities planned fall within role

VI. Identify Self-Assess individual need in relation Development Needs to requirements of job responsibilities

- * Think of future personal developmental needs that may arise in the course of career
- * Assess availability of avenues for improvement
- * Spell out clearly what inputs you may need and from which source

VII. Discuss Proposed Work-Clarify result areas in relation to Plan with Superior overall thrust of department/office

- * Improve perspective in relation to overall organisational aims
- * Share concerns and priorities
- * Sharpen activities
- * Better understanding of one's own developmental needs

VIII Review by Self-Looking at progress of activities in relation to time-schedule

- * Assessing impact of activities
- * Assessing causes for variations, if any
- * Planning out corrective strategies
- * Re-examine time schedules if necessary

IX. Review by Superior-Sharing views on progress of activities and impact

- * Analysis of causes for failure if any
- * Sharing views on corrective measures required
- * Discuss rescheduling where necessary

*PPR in the National Dairy Development Board (NDDB)**

Making a modest beginning in the field of dairy development in the late sixties the NDDB has now emerged as an organisation of national importance with multifaceted activities. The NDDB continues to focus its activities on promotion of viable producer owned and controlled organisations primed to produce, procure, process and market milk and its products as well as other commodities. Each officer in NDDB is expected to play a significant role in achieving the objectives of the Board.

NDDB introduced a new system for planning, analysing and appraising the performance of its executives from the year 1989. This system is called the Performance Planning and Review Systems. This system was designed primarily by an internal task force through a process of consultations and involvement of a sizeable group of its executives. The members of the task force represented different disciplines/departments and the HRD department orchestrated this effort.

Objctives

The PPR is designed to be forward looking and developmental in its application. As against appraising an individual employee's performance after it has taken place without planning, the PPR requires that the performance for every employee be planned ahead of time, expected results agreed to at the outset, and performance assessed on the basis of these plans and agreements. This is considered as a dynamic and ongoing process in which continuous dialogue between the employee and his reporting officer is critical. The PPR has the following objectives:

1. Bring about clarity of the role of each officer.
2. Help officers plan and review their work through a participatory process and thereby increase job satisfaction.
3. Facilitate communication at all levels.
4. Improve the quality of data available for personnel decisions.
5. Identify training and development needs on a continuing basis, evolve training plans and facilitate development decisions.
6. Enable the officers to be responsible for the development of their subordinates.

---

*Permission given by HRD Department, NDDB to describe the PPR System is gratefully acknowledged.

Beliefs

The Performance Planning and Review System in NDDB is based on the following beliefs:

1. It is the employee who creates excellence and dynamism in an organisation.
2. Employees' competencies should be developed on a continuing basis for their own growth and growth of the organisation.
3. Competency development takes place on the job when employees facilitate each other's performance.
4. Planning performance is an important managerial responsibility enhancing the ability of each employee to contribute to his organisation.
5. Communication, openness and participation, are valuable for human resource development.

Components

In order to achieve the above mentioned objectives the PP&R Forms and Manual are divided into the following components:

1. Performance Planning

This is the first stage of the process where a performance plan, in term of key tasks, is jointly developed by the Reporting Officer and the Officer. The plan is worked out in terms of results expected, performance standards, per formance measures and target dates for a period of one year.

2. Performance Review

The performance review provides opportunity for the Officer and the Reporting Officer to assess the results achieved in relation to the original plan. Performance facts form the basis for this discussion. Performance review also provides input for future planning.

Review need not be restricted to a 12 month cycle but can be done as frequently as the need arises and can be initiated by either the Reporting Officer or the Officer. It is a means of communication on a continuous basis. A mid-year review is recommended as an informal stocktaking for corrective action. The records of such reviews should be retained by the Reporting Officer.

An important aspect of the performance review is self-review. Self review, to be filled in by the Officer has been structured to give the Officer an opportunity to report on his performance, his outstanding achievements, the difficulties faced, and his suggestion for improving performance.

Following a review discussion the Reporting Officer will assign an assessment of performance for each key task.

3. Attributes and Overall Assessment

These are job related skills and behavioural dimensions required of every officer of NDDB. The factors are rated on a 5-point scale. The rating is done by the Reporting Officer and thereafter communicated to the Officer. The attributes/factors assessed are: Leadership, Development of subordinates, Stress tolerance, Creativity, Cost consciousness, Internal relations, Initiative, Communication skills, Problem solving, Job knowledge, Planning and organising, Discipline and dependability.

4. Training and Development Needs

This can be used at the planning stage and/or review stage. At the planning stages the training and development plan indicates what training is required to meet the performance objective. At the review stages careful consideration can be given to the overall performance achievements of the Officer including his potential, various managerial and behavioural dimensions, career aspirations as well as organisational requirements. This form can be filled in and forwarded to HRD Group as and when such needs are identi fied.

The role of HRD Group is to co-ordinate formal training and development programmes. Line managers are responsible for the training and development of those reporting to them.

5.0 Critical Incident Log

While reviewing the performance of subordinates, managers often rely on recent events - those which can be easily remembered. A manager's life is hectic, often fragmented by interruptions and crisis. As a result they miss continuous historical documentation of a subordinate's performance. This situation forces them to recall recent incidents of performance to conduct assessment at the end of a review period.

The subordinate may have met a significant goal or made a major contribution early in the review period which is forgotten at the end of six months or a year.

Subordinates, on the other hand, who are aware that their Reporting Officer only values accomplishments made during the last part of the review period, may save their energies and work hard only then. They may be careful not to make any errors during this period since they realise that mistakes are remembered as readily as accomplishments.

In order to minimise the effect of this recent approach, often called the "halo effect", it is helpful for the Reporting Officer to maintain a critical incident log or diary. Here he/she can briefly record important incidents which have a bearing on the ability of the subordinate to perform the key tasks agreed to at the time of performance planning. It is recommended that this be done on a monthly basis.

Such a critical incident log could also be kept by the Officer and used with the Reporting Officer's log at the time of review to establish performance facts.

Introduction of the System

The HRD Department of NDDB has prepared a detailed manual explaining various components of the system. For example, the manual explains in detail how the performance is to be planned in a participative way identifying key tasks, establishing weightages, sharing performance expectations and taking into consideration a variety of situational facts. The Training and Developmental needs are also expected to be planned in the beginning of the year rather than at the end.

The NDDB introduced this system only after an organisation-wide education workshops conducted by the HRD Department.

*Performance Appraisal System in Sundram Fasteners Limited**

Sundram Fasteners is a member of the TVS Group of companies, who are the largest automotive ancillary group in India. They are the

* Note prepared by Smt. Usha Krishna, reproduced from HRD Newsletter, 1986, No.4, pp.10-11.

largest manufacturer of high tensile fasteners in India. They make about 4,000 different products. They mainly cater to the requirements of commercial vehicles, tractors, two-wheelers, stationary engines, machine tools, auto ancillaries, electrical/electronic industries, defence and other priority sectors.

Sundram Fasteners started its commercial production in the year 1966. They diversified into cold extrusion in 1976. The second fastener plant was opened near Madurai in 1981. In 1982, they finalised a technical collaboration with M/s. Neumeyer Flies spressen GmbH, West Germany, for cold extrusion. The same year they went public too with an Authorised Capital of Rs.500 lakhs. In 1983, they diversified into the manufacture of Power Metal Products (sintered products) in technical collaboration with M/s. Sintermetallwerk Krebsoege GmbH, West Germany. This unit has come up in Hosur near Bangalore.

The total number of employees are 1,200 (400 in Madurai, 600 in Madras and 200 in Hosur). Out of this, the staff in the middle management and above are about 170 and they have so far covered the PAS only to this cadre.

The HRD is placed in the Corporate Planning and Development wing since it is considered as a part of the overall organisational growth process with focus on people related issues. This was aimed at middle management and upwards because people at this level are key corporate resource, occupying critical position. They have a significant number of levels under them to influence and effect change. Also, the level of frustration was high at this level, due to alienation of this group in the past - the lower levels had the unions and the top level had direct contact with the top management - and it was this middle level that had been neglected. The key areas of responsibility undertaken by HRD were: Organisation structure (focussing on reporting relationships and responsibilities), Job description (describing key responsibility areas), Manpower Planning (focussing on long term requirements), Recruitment/Placement, Performance Appraisal System (focussing on developing individuals for effective performance), Training and Development, Management of Salary and Perquisites, and finally Career Planning. Finalisation of organisation structure preceded the introduction of PAS.

Job descriptions were prepared clearly specifying key areas of responsibility. Corporate philosophy was finalised to act as a framework for the Appraisal System. Extensive research was undertaken spreading over 1 1/2 years and studying the various systems available both in India and abroad. After the system was evolved in tune with the culture of the organisation it was tested beforc launching. Through workshops the system was communicated to all employees. The continued participation by the top management including the Chairman & M.D., at every workshop, reinforced the commitment to the system.

The PAS aims at promoting desired values of openness, trust and team building. Its objective is to help an individual's effectiveness and growth through constructive feedback and counselling. The appraisal covers the assessees, his immediate supervisor, acting as first assessor and first assessor's immediate supervisor, acting as second assessor. It comprises of semiformal session quarterly between the assessee and first assessor. Then there is the formal, annual session between the assessee, first assessor and second assessor. A representative from the Corporate Planning and Development Department is present in all the assessments to give feedback to assessee and asessor. He really acts as a facilitator. The criteria for measurement of performance are divided into (a) Task related areas, (b) Skills related areas, (c) Personality attributes. In the task related areas, the achievement of results, output of work (quantitative) and the quality of work (qualitative) are taken cognisance of.

Skills related areas can be divided into three parts: (i) Conceptual skills, (ii) Human skills and (iii) Functional skills. In conceptual skills, a person's different skills like proactive, integrity, analytical, planning and total perspective are taken into consideration. In human skills, his leadership qualities, ability to inspire and motivate, his inter-personal relationships, co-operation and tact, training and development of subordinates, appraising ability, communication and resolution of conflict are the main areas of consideration. In the field of functional skills, job knowledge, planning, organising and decision making are considered important. Weightage is given for different criteria.

In the Personality attributes, the qualities of openness, empathy/ sensitivity, integrity, flexibility, positive outlook, perseverance, creativity, capacity to withstand stress, discipline, commitment, dependability, loyalty, self-confidence and of course appearance and looks.

All these factors have been taken in the PAS. Ratings against individual items, is done a 10 point scale as follows: Excellent 9-10; Good 7-8; Competent 5-6; Average 3-4; Poor 1-2. Varying weightage is given for different criteria of performance. There is a provision for descriptive comments by assessors and records of appraisal interview. Linkages of

PAS to rewards has yet to be taken up. The appraisal system has built in flexibility to extend the coverage both upwards and downwards.

Activity Planning and Faculty Appraisal at Indian Institute of Management, Ahmedabad (IIMA)

The foundation for faculty work planning and appraisal at the Indian Institute of Management, Ahmedabad was laid in late sixties by Prof. Ravi J. Matthai who was Director of IIMA at that time. The Faculty Evaluation System was evolved through discus sions by the faculty and formalised in 1971 (Matthai, 1974).* This system has been described by Matthai in detail in a note prepared by him in 1971. Describing the background behind this note Matthai wrote "Faculty members wanted to know where they stood". They wanted to know more specifically how to allocate their time between academic activities and how to plan their work such that their plans would be acceptable to the Institute. They wished to know more explicitly their "rights and obligations", what was permissible and what was not. From the description given by Matthai and on the basis of the experiences of the author the system existing in practice at IIMA is described below.

Work Planning

Every faculty member is expected to plan his work a year in advance. Normally the work for the academic year begins in June every year and end in April the next year. Academic activities the faculty member expects to undertake from June onwards for that academic year are planned in February-March of that year. Every faculty member is expected to do six academic unit equivalents of work in a year. Teaching a section of 60 students over 30 sessions and all the associated preparation, assessment etc. is considered as one unit of academic work. Its equivalence in research, case development are left to be established by each faculty member from time to time. Its equivalence in administration is established by the Institute. For example, it is assumed that the Chairman of the Post Graduate Programme is involved in about three academic unit equivalents of administration or insti tution building work. Consulting is not counted as a part of this workload of six unit equivalents. Each faculty member is required to plan his work in terms of teaching

***Matthai, R.J., a note of Faculty Evaluation, in R.J. Matthai, U. Pareek and T.V. Rao, Institution Building in Education and Research: From Stagnation to Self-renewal, New Delhi: All India Management Association, 1975.**

(in the Post Graduate Programme, Doctoral Programme, Executive Development Programmes and the Faculty Development Programme), research, case development and publications, academic administration and other professional work. Such plans are prepared through a discussion in the academic groups (areas, centres, etc.). Such groups also prepare their teaching plans taking into consideration the needs of the institution as well as the academic interests of the faculty. Individual faculty members also finalise their plans and send to the Dean who may consolidate, identify gaps in terms of institutional needs and discuss with some faculty if necessary to fill the gaps.

Such advance activity planning provides a sense of direction for faculty in terms of their activities.

Faculty Evaluation

The activity planning and faculty evaluation are somewhat inde pendent activities at IIMA. Faculty are not evaluated in terms of what they have planned but more in terms of what they have done and the quality of contributions made in each activity (teaching, research, administration, publications, consulting, etc.) The evaluation period for faculty member may be from July to June or from January to December depending on the closeness of his date of joining to July or January. When his annual evaluation is due each faculty member is expected to prepare a detailed note listing various activities (teaching, research, publications, academic administration, professional work, etc.) he had done during that year. The faculty member may also express his views and attach reports, publications if any for review by the Faculty Evaluation and Development Committee (FEDC). The FEDC is chaired by the Director and has four other faculty members on it. These faculty are chosen by the Director taking into consideration confidential suggestions by the faculty. The composition of the FEDC keeps changing every two years. The Dean is an additional member of the Committee.

The FEDC reviews the work done by every faculty member. Promotion decisions are taken by this Committee on the basis of a comprehensive review of the faculty member's work for three years or more. In such cases published works and research reports etc., of the faculty member are also sent to external referees for comments on the quahty of work.

Participant Evaluation

In addition to self-reporting and evaluation by the FEDC a significant source of feedback for development of every faculty member is the student/participant evaluation. The students of the Post Graduate Programme at IIMA conduct an independent evaluation of each course and faculty members teaching that course. The students prepare and administer a questionnaire to the student body every year requiring them to assess each course they took and each faculty member that taught them. Such an assessment is made on various dimensions like the relevance of the course, quality of teaching, resourcefulness of the faculty, teaching method, learning value, etc. The student assessment of the faculty and courses are then tabulated and the data are circulated to all faculty. Thus every faculty member has knowledge of how effective he had been and his relative standing vis-a-vis his colleagues. These data are freely distributed to all faculty and is an excellent source of feedback to faculty. Awards are given to faculty whose teaching is outstanding every year.

In the Executive Development Programmes, the faculty themselves design a questionnaire and collect feedback from the partici pants. Such feedback and evaluation is tabulated and circulated by the course coordinator to all teaching faculty of that programme. This serves as another important source of evaluation to faculty.

In sum, annual activity planning, self-reporting, student/partic ipant evaluation and review by a committee are the components of the Faculty Appraisals at IIMA. Any interested reader may get more details from Ravi Matthai's note (Ravi Matthai, 1974).

Chapter 20

MONITORING PERFORMANCE PLANNING ANALYSIS AND DEVELOPMENT SYSTEMS

If performance appraisals have to achieve the variety of developmental objectives outlined in this book, the appraisal system need to be designed well and its implementation monitored well. Most appraisal systems are well designed but do not get implemented well due to poor monitoring and follow-up. Line managers do not put in enough effort in implementing the system for the following reasons:

1. It is one of the activities that can be postponed without any visible damage to their productivity, effectiveness or performance.
2. It has not yet become a part of their work-life and it has not become a habit like regular daily or weekly meetings on production planning etc. It is an infrequent thing taking place once a year or twice a year.
3. Line managers move from one crisis to another having limited time for such developmental activities.
4. Organisations have not yet fully established a HRD culture in which not having performance planning and review discussions is considered as poor management or a stigma.
5. There are difficulties in facing each other and frankly talking about each others performance and there is a fear of hurting each other or anxiety of not being able to handle the consequences of 'openness'.
6. There are no systemic ways in which these are monitored, data are used and feedback provided to line managers. It is considered as a ritual to be completed some how than an opportunity to be used.

Only some of these sources can be eliminated through good monitoring and follow-up. When the implementation is monitored, it establishes the significance of the PPA & D system in the work-life and as an instrument of building people, provides continuous attention of the top management and senior executives and demonstrates that the data generated in the PPA & D system are used for various developmental and managerial decisions.

Such a monitoring needs to be done comprehensively for a few years until the system becomes a matter of habit and a part of worklife. Such monitoring needs to be done using different methods and by different agencies. Such monitoring and follow-up may aim at the following objectives:

1. Providing necessary guidance and support for the appraisee-appraiser pairs to be able to implement the system well (i.e., to plan the performance well, analyse it, have good performance review, identify development needs, generate useful data and enjoy the benefits of PPA & D).

2. To establish the significance of the PPA & D by analysing the data and providing feedback at departmental/group level.

3. To serve as a reminder or pressure point to employees who are accustomed to work under such pressure until it becomes a part of their routine. This also enables them to find time for this purpose.

The following methods can be used for monitoring purposes.

1. **Individual contact**: This is to find out the implementation status through interviews and provide guidance wherever necessary. In this method the personnel and HRD staff play a lead role by individual by contacting employees and interviewing them to find out the implementation status, benefits, problems etc. It is preferable to contact all individuals. If the group is large it may be useful to contact all reporting or reviewing officers or a sample of them. An interview schedule may be developed.
2. **Analysis of Forms**: Analysing the forms received from the employees to find out trends, problems etc., and feeding the data back to line managers for use is another significant way to monitor.

The performance plans/KPAs/Tasks/Targets etc., maybe compiled department-wise to see whether there are any missing

KPAs/tasks/targets and how the parts are adding up to a whole. The performance analysis data may be compiled department-wise to identify most frequently mentioned inhibiting factors and the data may be fedback to the departmental heads. The developmental needs could be tabulated to identify the department-wise training needs and take developmental decisions. The ratings could be analysed to identify biases, interdepartmental variations, etc., and initiate corrective action.

3. **Line Manager Task Forces or Departmental Task Forces**: An organisation-wide or department based task forces can be formed to monitor the implementation. Such task forces may evolve their own methods of monitoring including a combination of individual contacts, questionnaire surveys, short review workshops, analysis of forms, etc. When line manager task forces are formed employees tend to see a high significance attached to the system than when the personnel/HRD department alone monitors the implementation.

4. **Departmental Review Meetings**: Each department could set aside a day or half-a-day every year or every six months to review the implementation of the PPA & D. In such departmental reviews all the employees may participate. Commonly experienced difficulties could be identified and technical assistance sought to help them overcome these. Such reviews tend to improve the significance of PPA & Ds. Each employee is normally required to give his views in such meetings. This also acts as a pressure point.

5. **Questionnaire Surveys:** This is a most commonly used and a very useful method. In this method a follow-up questionnaire is designed and sent to all employees. The questionnaire may deal with one aspect or comprehensively deal with all aspects of implementation. It may solicit factual information as well as perceptions, feelings and reactions. It could be collected anonymously to get frank and free data or may be collected by name to get factual information and provide feedback. It is useful to collect infor mation from all with the help of the questionnaire.

6. **Presentation to Top Management or Heads of Departments**: This is not a separate method but can be used as a potential mechanisms to communicate the significance of data generated

in the PPA & D exercises. In this method the Personnel/HRD department staff or Line Manager or task-forces review the implementation and make a presentation of their recommendations for improving it. Analysis of data and questionnaire surveys also could be presented to them. Such presentation help top management to become aware of various issues and also communicates to the employees the top management in volvement. Such presentations should be followed by some action or atleast a communication of the implementation status and concerns of top management to all employees.

Component Monitoring :

Monitoring may be done for the entire system every year or for every significant component of the system. Table 21.1 gives a schematic presentation of the monitoring matrix highlighting the use of different methods for monitoring each of the components. A monitoring plan could be worked out using the inputs given in this table depending on the needs of the organisation and the stage of its implementation.

Comprehensive Reviews and Renewal

Any system becomes a part of the routine after some time. In the initial stages there is some euphoria or excitement but after about three years it dies down and becomes a routine. Unfortunately both positives and negatives get settled down in this routine. In other words the system with all its side-effects and inadequacies becomes a routine. There is normally scope for improving the system or its implementation. By about the third or fourth year people are able to experience the inadequacies, imperfections, problems and difficulties in the system and its implementation. They are also able to articulate these well. It is then time to review the system and renew it. Howsoever excellent a system may be, it is useful to review it once in five years. Such review and renewal exercises may be conducted internally by an interdepartmental task force or if necessary by an external agent. Such renewal exercises may use various methods like individual interviews, questionnaire surveys and workshops. Such a renewal exercises and consequent decisions go a long way to keep the spirit of PPA & D systems alive and benefit the organisation a good deal.

It should be remembered that in the ultimate analysis PPA & D systems are not merely appraisal instruments but instruments to improve management practices and build professionally effective management culture.

PPA & D MONITORING MATRIX

Monitoring Method	PPA & D Dimension Monitored					
	Perf. Planning	Self Appraisal and Perf. Analysis	Perf. Review Counsel-ling	Develop-ment Needs	Ratings	Review and Follow-up
1. Individual contact, guidance and inter-views	For guidance and quality improve-ment	To improve quality and depth	Facilitate good PRDs and counse-lling	To help articulate dev. needs	To improve quality of ratings (appraisers only)	With review officers/ committees to assess effective-ness
2. Analysis of forms	To see trends examine quality and relevance to org. goals	To analyse support require-ments and collate inhibiting factors	–	To identify training needs and other devt. needs	To identify biases, le-niency and other trends	Follow up of devt. decisions
3. Line Manager/ Task Forces or Depart-mental Task Forces	"	To under-stand and improve factors affecting perfor-mance	To assess commit-ment and serious-ness	To identify trg. and other dev. needs	To identify develop-ment needs reduce biases	–
4. Depart-mental Review Meetings	"	"	To improve quality	"	"	–

Monitoring Method	PPA & D Dimension Monitored					
	Perf. Planning	Self Appraisal and Perf. Analysis	Perf. Review Counsel-ling	Develop-ment Needs	Ratings	Review and Follow-up
5. Question-naire re-surveys	To assess seriousness commit-ment satisfaction	To assess the effec-tiveness of self-apprai-sal process	To assess the effec-tiveness of PRDs	To assess the extent to which of dev. needs have been identified	To assess the diffi-culties, biases, and improve quality	To assess the effec-tiveness of review mechanisms
6. Presenta-tions to Top Manage-ment	To improve quality and related aspects	"	–	To take develop-ment decisions	To help them understand biases and make cor-rections	Variations in reviews

Chapter 21

RATINGLESS APPRAISALS FOR FUTURE

Appraisal systems require constant rejuvenation and renewal. If appraisal systems have to serve developmental purposes without creating any insecurity or defensiveness we need to learn to treat people as people and not as statistics. At best numbers should be used as aids. Multiple sources and methods of assessment and feedback should be encouraged in organisations. Subjectivity should be accepted as a part of life. Promotions should become a matter of routine rather than becoming sources of frustration. Work and working environment should be made more challenging and enjoyable rather than 'status' and 'power' associated with 'positions' and promotions. At the same time a good work culture and dignity of those who work should be aimed at. Trends are observable in these directions by a few companies who, are thinking of 'Ratingless Appraisals', 'Subordinate Appraisals', 'Internal Customer Assessment' and the like. Some of these trends are highlighted below and it is hoped that many organisations will move in this directions.

Sometimes a question is asked about the possibility and/or desirability of doing away with appraisal ratings. If one looks at the HRD philosophy of an organisation in its true sense it appears that in assessing the performance of an individual through ratings we are reducing the person and his entire year's work into a few numbers. It appears that reducing the human being to a statistic and using the statistic for all decisions that are important to him is anti-HRD or atleast not in conso nance with the HRD philosophy. Therefore, the question is if there can be numberless or ratingless appraisals.

The argument against this is that without the numbers it is difficult for someone at the top to take decisions about whom to reward for good performance. When the final choice comes 'numbers' or 'ratings' seem to matter a lot, yet these very ratings are perceived as anti-HRD. If the numbers are not there, reward administration becomes difficult, perceptions of subjectivity increases and appraisals may not be valued much by employees.

There is no simple answer to the problem. The following seems to be some of the conditions under which performance ratings could be eliminated altogether from the appraisals.

1. Performance rewarding is not by a central team but is decentralised to the level of reporting or reviewing officers, i.e., at each level the appraisee's reporting officer or a reviewing officer two levels above him in the organisational hierarchy decides the methods of rewarding and whom to reward.
2. If a central team or review committee that decides rewards takes such decisions after discussions with each reporting officer and if necessary the appraisee in select cases.
3. If the appraisal system shifts the focus from individual to team appraisals.
4. The HRD philosophy and practices are very well integrated into the organisation, everyone trusts each other and rewards do not matter as every individual works with commitment and devotion irrespective of rewards.
5. There is no reward system and everyone gets the same reward.
6. There are several mechanisms of recognising employee contributions and performance appraisal reports is only one of them.
7. When the organisation is moving in the direction of having a flat structure (hierarchy-less organisation).

These are only some of the alternative conditions for making appraisals ratingless. In any case when appraisals do not have ratings there will be some form of assessment. This may be qualitative assessment. It would require more attention to be paid to everything that is written in the appraisal by the appraisers for any other decisions. As of now Indian organisations have not come to the level of ratingless appraisals but it is hoped that as HRD gets stabilised and internalised the number game would stop and human beings get treated as human beings.

In large organisations there are still serious difficulties in moving in this direction.

Subordinate Assessment

Recently TISCO has started experimenting with subordinates ap praising their reporting officers. Development takes place only when an individual perceives a gap between what he should do or what he would like to do and what he actually does. Or a development need is indicated when an individual experiences or perceives a gap between the impact he likes to make and the impact he actually makes. Such gaps are first steps in HRD. Subordinates, colleagues, reporting officers and other seniors are some sources of creating such awareness in employees. Subordinate appraisals, peer appraisals are very useful instruments. However, until such time Indian executives become mature and capable enough to receive feedback from subordinates, subordinate appraisals should be made voluntary. The author has come across several managers who collect anonymous feedback from their subordinates on their styles etc. to improve themselves. There are executives who also discuss such feedback with their subordinates. It is hoped that such managerial practices will multiply in future.

Anonymous Feedback From Significant Others

A few years ago an experiment was started at the Indian Institute of Management, Ahmedabad in the form of an Executive Development Programme on "Top Managers Styles and Organisational Effective ness". In this programme top level managers from different organisations were required to register for the programme atleast three months in advance. They were also required to supply (nominate) along with their registration names and addresses of atleast 10 persons who worked with them in the past and whose assessment the participant valued. Questionnaires requiring the nominees to give their assessment of the candidate were sent to the nominees. The questionnaires dealt with the leadership and supervisory styles, delegation, decision making, effective performance of different roles, strengths, weaknesses, learning styles etc., of the participants.

The feedback or assessment was required to be sent anonymously and directly to the programme coordinator. The responses received for each candidate were tabulated and during the programme each participant was handed over the consolidated feedback he received from his nominees. Such handing over of the feedback was done after giving adequate conceptual inputs and preparing the person to receive and use feedback. This feedback was given also after self-assessment by each candidate. Subsequent to the feedback opportunities were provided for skill development in the workshop.

This experience gave very satisfactory results and subsequently has been adopted as a good model for development of senior executives by several organisations.

REFERENCES

Bernardin, H.J., 1977, Behavioural Expectation Scale versus Summated Scales: A Fairer Comparison, *Journal of Applied Psychology,* 62, 422-428.

Bernardin, H.J. and Cardy, R.L., 1982, Appraisal Accuracy - the Ability and Motivation to Remember the Past, *Public Personnel Management Journal,* 11(4), 352-357.

Bernardin, H.J., Cardy, R.L. and Carlyle, J.J., 1982, Cognitive Complexity and Appraisal Effectiveness: Back to the Drawing Board, *Journal of Applied Psychology,* 67(2), 151-160.

Bernardin, H.J., and Smith, P.C., 1981, A Clarification on Some Issues Regarding the Development and use of Behaviourally Anchored Rating Scales (BARS), *Journal of Applied Psychology,* 66(4), 458-463.

Borman, W., 1979, Format and Training Effects on Rater Accuracy and Rater Errors, *Journal of Applied Psychology,* 64, 410- 121.

Cantor, N. and Mischel, W., 1977, Traits as Prototypes: Effects on Recognition Memory, *Journal of Personality and Social Psychology,* 35, 38-48.

Decotiis, T. and Petit, Andre, 1978, The Performance Appraisal Process: A Model and Some Testable Propositions, *Academy of Management Review,* 63.

Dunnet, M. and Borman, W, 1979, Personnel Selection and Classification Systems, *Annual Review of Psychology,* 30, 477-525.

Feldman, J.M., 1981, Beyond Attribution Theory: Cognitive Process in Performance Appraisal, *Journal of Applied Psychology,* 66 (2), 127-148.

Flanders, Ned., 1970, *Analysing Teacher Behaviour,* Reading, Mass: Addison Wesley.

Friedman, B.A. and Cornelius, E.T., 1976, Effects of Rater Participation in Scale Construction on Psychometric Characteristics of the Rating Scale Formats, *Journal of Applied Psychology,* 61, 210-216..

The Academy of Human Resource Development and such other agencies intend providing such development experiences. Organisations are also using increasingly their HRD departments to conduct such development-oriented assessment and feedback services.

An important pre-requisite for such assessment is that the data should be used only by the individual and not by the organisations. It is hoped that in years to come such type of development oriented appraisals become quite common and useful. In all these ratings should play much lesser role and the feedback should become a learning experience.